Three Jesus Certitudes

Three Jesus Certitudes

Pacifism, Feminism, and the Birth of Christianity

LEONARD J. SWIDLER

CASCADE Books • Eugene, Oregon

THREE JESUS CERTITUDES
Pacifism, Feminism, and the Birth of Christianity

Copyright © 2018 Leonard J. Swidler. All rights reserved. Except for brief quotations in critical publications or reviews, no part of this book may be reproduced in any manner without prior written permission from the publisher. Write: Permissions, Wipf and Stock Publishers, 199 W. 8th Ave., Suite 3, Eugene, OR 97401.

Cascade Books
An imprint of Wipf and Stock Publishers
199 W. 8th Ave., Suite 3
Eugene, OR 97401

www.wipfandstock.com

PAPERBACK ISBN: 987-1-5326-0427-0
HARDCOVER ISBN: 987-1-5326-0429-4
EBOOK ISBN: 987-1-5326-0428-7

Cataloging-in-Publication data:

Names: Swidler, Leonard J., author.

Title: Three Jesus certitudes : pacifism, feminism, and the birth of Christianity / Leonard J. Swidler.

Description: Eugene, OR: Cascade Books, 2018. | Includes bibliographical data and indexes.

Identifiers: 987-1-5326-0427-0 (paperback). | 987-1-5326-0429-4 (hardcover). | 987-1-5326-0428-7 (epub).

Subjects: LCSH: Jesus Christ. | Bible. Gospels—Criticism, interpretation, etc. | Feminism—Religious aspects—Christianity. | Women—Religious aspects—Christianity. | Women in Christianity—History—Early church, ca. 30–600. | Nonviolence—Religious aspects—Christianity.

Classification: BT704 S95 2018 (print). | BT704 (epub).

Manufactured in the U.S.A.   07/23/18

Contents

Introduction | 1

1 Jesus and Yeshua | 5

2 Yeshua: Nonviolence and Pacifism | 25

3 Yeshua Was a Feminist

Excursus I: A Leap Ahead to a Female Holy Spirit | 71

Excursus II: Whence Evil? and, Is Woman Superior to Man? | 74

4 Yeshua's Women Followers Created Christianity | 82

5 Pacifism, Feminism, Women Evangelists: A Virtuous Triangle! | 164

Bibliography | 173
Index | 177

Introduction

THE ARGUMENT OF THIS book comprises three steps.

1. Two major characteristics of Jesus stand out starkly against the culture of his time: The first is his commitment to nonviolence—*Jesus's pacifism*.
2. His fundamentally related commitment to equality for women—*Jesus's feminism*.
3. Intimately connected to both characteristics, but especially the latter—*Women followers of Jesus gave birth to Christianity!*

First two steps: Precisely because Jesus's two positions of *pacifism* and *feminism* were antithetic to basically all human cultures from the beginning of history to his time—and unfortunately also for two millennia afterward!—we can be historically more certain of them than any other historical facts about Jesus. And yet, most ironically, it was also precisely these two most certain characteristics of Jesus that went unfollowed, indeed, one of them was de facto suppressed until just decades ago, his feminism; only very recently has it been rediscovered—hidden in plain sight![1]

However, the two clearly belong together; one implies the other. Humans are the most developed of all the beings we know—being bodies that can think abstractly and hence choose freely; that is, they are rational and free. That means that humans are potentially capable of seeing that every human ought to be free up to the point where his/her freedom would inhibit other humans' freedom. This immediately implies that because violence limits human freedom, humans are morally bound to be nonviolent, "pacifist," toward others and themselves—short of when not to be violent

---

1. See Swidler, "Jesus Was a Feminist," reproduced dozens of times in many languages. See below for further discussion. For an expansion of this brief essay, see Swidler, *Jesus Was a Feminist*.

Three Jesus Certitudes

would cause even more violence. However, since both women and men are full humans, *each* morally must be allowed freedom up to the point where it would inhibit other humans' freedom—i.e., to be a "feminist." This may seem somewhat abstract, but I believe that it is nevertheless clear to all modern persons who accept the idea of human rights: Without "feminism," half the humans of the world would be shorn of their human rights, and this would be (and largely still is!) an egregious act of violence.

Third step: The third-step thesis of this book is potentially even more unnerving: If we were missing the information about Jesus that has come to us from women, there *would be no Christianity!* I will lay out below the striking evidence that protoversions of two of the four canonical Gospels were produced/sourced by women (Luke and the Fourth Gospel), and that massive amounts of the information in the other two Gospels (especially Matthew) came from women. Hence, if all the information about Jesus, his teaching and actions, that came from women were missing, Christianity would never have been born, or would have died almost aborning.

One could imagine, *per impossibilem*, that if all the material not handed on by women about Jesus's teaching and life were nevertheless gathered together and written down, and if the missionary activities of Paul, Barnabas, Silas, Timothy, and others did occur, which the New Testament details (but if we learned of these activities *sans* the work of all the women listed, and those not, in the New Testament), *perhaps* some kind of religion around Jesus would have arisen. However, it would have been anemic, and doubtless in a few short centuries would have faded from all but human memory, as Mithraism did, and numberless other cults popular for a century or few.

To begin, I will lay out the evidence for Jesus's pacifism and feminism and something of their implications and then most briefly show how they mutually coinhere, starting with Jesus's pacifism because the written material about it is quantitatively much less than that for his feminism. In this process I will lay out the extraordinary role women followers of Jesus had in passing on the information about Jesus: my argument will lead to the conclusion that without them, *there would be no Christianity!* Put positively, *Women were the founders of Christianity!*

There is no argument among scholars concerning Jesus's commitment to nonviolence—what I'm calling his pacifism; the argument came throughout most of Christian history about what its implications are for living as a follower of Jesus. Concerning Jesus's treating women as the equals of men, that is, what I'm calling his feminism, the story is quite different. Clearly

Jesus's women followers were keenly aware of his revolutionary egalitarian relations with women, but within a few short decades after his death Jesus's feminism was not only completely forgotten, but it was even vigorously suppressed! As ongoing contemporary evidence I offer briefly the recent life facts.

As I noted briefly above, in January 1971 I published an article titled "Jesus Was a Feminist" in a little known magazine, the *Catholic World*. Within a short time it was reproduced in at least two score different publications in at least ten different languages. The echo of that tiny article continues to this day! Just three most recent examples of the last forty-plus years: A few years ago I was at a meeting in the World Council of Churches in Geneva, Switzerland, and when we went for lunch in the cafeteria, I got in line and happened to be behind a quiet looking, fifty-something white male. I put my hand out and said, "Hi, I'm Leonard Swidler." He looked at me and said: "*The* Leonard Swidler?" I stammered, "Yes." He stretched out his arm, pointed his finger at me, and in a stentorian voice proclaimed: "Jesus Was a Feminist!" I gasped, "Where did that come from?" He said that some thirty years prior his theology professor at his seminary in Chicago gave the class my article to read. I judged that it clearly must have seared itself into his memory all those years ago for him to have declaimed my name and article out of the blue decades later!

It just doesn't stop. A little over a year ago at the annual conference of the North American Academy of Ecumenists, held at the headquarters of the Evangelical Lutheran Church in America, I found myself waiting for hot water next to a thirtysomething woman professor at a Lutheran seminary who had just spoken on a panel, and again offered my hand and said that I was Leonard Swidler. She looked at me, hesitated, and then said, "The 'Jesus-Was-a-Feminist' Leonard Swidler?" I gulped once again, and . . . She went on to tell me how the article shaped her life and led her to be a theology professor.

Then just last year, once again out of the proverbial blue I received an e-mail from a fifty-some-year-old successful Catholic businesswoman who said that in the 1980s while at college, she was so struck by my article that she cut it out and taped it in her Bible; then just last year, it had gotten so worn that she decided to make new copy of it—then the idea struck her that she could look me up on the Web and write and thank me; she wrote that the article encouraged her to strike out on her own and helped sustain her as she became a very successful, ethical woman in business.

Three Jesus Certitudes

I recall all this because what is so extraordinary is that my 1971 article was no breakthrough work of massive scholarship. I simply did what any undergraduate working on a term paper would do: I merely took all the sources we have on the life of Jesus—the four Gospels—and read through them again, jotting down on three-by-five notecards wherever there was something about women; I then sorted the cards according to topic, and voila! "Jesus Was a Feminist"! Jesus never did or said anything negative about women, but on the contrary constantly went out of his way to treat women—in countercultural fashion!—fundamentally as human beings, equal to men, which is the definition of a feminist. That secret for almost two thousand years was simply hiding in plain sight!

The third step is at once similar and more controversial, as well as more inchoative, and therefore leaves more work to be done by future scholars. I am talking about my claim here that the information we have about Jesus is so massively dependent on Jesus's women followers, that without it we would have no Christianity. To put the same assertion positively, the women followers of Jesus created Christianity! As I recently again pored over the Gospels, and the rest of the New Testament, I had something of a combined déjà vu and eureka experience, realizing just how much about Jesus we know only because women experienced his—especially for them—liberating life and teaching, and therefore their hearts and memories were seared by it, and they passed it on in either oral or written form or both! Without Jesus' women followers who experienced, remembered, told, wrote, and promoted what Jesus did and taught, there would be no Christianity!

Before I can turn to the heart of our study here—the Gospels—I first need to lay the groundwork by briefly investigating (1) the naming of Jesus, (2) the meaning of sacred Scriptures, and (3) the quest for the historical Jesus.

1

Jesus and Yeshua

WHAT'S IN A NAME?

THE NAME JESUS IS simply a Latin form of the Greek Iesous. Actually Iesous is not originally a Greek name but rather a Greek form of a Hebrew name, Yehoshua (the biblical name Yoshua), which means "YHWH is salvation." (The Hebrew name YHWH, probably pronounced "Yahweh," means "I am who am"; it is God's self-given name from the burning bush story in Exod 3:14.) It is not difficult to see how the name Yehoshua, which in colloquial parlance would sometimes be abbreviated Yeshua or even Yeshu, was transliterated into the Greek name Iesous and the Latin name Jesus. Unfortunately, in the movement of the name Yeshua from its original forms into the various languages used by Christians and others, something important has been lost. First of all, Jews no longer use the name Yeshua, nor indeed do Christians. In fact, both the Hebrew and Greek forms as proper names disappeared from usage after the first century.[1] As a result, both Christians and Jews automatically think of Jesus as the name of someone other than a Jew. This simple fact tends to cut Christians off from the taproot of their religion, the Hebrew-Jewish tradition. On the other side, it also tends to cut Jews off from a very important son of their tradition, one who has become the most influential Jew of all history, surpassing in historical impact even such giants as Moses, David, Marx, Freud, and Einstein.

1. See Foerster, "*Iesous*."

Three Jesus Certitudes

The name *Yeshua* is made up of two parts. The first part, "Ye" is an abbreviated form of the proper name for God in Hebrew, *YHWH*. The second part, *shua*, is the Hebrew word for "salvation." Where the root meaning of the Indo-European words for *salvation* is fullness, wholeness, the root meaning of the Semitic word used here, *shua*, is that of capaciousness, openness. *Salvation* in Semitic languages then means the opposite of being in straits; it means being free in wide open space. This makes it close to, though not precisely the same as, the Indo-European root meaning. The word *salvation*, however, is one that to a large extent been significantly altered in the Christian tradition from its meaning in Israelite religion and its root meaning in Greek and Latin. It has for the most part been given a restricted meaning since the third century CE, namely, that when believers in Jesus Christ die, if they have remained faithful, they will go to heaven. But that is not at all what the word basically means. In its Latin form, *salvatio*, it comes from the root *salus* (the Greek term is *soterion/soteria* from *saos*), meaning "wholeness," "health," or "well-being"; hence, cognates as "salutary," "salute," and "salubrious" in English. The same is true of the Germanic root of the word *Heil*, which adjectively also means "whole," "hale," "healed," "healthy." Indeed, this is also where the English word *holy* comes from. To be holy means to be whole, to lead a healthy, whole, a full life. Further behind the German *Heil* lies the Greek *holos*, meaning of course "healthy," "whole," "holy." When we lead a whole, full life, we are holy, we attain salvation, wholeness, holiness.

The Jewish scholar Geza Vermes confirmed this Semitic understanding of salvation as being current with Yeshua and his contemporaries when he pointed out that they linked together physical and spiritual health: "In the somewhat elastic, but extraordinarily perceptive religious terminology of Jesus and the spiritual men of his age, 'to heal', 'to expel demons' and 'to forgive sins' were interchangeable synonyms."[2]

The name Yeshua, then, means "YHWH is wholeness/salvation"; and the name YHWH is the Hebrew proper name of the one and only God who created everything that exists. (YHWH most probably means "I will be who I will be" rather than "I am who am.") We are so used to the concept of monotheism today that we do not realize what an extraordinary breakthrough this insight was in the history of humankind. It had massive immediate implications for how one related to all other human beings and all reality.

---

2. Vermes, *Jesus and the World of Judaism*, 10.

If I lived in a nation that had its own god or gods, and all other nations also had their own god or gods, then the ethical rules that were developed by my god's religion would not necessarily be applicable to those persons and things under other gods, and vice versa. Hence, there was not one ethics valid for all human beings and for all the earth—until the insight developed that there was in fact one creator God of all human beings and all reality. So, then, the very name Yeshua is an assertion that YHWH is the source of wholeness for all human beings, for all things. It is a name that carries the very heart of the great contribution of the Israelite people to humanity, ethical monotheism.

Of course many Jewish men were named Yeshua besides Yeshua of Nazareth. However, a special appropriateness lies in the fact that Yeshua of Nazareth was given this name, for it is through him that billions of non-Jews came to the Jewish insight of ethical monotheism, came to YHWH, came to salvation, wholeness.

For all these reasons I will in this reflection use the original Hebrew name, Yeshua.

UNDERSTANDING SACRED SCRIPTURES

From the earliest history of Christianity, those who understood themselves to be followers of Yeshua (or *Iesous* in Greek or *Jesus* in Latin) felt called by his example to oppose violence. They refused, for example, to be soldiers. However, this widespread commitment to nonviolence, "pacifism," faded quickly after the Roman emperor Constantine declared Christianity licit (via the Edict of Milan in 313 CE), and in practice quickly made the Christian church an effective arm of his Roman Empire, with its military legions fighting to expand and maintain its frontiers. Indeed, a few decades later in 391 CE, Emperor Theodosius declared Christianity the *only* licit religion of the empire! Likewise, the "feminism" of Yeshua was not only forgotten but even vigorously flouted already just a few decades after his death. Hence, the early—and lasting—massive Christian traditions of violence and misogyny in the name of Yeshua present an initial challenge to my biblical claim of Yeshua's pacifism and feminism. How in the face of these very early and very common Christian practices of violence and women's subordination can one claim that pacifism and feminism were indubitable, core values of Yeshua?

Three Jesus Certitudes

This challenge leads me to first lay the groundwork for how we in the twenty-first century can properly study and understand sacred Scriptures, or, indeed, any documents, especially those from ancient foreign cultures in other languages. We must remember that Yeshua was born over two thousand years ago and grew up in a culture very different from that of 99.9 percent of Christians today. Furthermore, his culture was one that the vast majority of contemporary Christians see through the astigmatic lenses of anti-Judaism (religious hatred) and antisemitism (racial hatred). (This nonhyphenated spelling is correct for this nineteenth-century euphemistic neologism meaning "Jew-hatred"; it has nothing to do with other "Semites.") How to correct for that astigmatism and come reasonably close to seeing what Yeshua did and understanding what he said as he meant it (which may not be how the pious clergy and laity during much of Christian history understood it) is what Scripture scholars have been working mightily to make increasingly possible for us during the past two hundred fifty years or more.

Not all religions have sacred scriptures, but many do. In most instances religious traditions were originally in oral form and were transmitted by word of mouth, sometimes for generations. Only later were they committed to writing. Then they were meticulously copied by scribes and other learned members of the religion and often memorized by various adherents. Since it is believed that such holy writings have insights of enormous or even decisive significance for the life of the followers, they had to be applied to concrete situations. This required interpretations as to the meaning of the text. The study of the text and its meaning belong to the oldest known form of religious scholarship.

There were basically two ancient methods of interpretation, which are still widely used by many religious people and leaders: the so-called *literal* and the *allegorical*. Following the so-called literal method meant that the reader or listener would simply take the meaning of the words as commonly understood *at the time when the reading and interpretation was done*. No attempt was made to discover either the "real meaning" as intended by the author, or some metaphorical use of language; generally, the interpreter was satisfied that what met his eye was the real meaning of the text.

Despite its prevalence in at least in some religious traditions, a so-called literal interpretation causes grave difficulties for the religious community. It is proverbially weak in interpreting poetry and mythology or any kind of parabolic or metaphorical use of language. Too frequently the result of a literal reading is that the interpreter reads *into* the text a meaning that seems apparent in the reader's time, or a meaning that is desired, particularly by a method such as cross-referencing (that is, interpreting the meaning of one text by another, which may well be historically much later in origin). Thus, so-called literal understandings of a text are not *ex*egesis (literally, "reading *out*" of a text what the author put into it), but *eis*egesis (literally "reading *into*" a text what is not in the text, but comes from the readers's head). It is also evident that scriptural literalists tend to be very much at odds with one another, depending on how much weight they give to one segment or another of the scripture, which, they maintain is an unchanging, divine text, the divine word. Generally, literal interpretation has also tended to result in a harshly opinionated hardening of lines, resulting in mutual condemnations and excommunications.

The *allegorical* interpretation proceeded from the assumption that in addition to the surface, evident meaning of the text there is also a deeper, often hidden, meaning, or even several layers of meaning, of the text: persons, things, events in the text stand in symbolic fashion for something else. Sometimes very intricate, perhaps even convoluted approaches were developed supposedly in order to get at the "deeper meaning," which, it was said, eludes the casual reader. Many mystics of nearly all religious traditions embraced this allegorical approach. For instance, various Sufi orders of Islam have the tradition by which the *sheikh* or teacher of the order teaches the followers increasingly deeper meanings of the text, which are believed not to be accessible to the uninitiated.

A number of influential historical groups and individuals of various traditions were quite fond of the allegorical method (e.g., Jewish Cabala, Jewish and Christian gnostics, individuals like St. Athanasius and Saint Augustine). For example, both the rabbis and Christian fathers interpreted the Hebrew scriptural text the Song of Songs not as a sensuous wedding poem (which it was) but as an allegory of the love of God (the bridegroom) for God's people (identified as Israel or the Christian church, depending on whether the allegorist was Jewish or Christian).

The allegorical method of interpretation is helpful when dealing with an *intended* allegory or metaphor—as, for example, when Yeshua says, "If your eye offends you, pluck it out!" or when John the Baptist says of Yeshua, "There is the lamb of God" (John 1:36). But the allegorical method distorts the meaning of those texts meant to be taken in a straightforward fashion.

Then the allegory can present a radical departure from the intended meaning of the text.

The Christian Middle Ages specified and named two more ways to understand sacred text, though Christians were not the first or only ones to use them: the *anagogical* and *tropological* understandings of a text. Both understandings had more to do with the then-contemporary reader of the sacred text than with the author's intended meaning in the text's original *con*-text.

The *anagogical* meaning (from the Greek, "to lead up") is the "higher," "spiritual" meaning of the text as understood and applied by a *contemporary* reader. The *tropological* sense (from the Greek, "transferred meaning") is the *moral* meaning of the text as understood and applied by the *contemporary* reader. Clearly if a sacred text is to have any influence on later people's lives, it will have to be applied to the contemporary situation, and that is what these methods of interpretation attempted to do. The danger involved in them is that the original text can be gravely distorted in meaning. Instead of being an *ex*egesis, such a method of interpretation can very easily become an *eis*egesis; instead of being a *drawing out* of the meaning in the text, it can easily become a *reading in* of an extraneous meaning not at all in the text.

Historical criticism studies the historical circumstances that surrounded the writing of the text, but also places under historical scrutiny the claims of the content of the text. This means that a careful study is undertaken of the conditions existing at the time when the text was written, which helps provide a more accurate sense of why and when the author wrote.

It should be noted that there is a great difference in the way ancient historians recorded the past and the way modern scholarly historians practice their craft. Professor Lawrence Boadt provided the following comparison chart:[3]

A Comparison of Ancient and Modern Methods of Recording Historical Events

Ancient Israelite Historian	*Modern Scientific Historian*
Records the traditions of the tribe or nation as they interpret them.	Attempts to reconstruct past events objectively and accurately.
Uses oral sources with few written records or lists.	Relies on documents and written records almost exclusively.

3. Boadt, *Reading the Old Testament*, 57.

Ancient Israelite Historian	Modern Scientific Historian
Often includes several parallel versions of the same story.	Sorts out the conflicting accounts in order to find the single original one.
Does not have much exact information of dates and places, and so gives rough approximations.	Carefully searches out the correct chronology of events.
Relies strongly on fixed types of literary descriptions or motifs that can be applied to all similar situations.	Seeks to get behind literary genres, narrative modes to learn out what truly happened.
Uses a common-sense approach to describing human behavior and does not guarantee every fact.	Uses all the critical tools and means of information to check sources and their claims.
Uses past history to explain convictions for the present time or for a particular point of view.	Writes history without special bias or undue emphasis on only one side of the picture.a

Literary criticism relies on a series of methods that helps determine the origin (author, date, place), purpose, composition, style, plan of writing, and content of a specific text. We can discern *source, form, redaction, audience, criticism*, and several others. I will look briefly only at these four.[4]

Source criticism is one of the oldest critical approaches. It is a tool by which scholars are able to decipher whether there are earlier written documents on the basis of which the present text was composed and how and when a text was composed. It has been discovered that in many instances the version of a text that survived was composed from several earlier sources that the last author or editor wove together. In the ancient past it was not customary to acknowledge the existence of previous sources or their authorship. Source criticism makes it possible to hypothetically reconstruct the process of composition, separate the different sources, and date them (though authorship usually remains anonymous). The need for source criticism arose when it was evident that a given text contained contradictory styles of writing and data or repetitions appearing side by side.

A clear example of a relationship between a later document and an earlier one—in this case of the "Old" Testament on the "New" Testament—is the prayer uttered by Mary, the mother of Jesus, often named by the initial word of Saint Jerome's Latin translation: *Magnificat* (Luke 1:46–55).

---

4. Further detailed information can be found in Swidler and Mojzes, *The Study of Religion*.

It has been shown to be an amazing paraphrase of the Song of Hannah (1 Sam 2:11–20).

Form criticism. Scholars studied the customary forms in which content is packaged. Messages come in distinct forms; a business letter differs from a love letter, which in turn differs from a greeting sent to friends while vacationing. Form critics were able to distinguish between miracle stories, parables, pronouncements, speeches, laws, short stories, myths, legends, and so forth. It is essential that one distinguish the form a message takes in order to understand the message accurately.

Form critics have also pointed out that the ancients used mythological forms to convey profound truths and values, and that consequently those ancient texts will be completely misunderstood if they are mistakenly interpreted in a literal manner. Thus form critics have led the attempt to figure out for contemporaries the profound message cast in ancient mythological language by explaining its meaning in contemporary language. Such processes have helped us understand that myths are not lies or primitive understandings of phenomena from people with no scientific knowledge, as was once thought. Thanks to form critics, we have become aware that mythological language is sometimes the most appropriate vehicle for transmitting profound insights: this may be as true today as when the myth was created.

Redaction criticism. *Redactor* is another word for "editor." Redaction criticism points out that the editors were not merely collectors of source material, but were selectors and arrangers of the material according to some consistent internal principle that they promoted in their final work. Such editors had a distinct purpose and audience in mind. For instance, Yeshua gave a sermon, which in Matthew's Gospel was delivered "on a mountain," and hence is famously known as the Sermon on the Mount. However, according to Luke's Gospel, Jesus delivered the sermon "on the plain." A comedian might ask, where is the gospel truth! The answer was discerned by redaction criticism. The author of Matthew's Gospel clearly from his heavily Hebraic Greek and from the fact that he alone time and again writes, "this was done to fulfill what the prophet said," was a very learned Jew writing for Jews who knew the Torah. Matthew was telling his Jewish readers that just as Moses taught the Jewish people from a mountain (Sinai) how to live, so too Yeshua was teaching the Jewish people how to live—from a mountain! Matthew did not have to say that Yeshua was a new Moses; he needed only place Yeshua on a mountain to give his core teaching—the Sermon on the Mount! Luke wrote in Grecian Greek, and could not assume that his readers would know the Torah. So, he had no reason to locate Yeshua on a mountaintop to deliver his key teaching—the Sermon on the Plain!

Audience criticism asks the question: What did the terms, images, and such in a document mean to the *audience* for whom the document was originally intended? The answer can make a huge difference in understanding the text. For example, Yeshua is referred to as the "son of God" in the Gospels. *Audience criticism* asks whether that term was intended the way Hellenistic Gentiles would have understood it (that is, to designate a supernatural being) or as Jews and those under Jewish influence would have understood it (that is, to designate someone who lived according to God's will) so that as the Jew Yeshua said to other Jews, "That you may become sons of your Father in heaven" (Matt 5:45).

Since the Gospels were written almost entirely for Jews or those attracted to Judaism, for everywhere Paul, Barnabas or other missionaries went to preach the "good news of Yeshua" (as the term "gospel," from the Anglo-Saxon *Gutspiel*, means), they always went to the synagogues, the correct answer here obviously is that the reference in the Gospels to Yeshua as the "son of God" was understood (by the Jewish *audience*) in the Jewish manner, as designating someone who lived according to God's will, and not in the Hellenistic manner as a supernatural being.

YESHUA, THE SOURCE OF CHRISTIANITY

Most adherents of a religion are born into it. However, with the rise of modernity with its focus on freedom and critical thinking, which is greatly fostered by the mass education that modernity has generated, more and more people are choosing whether or not to believe and practice a religion, and with what degree of intensity. Thus, for example, the more fully human I become, the more I must *consciously* choose whether or not I will be a Christian.

If I am going to choose to be a Christian, the first thing I need to do is to clarify for myself what it is I am choosing. In the past, the contours of the choice to be a Christian were pretty well drawn out for us—first by our parents, and then as we grew older, by our teachers and priests or ministers. We were told in greater or lesser detail that *this* is what *the church* teaches. With modernity, however, and the rise of the importance of our thinking and deciding for ourselves, whether in government (democracy) or work and business (capitalism), we increasingly learned that we are a generation of humanity who has "come of age," as Pope St. John XXIII put it. His successor, Pope Paul VI, noted that dialogue "is demanded by the pluralism of society and the *maturity man has reached* in this day and age. Be he religious or not, his secular education has enabled him to think and speak."[5]

So, an obvious question any thinking Christian, or would-be Christian, has to put to her- or himself is this: What is the foundation, the starting point of Christianity? When one thinks through the unquestioned childhood answers that were given unrequested and thereafter remained largely unchallenged, the many answers all come down to a single point in the end: Yeshua (who, of course, was called Jesus), who lived in Israel some two thousand years ago.

Now this may seem a simple and straightforward answer to an obvious question. However, if followed through seriously, it leads to serious questioning concerning many of the doctrines "born" Christians were taught, and therefrom many of practices. First, one notices that the word *Christ* is simply an English translation of a Greek translation (*Christos*) of a Hebrew term, Messiah (*Meshiach*), which indeed means an anointed person who has been given a very special social responsibility, such as the king or queen. In this case, the Messiah was to be given by God the responsibility of driving the occupying forces of Rome out of Judea and reestablishing the kingdom of Israel. That is why the Roman governor, Pilate, asked Yeshua whether he was a king, and had him executed as one—with a sign over his cross "written in Hebrew, Latin, and Greek" (John 19:19): it read, *Yeshua ha Notzri Melek Yehudim*; *Iesus Nazarenus Rex Iudaeorum*; *Iesous ho Nazoraios ho Baseleus ton Ioudaion*; Jesus of Nazareth King of the Jews.

So, then, just who and what was Jesus, Yeshua? The question is simple, but the answer will be extremely difficult to work out. The problem is that almost the only information we have about Yeshua comes from the four canonical Gospels in the New Testament, and, despite their prima facie appearance, they are not biographies or histories of Yeshua. Rather, they are essays written by second- or third-generation followers of Yeshua, built on various sources, and each oriented toward specific missionizing goals (more of that below).

I am not going to try to present here a thorough analysis of contemporary biblical scholarship. Rather, I will attempt to present what I consider

---

5 Pope Paul VI's first encyclical in 1965: *Ecclesiam suam*, no. 9 (italics added).

a reasonable analysis and consequent conclusions of what I find in today's New Testament scholarship. I will not, e.g., detail the scholarly arguments that a particular gospel was written at one extreme (in 55 CE) or that another Gospel was written at another extreme (in 140 CE). I will stay with the scholarly consensus. All the texts of all the books of the Bible, as well as the apocryphal biblical writings, and a bewildering wealth of interpretative material, can now be found on line in a compilation by Peter Kirby at www.earlychristianwritings.com/, as well as at www.earlyjewishwritings.com/.

Saul/Paul Is of Little Help in Finding Yeshua

Unfortunately, the oldest writings in the New Testament, those of St. Paul (Saul) of Tarsus, said hardly anything about Yeshua but spoke almost exclusively of *Christos*. Paul never met Yeshua, though he met many of the principal eyewitnesses of Yeshua. And yet, Paul, with one tiny exception, never passes on any of the teachings of Yeshua, nor does he write of any of Yeshua's life actions other than his crucifixion (which of course is not really an action *of* Yeshua but what happened *to* Yeshua) and thereafter his being raised up *by* God. As I said, Paul's focus was almost exclusively on the title *Christos*, which most often he fills with otherworldly, cosmic meaning.

From Paul one never learns that Yeshua spent his adult life studying (possibly with the two great rabbis, Shammai and Hillel), and then as a rabbi (teacher) himself. As I wrote over a quarter of a century ago:

> The deaths of Hillel and Shammai are placed around the year 10 CE and 30 CE, respectively, and the birth of Yeshua around 4 BCE. If these dates are reasonably accurate, it is even possible that Yeshua sat at the feet of either Hillel or Shammai themselves or both, especially when one recalls that Jewish lads came of age religiously and otherwise at the age of twelve. That Yeshua was already steeped in religious learning by that age is recorded in Luke 2:40–52, where it is said that Yeshua was filled with wisdom and that he spent three days with the rabbis (*didaskalon*, "teacher," which is the term Luke uses here, is of course what *rabbi* means and is the Greek translation for *rabbi* used throughout the Gospels in general) discussing religious matters with them and astonishing them [did the "them" include either or both Hillel and Shammai?] with his answers.[6]

---

6. Swidler, *Yeshua*, 46.

However, in the four Gospels, especially the first three, the so-called Synoptics (Greek: "with the same viewpoint"), being a rabbi, a teacher, was mostly what Yeshua was. How could such an important communicator of "Christianity" as Paul not pass on what most other followers of Yeshua experienced him as? The answer seems to be that Paul was bowled over by his own experience of the crucified Yeshua's resurrection rather than by Yeshua's teaching and modeling actions (neither of which he experienced). Most of the other writers of the New Testament were focused on the latter. Doubtless Saul/Paul was a "Hebrew of the Hebrews," as he himself claims (Phil 3:5), but he was also an educated Hellenist, at home in that culture. It seems quite likely that the Greco-Roman mental world with its focus on the cosmic context of the gods and a "divine" Roman emperor influenced him to interpret his "encounter" with the risen Lord on the road to Damascus in a way both sympathetic to and symbiotic with the Hellenistic world. (Tellingly, Paul addresses the one he sees on the road as *Kyrios*—"Lord"—not *Didaskalos*—"Teacher" or "Rabbi" [Acts 9:4].) In any case, we cannot look to Paul and his writings to learn much more about Yeshua other than that he was crucified and subsequently raised up to a life with God.

A few shadowy allusions to the historical Yeshua appear in some of Paul's letters. In addition, there are numerous Pauline references to Christ or Jesus Christ or Christ Jesus, which are not even shadowy reflections of the historical Yeshua but theologized implications of what, not Yeshua, but rather *Christos*, meant to Paul. For the sake of completeness, I will gather the "shadowy" historical allusions, and a sampling of the theologizations together here.

Paul's "Allusions" to the Historical Yeshua[7]

Shadowy Historical Allusions

1 Corinthians 7:10–11. "I enjoin, yet, not I but the Lord that a woman not separate from her husband." Paul, like many subsequent Christian Scripture scholars, seemed to have been unaware of the rabbinic dispute I discuss below, but nevertheless nullified what he mistakenly thought was the teaching

---

[7] I am deeply grateful to Professor Peter Spitaler, chair of the theology department of Villanova University, for the references to the following Pauline material and a splendid analysis of contemporary Pauline scholarship on the subject.

of Yeshua, that there could never be divorce and remarriage, a little later in 7:12: "I, not the Lord, say, . . ."

Romans 9:5. When writing of the Israelites, Paul says it is from them that "the Christ [not Yeshua or Jesus or even the *messias* in Greek, but *ho christos*] came according to the flesh."

Romans 15:3. "For Christ [not really simply *christos*, but **ho** *christos*, *the* christ] did not please himself."

Galatians 3:1. "O foolish Galatians . . . to whose eyes Jesus Christ was presented as having been crucified."

Galatians 4:6. "God has sent the spirit of his son into our hearts, crying Abba, Father." This repetition of the Hebrew and Greek, Abba, Pater, which appears in the much later-written Gospels, must have already by the time Paul was writing in the 50s been a cliche associated with the historical Yeshua.

1 Corinthians 11:23–26. "For I received from the Lord what I also handed on to you, that the Lord Jesus on the night he was betrayed took a loaf of bread . . . Do it in memory of me." Already by Paul's time—long before they were written down in the three Synoptic Gospels—these words uttered by Yeshua at the "last supper" had been memorialized, turned into liturgical formulae, and passed on.

Theologizations

Romans 3:24–25. "Christ Jesus whom God put forth as an atonement through faith."

Galatians 3:13. "Christ redeemed us from the curse of the law by becoming a curse for us."

2 Corinthians 5:21. "For our sake he made him to be sin who knew no sin, so that in him we might become the righteousness of God."

2 Corinthians 8:9. "Our Lord Jesus Christ, though he was rich, for your sakes became poor so that by his poverty you might become rich."

If these shadowy allusions to the historical Yeshua are the sum total of what Paul in his letters records of the historical Yeshua, and the rest of his references to Yeshua are all his *Christos* theologizations, then this review of the Pauline record reinforces all the more my conclusion that we cannot look to Paul for any significant historical information about Yeshua.

Roger Haight, SJ, summed up the relationship between the preaching of Paul and the Gospels thus: "A sense of historicity is leading theologians and Christians generally to put more stock in the saving power of Jesus' public career and ministry, in contrast to the almost exclusively dogmatic Pauline concentration of the dynamics and power of salvation in Jesus' death."[8]

The Quest for the Historical Jesus

The First Quest for the Historical Jesus

Learning in the West began to revive in the High Middle Ages, and continued to advance in the centuries of the Renaissance, and burst dramatically forth in the seventeenth-century scientific revolution, followed by the eighteenth-century Enlightenment. It was especially then that the new scientific mentality began to be applied more and more broadly to the understanding of ancient scriptures, in particular the Bible. An early major voice in this biblical scholarship was Hermann Reimarus (1694–1768). His work in this area—*Apologie oder Schutzschrift für die vernünftigen Verehrer Gottes (Apology for Devout Devotees of God)*—was, out of fear, published only posthumously by a colleague, Gotthold Lessing. Thinkers began to seek for a more scientifically based picture of the historical figure of Yeshua ha Notzri, underneath the church doctrine and tradition and the beliefs about him often expressed in significant portions of the New Testament. It was very much this burgeoning "quest for the historical Jesus" that drove the development of the scholarly tools to better understand ancient documents, particularly the Bible.

The eighteenth century gave birth not only to the so-called Age of Reason, the Enlightenment, but also to a growing interest, as noted above, in writing history based on rational, scientific principles. This movement only grew stronger in the nineteenth century, led especially by German scholars such as Leopold von Ranke—known as the father of scientific history—(1795–1886), who strove to research and write history *wie es eigentlich gewesen*, "as it really was"! This led to a many-decades-long battle among scholars about the "historical" Jesus; of those who used the newly developing historical techniques, some made claims that Jesus never really existed whereas others composed full "lives" of Jesus. This quest for the

---

8. Haight, *Jesus, Symbol of God*, 58. Elisabeth Schüssler Fiorenza also indicates that Paul's conception of God must be subordinated to that of Yeshua's (see *In Memory of Her*, 101).

historical Jesus came to a clamorous end in 1906 with the book *The Quest for the Historical Jesus* (*Geschichte der Leben-Jesu-Forschung*) by the famed scholar Albert Schweitzer (1875–1965), who claimed that it is impossible to get behind the "Christ of faith" to reach the "Jesus of history." He was confirmed by the somewhat younger, widely influential scholar Rudolf Bultmann (1884–1978), whose house I visited in Marburg in the late '60s and whose daughter served me tea. (Bultmann and his wife were away on vacation.) Bultmann proceeded to say, not only can we never reach the Jesus of history, but we do not even need to! The gospel, the "good news," is simply God's call, "proclamation" (*kerygma*) to humanity, which we must "demythologize" and rearticulate in contemporary language (which Bultmann took to be then current existentialist philosophy). Thus ended the *first* quest for the historical Jesus.

The Second Quest for the Historical Jesus

Subsequently the modern quest lay relatively dormant for almost half a century, until 1953, when Bultmann's prize pupil, Ernst Käsemann (1906–1998), launched the *second* quest for the historical Jesus with his inaugural address, "The Problem of the Historical Jesus," at the University of Marburg. (Käsemann also later taught at my alma mater, the University of Tübingen.) Contrary to his *Doktorvater*, Rudolf Bultmann, he claimed that, we can learn to know the historical figure Yeshua behind the Christ of faith. In his inaugural address Käsemann laid out several principles that would allow contemporary readers of the Gospels to discern which words and actions most likely should be attributed neither to contemporary Jewish culture and beliefs nor to the nascent Christian church but to the historical figure of Yeshua. These serious, scientific principles found immediate, widespread reception among scholars and were quickly applied, and even augmented.

The most prominent of such criteria included the following: (1) the criterion of discontinuity, (2) the criterion of embarrassment, (3) the criterion of multiple attestation, (4) the criterion of coherence, and (5) the criterion of linguistic suitability.

The criterion of *discontinuity* (sometimes referred to as the criterion of double discontinuity) is that if Yeshua is cited as saying or doing something that from other evidence is known to reflect the Jewish culture of the time or what the early Christian church fostered, then the likelihood of its stemming from Yeshua is called into question. However, if the saying or action of Yeshua is contrary to both, then it should be attributed to the authentic Yeshua. Yeshua's repeated prowoman statements and actions are prominent examples of words and deeds that were directly opposed to the Jewish customs of the time[9] and also that were massively denied by the early Christian church (more about this below).

The second criterion, that of *embarrassment*, is similar but not precisely the same. If something is attributed to Yeshua—either action or saying—that would be an embarrassment, especially to the Christian church, then it very likely really does stem from Yeshua. An example of something that passes the criterion of embarrassment is the story about the woman caught in adultery and dragged before Yeshua to be condemned. (He didn't condemn her!) In our Bibles today the story is found in John 8:31–41. However, the story is not found in the oldest manuscripts of the New Testament. As a result of diligent detective work on the part of a generation of "scientific" biblical scholars, it is clear that the story was originally located in Luke's Gospel (after Luke 21:38), where it fits perfectly, but was torn out and eventually later stuck in John, where it doesn't fit; nevertheless, it was thereby saved for posterity. The story of Yeshua not condemning adultery was apparently too embarrassing for many early Christians to stomach and pass on—but others later on couldn't stomach completely suppressing what appeared to them, nevertheless, to be something Yeshua actually did.

The third criterion, that of *multiple attestation*, comes into play when words or actions are attributed to Yeshua in several different places. For example, Yeshua was said to be executed by crucifixion (not stoning, the traditional Jewish form) in the early letters of Paul (who apparently died in the 50s) and in the Gospel of Mark (written around 70) and in the Fourth Gospel (which scholars largely agree was written independently of Mark, and much later, around the year 100).

The fourth criterion, that of *coherence*, asserts that if some action or statement fits together with (coheres with) another statement or action of Yeshua already affirmed as authentic, the parallel statements or actions are also judged proportionately authentic.

The fifth criterion, that of *linguistic suitability* affirms the authenticity of a statement attributed to Yeshua if it makes sense in Aramaic. For example, in Matt 16:18 Yeshua says to Peter, "You are Peter, and upon this rock I will build my community." To those of us who speak a Teutonic-rooted language, like the Scandinavian, German, and English languages,

---

9. See Swidler, *Status of Women in Formative Judaism*.

the statement doesn't make any sense. However, what the Greek New Testament has as *petros* ("rock"), in Aramaic is *kepha* ("rock"). There was obviously a wordplay here where Yeshua said to Simon: "You are *Petros/Kepha* ("Rocky"), and upon this *petros/kepha* ("rock") will I build my community." The wordplay works not only in Aramaic and Greek, but, fortunately for Western Christendom, also in Saint Jerome's Vulgate Latin: *Tu es Petros et super hanc petram aedificabo ecclesian meam* (printed in massive letters in the apse of Saint Peter's Basilica in Rome).

New Testament scholars of the '50s and '60s developed more criteria for specifying scientifically from the Gospels the actions and sayings of the historical Jesus. These scholars rounded out the second quest for the historical Jesus.

However, two changes occurred in the 1960s that drastically changed the scholarly landscape of Jesus scholarship. The first change came with the Second Vatican Council (1962–1965) and its decree called *Nostra Aetate*, which signaled a change in the attitude of the Roman Catholic Church toward Jews and Judaism. Abandoning a long-standing and pervasive anti-Judaism (and even a level of antisemitism), with the Second Vatican Council the Catholic Church made a serious commitment to dialogue with Jews and Judaism.

The second change also began to occur starting in the middle 1960s. Jews finally began to publicly talk among themselves, and then also with Christians, about the horrors of the Holocaust. Christians met this talk with an insistence that such a horror could never again even be conceived (let alone de facto carried out) in the then most highly educated Christianized country in the world. (Germany had invented the PhD and before that the Holy Roman Empire of the German People.)

The Third Quest for the Historical Jesus

This then led to the launching of the third quest for the historical Jesus. One of the negative results of applying the criterion of dissimilarity vis a vis the contemporary Jewish culture was that it tended to pull Yeshua out of his Jewish culture. Thus, for example, even though Yeshua was addressed as Rabbi, that fact tended to be suppressed because the New Testament was written not in one of the Semitic languages Yeshua spoke—Hebrew or Aramaic—but in Greek (which functioned then in the Roman Empire as a lingua franca, much as English does today around the world). Hence,

Three Jesus Certitudes

whenever in the Gospels Yeshua is addressed as Rabbi (which in Hebrew/Aramaic means "My Master," or "Teacher"), the Greek term *didaskolous* ("master" or "teacher") is used. As a result, a gospel reader in a modern language, or even in the New Testament's Greek, does not time and time again hear or see that Yeshua was addressed as Rabbi, addressed as a Jew.

Hence, with the Christian turn toward dialogue with Jews and Judaism, and likewise Jewish engagement in dialogue with Christians, the third quest for the historical Jesus burst forth, continues to the present day, and doubtless will on into the future. Consequently Christian scholars are increasingly striving to perceive and understand Yeshua precisely as Jewish—which he really was!—for Yeshua did not reject being a rabbi, did not reject Judaism. All that rejection happened later, not by his apostles, not by Paul, not by Mary Magdalene, not by Yeshua's mother Mary, not by his brother James—but by later Christians.

In an amazing way, this new quest was led by Jewish scholars, a growing number of whom made themselves into New Testament scholars.[10] They argued that the criterion of dissimilarity should not alienate Yeshua from Judaism: "The fact that he [Yeshua] often presented a contrast with his milieu also makes him Jewish, for I know of no luminary of Judaism from Moses onwards who did not provoke lively opposition from among the Jewish people."[11]

In fact, as the Jewish New Testament scholar Pinchas Lapide stated starkly,

> His people did not reject Jesus.
> Jesus did not reject his people![12]

Christian (and Jewish) scholars began to see that the only correct way to understand Yeshua was to see him as the rabbi, the Jew, that he was. Hence, more and more Christian scholars began to take the study of things Jewish, including early rabbinic writings such as the Targumim, Mishnah, Tosefta, and Talmud seriously, as well as archeological information.

The attempt was and continues to be made to study the historical Jewish context of the first century, and *then* to try to understand Yeshua within it. Quite a stunningly different Yeshua stands forth against this

---

10. See Homolka, *Jesus Reclaimed*; Homolka, *Jesus von Nazareth*.

11. Küng and Lapide, *Brother of the Lord?*, 25. I was fortunate early in my career to become good friends of both Hans Küng and Pinchas Lapide (and even translate some of their work into English). This doubtless influenced my subsequent scholarship.

12. Lapide and Luz, *Jesus in Two Perspectives*

background, than what many Christians saw before. For example, in the past, many Christians attempted to portray Judaism as a religion of wrath and harsh judgment, and the religion of the Christian Jesus as one of love. After all, Christians traditionally pointed out that according to Matthew's Gospel (Matt 22:34), when Yeshua was asked about the greatest commandments, he said that they were *love* of God and *love* of neighbor—go and practice (Luke 10:28). Amazingly, these Christian scholars, and the average teachers around the world who followed them, somehow did not notice that in Luke's Gospel it was not Yeshua who uttered those two greatest commandments, but the questioning Jewish lawyer (Luke 10:27)! Further, those two commandments were simply quotations from the much earlier Jewish Scriptures—the Torah (Lev 19:18; Deut 6:5)! Still further, it was not even the Matthew's Yeshua (or Luke's lawyer) who first linked the two commandments together. Already over a hundred years before, several different Jewish writers specifically linked the two together![13]

Christian scholarship, often aided by Jewish scholarship, since the 1980s increasingly, then, has been vigorously pursuing this third quest for the historical Jesus. I offer one of my own books from the 1980s as an example of the early part of this quest: *Yeshua: A Model for Moderns*.[14] My Jewish New Testament scholar friend Pincus Lapide wrote this in the foreword to the German version of this book: "Here is a masterwork that finally deals seriously with the three facts about the Nazarene which until now have been largely dismissed as theologically irrelevant in Christianity: His 'true humanity,' his being a fully believing and practicing Jew, and, not least, despite his being raised to be the Christ for the Gentile Church, in light of the unredeemed reality of this world, his not being the awaited Messiah of the Jews."[15] To this I finally add a quotation from another contemporary

---

13. These linkages are found in various of the Pseudepigrapha (noncanonical Jewish writings in Greek): "Love the Lord and the neighbor" (*Testament of Issachar* 5:2); "I loved the Lord and every human being with my whole heart" (*Testament of Issachar* 7:6); "Love the Lord in your whole life and one another with a sincere heart" (*Testament of Dan* 5:3); "Fear the Lord and love the neighbor" (*Testament of Benjamin* 3:3); "And he commanded them to keep to the way of God, do justice, and everyone love his/her neighbor" (*Jubilees* 20:9); "Love one another my sons as brothers, as one loves oneself . . . You should love one another as yourselves" (*Jubilees* 36:4).

14. Swidler, *Yeshua: A Model for Moderns*. In this book I made heavy use of Jewish New Testament scholars, including Vermes, *Jesus and the World of Judaism*; and Sigal, *The Halakhah of Jesus of Nazareth*.

15. Lapide, "Vorwort," 5.

Three Jesus Certitudes

Jewish scholar, Schalom Ben-Chorin, as Christian and Jewish evidence of the third quest for the historical Jesus:

> Jesus is for me an eternal brother—not only my human brother, but my *Jewish brother*. I sense his brotherly hand clasping mine and asking me to follow him. It is not the hand of the Messiah, this hand marked by a wound; it is certainly *no divine hand*. It is rather a *human* hand, in whose lines the deepest sorrow is inscribed.... His belief, his unconditional belief, his simple trust in God the Father, his willingness to humble himself completely before the will of God—that is the attitude of which Jesus is the supreme example, the attitude that joins us, Jews and Christians, together. The belief *of* Jesus unifies us, the belief *in* Jesus divides us.[16]

It is in that context that we will now proceed to look for the evidence of these two stereotypically Yesuanic characteristics: pacifism and feminism.

---

16. I was fortunate to be able to hear Schalom Ben-Chorin lecture, in German, at the University of Tübingen and later have a lengthy lunch conversation with him alone. It was in a summer during the 1980s, when I was doing some research at Tübingen and I saw the posters around the university for his forthcoming lecture. I went at the appointed time to the largest lecture hall in the university, only to find that it had already been jammed for the lecture before (which normally was sparsely peopled), but I made use of my hutzpah and stood near the lectern in the front. Ben-Chorin came in the hall a bit breathless, saying that he had just come from the airport in Stuttgart where all his luggage had been lost, including his formally written-out lecture—so would the audience please forgive him for having to speak extemporaneously. He then proceeded to deliver a stunning lecture (auf deutsch, natürlich) for the next hour and half—which was answered with a roaring standing ovation.

2

Yeshua
Nonviolence and Pacifism

GOSPEL EVIDENCE

ONE DOCUMENTED HISTORICAL CERTITUDE about Yeshua was his strong commitment to peace and nonviolence. Yes, he preached and taught in favor of the excluded, the poor, women, the despised, and children, but he did not do so by way of fomenting an armed rebellion. In fact, he chided the armed guards who came to arrest him, saying, "Am I leading a rebellion that you have come out with swords and clubs to capture me?" (Mark 14:48) He definitely was *not* the Messiah (the "Anointed One"—that is, the specially marked one) expected by many of the Jews of that time, including several of his own apostles. (The two I mean here are Simon the Zealot and Judas Iscariot, who was apparently a member of the *Sicarii*, a group of rebels even more violent than the Zealots.[1]) For the Messiah's role was to throw out the hated Roman occupiers and reestablish the kingdom of Israel, presumably by force: "Our hope had been that he would be the one who would *set Israel free*" (Luke 24:21)—which effort, in fact led eventually to the crushing of Israel and the destruction of Jerusalem by the Romans in 70 CE, and again in 115 CE, and yet again in 135 CE!

---

1. *Sicar* meant "hidden dagger," so in this case, "Judas Iscariot" meant something like "Switchblade Jude."

Three Jesus Certitudes

The ancient Jewish nation—or rather, the ancient Israelite nation—was like all other ancient nations, much given to violent warfare. Israel reached its greatest expansion under the kingship of Solomon in the ninth century BCE—only subsequently to split into two kingdoms: Israel in the north (including ten of the twelve tribes descendent from the twelve sons of Jacob, nicknamed Israel, "one who wrestles with God") and Judea in the south (the tribes of Benjamin and Judah). In the eighth century BCE Israel sided with Egypt in a war against Assyria, lost, and was largely dragged off into exile (giving rise to the phrase "the ten lost tribes of Israel"). A hundred-plus years later, Judea made a similar miscalculation to Israel's alliance with Egypt and so was dragged into exile by the Babylonians—only to be allowed by Babylon's Persian conqueror, Cyrus, to reestablish the subordinate nation of Judea seventy years later. Then the whole of the Near East was conquered by Alexander the Great around 330 BCE, and remained under "Greek" rule until Judea once again broke free in 167 BCE under the Maccabees. This independence again gave way to outside rule, this time within the expansive Roman Empire when Judea was conquered by Pompey in 63 BCE and remained part of the Roman Empire until conquered in the seventh century by Arab Muslims.

However, by the first century of the Common Era Jews were not located only in Judea. In fact, Salo Baron has judged that the population of the Roman Empire at that time was about one hundred million, of which perhaps eight million people were Jews, and of that number perhaps one and a half million lived in Judea, with the other six-and-a-half million scattered throughout the rest of the Roman Empire from the Persian Gulf to Scotland.

The messianic vision of Jewish political independence in the Holy Land and elsewhere led not only to the death of Yeshua but also to many, many millions of violent deaths—mostly of Jews, but also of hundreds of thousands of others at the hands of Jews—in the subsequent single century after the death of Yeshua. The bloodiest of the violent outbreaks occurred even before the first gospel was written, in the years 66–73 CE, in Judea and Galilea. The number of Jews killed by vicious infighting was almost as high as the number killed by Romans. Rage and violence seemed like rampant weeds scattered everywhere in the Jewish world at that time. Even though the Jewish historian Josephus reports that one million, one hundred thousand were killed in that first of the three Jewish-Roman wars, in the years 115–117 CE hundreds of thousands of Jews throughout the eastern half of the Roman Empire rampaged in rebellion from Libya, to Alexandria (the largest Jewish city in the world at that time) to the eastern Mediterranean islands, to the Near East and to Judea, killing hundreds of thousands of non-Jews, and suffering like casualties in the Kitos Wars. Not yet having exhausted the drive toward violence, the Jews of Judea rose up once more against Roman rule (130–135 CE) and violently established a messianic kingdom under Bar Kokhba (proclaimed the messiah by Rabbi Akiba in 132 CE), only to be once again crushed by Roman legions, with more hundreds of thousands of victims.

No Jews or Romans, of course, could foresee that bloody century to come in the year of Yeshua's violent execution around 30 CE, and so it was that Yeshua was thought then by many to be the future king of a Roman-free Israel. This was clearly the hope of the large crowd that welcomed him triumphantly into Jerusalem, shouting, "Hosanna! Blessed . . . is the *king of Israel!*" (John 12:13) just a few days before his Roman execution; perhaps the crowd itself triggered Yeshua's execution.

However, Yeshua had other thoughts, for he told the Roman ruler Pilate that "my kingdom is not of this world" (John 18:36), though eventually Pilate nevertheless had him crucified and had a sign nailed overhead saying that the crucified was Iesus Nazarenus Rex Iudaeorum (Jesus of Nazareth, King of the Jews).

Yeshua also told Pilate that were his kingdom of this world, he would have had legions of supporters fighting for him; but no, as I noted, Yeshua told Pilate, "My kingdom is not of this world." And to his followers who tried by the sword to prevent his being arrested, Yeshua said, "Put up your sword. Those who live by the sword shall die by the sword." (Matt 26:52). Further, he famously said, "Blessed are the peacemakers; for they shall be called the children of God" (Matt 5:9), and again, "Peace I leave with you, my peace I give unto you; not as the world gives, do I give you" (John 14:27).

It is difficult to know what Yeshua had in mind when on the one hand he constantly preached the arrival of the *basileia tou Theou* (the kingdom, or, better, the *reign* of God), and what he hoped would happen that last week of his life when he made his grand entrance into Roman-controlled Jerusalem, jam-packed with Jews from all over the world to celebrate the Passover, the memorial of Jewish *freedom* from their ancient Egyptian oppressors. Pilate had the reputation of executing any and all even vaguely potential "messiahs" or troublemakers. (The Gospels, all written after the devastating destruction of Israel by the Roman legions in 70 CE, paint Pilate in unwarrantedly gentle hues.) The Roman-appointed Jewish chief priests were thought of as quislings (and were largely liquidated by the Zealots and Sicarii in the 66–70 rebellion) anxious to repress any potential tumult: "It was Caiaphas who counseled the Jews that it was expedient that one man should die for the people" (John 18:14).

Yeshua obviously did not want to mount an armed insurrection, and he equally was not "sacrilegiously" planning his own suicide. Did he hope that the thugish Pilate would be replaced by a more just Roman governor? We have no evidence that he was thinking directly politically. Rather, he looked forward to a grassroots *inner* transformation of the rich and poor alike into becoming "poor in *spirit*" (*anawim* in Hebrew): that is, detached from both material property, and its lack—but with at least a minimum justice for all, especially the poor.

In brief, then, Yeshua was *not* intent on preaching the bringing in of the *basileia tou* **Israel**, the kingdom of **Israel**, but of the *basileia tou* **Theou**, the reign of **God**. Yeshua was focused on the *basileia* within/among you (*he basileia tou theou* **entos hymon** *estin*: "the reign of God is within/among you"—Luke 17:21). The Greek *entos* means both "within" and "among," and was clearly understood as both interior and interpersonal by Yeshua, not external or political: "My kingdom (*basileia*) is not of this world" (John 18:37). He said of his much-preached *basileia tou Theou* that we should "not to look for it here or there," but rather *entos hymon*—both *within* **and** *among* you!

The "revolution" Yeshua was seeking to foment was not an external, political one but was lodged first "within," and then was to be expressed "among" one's neighbors. In the wake of the "Fall of the Wall" in Germany in 1989, we spoke of a "Velvet Revolution," which overcame a seemingly impregnable fortress without bloodshed. Was such Yeshua's hope in the year 30 CE? It worked out in the end to be vastly more!

CHURCH RESPONSE TO YESHUA'S PACIFISM

Thus on that Good Friday two thousand years ago Yeshua's nonviolent life was violently snuffed out, an apparent total failure. But in the end, this nonviolent life inspired his followers to imitate him in seeking justice in a nonviolent manner, in a subsequent cascade of "Velvet Revolutions." Against all apparent odds, more and more people in the Roman Empire looking for meaning in life found Yeshua's teaching and self-giving example so attractive that millions became his followers. Despite Roman persecutions—climaxing in the longest-lasting and most violent one at the beginning of the fourth century under the emperor Diocletian (ironically one of the very few Roman emperors who peacefully retired and died of natural causes)—Christianity became so widespread that the next emperor, Constantine, reversed course and declared Christianity a *licit* religion, and in effect made it an arm of his mighty Roman Empire, which was to last with his new city Constantinople as its capital for another thousand years!

In those first three centuries of the "Christian Era" Yeshua's followers were strongly in favor of religious liberty and nonviolence, rejecting the very idea of a Christian soldier. However, after Constantine's conversion to Christianity, many Christian theologians dropped the idea of religious liberty and instead argued that the state had the responsibility to support the truth, which of course was Christianity. This development went to the extreme when in 391 CE Emperor Theodosius declared Christianity the *only* licit religion of the empire! Christians also no longer eschewed becoming soldiers, and when the Christian empire was attacked by various barbarians, Christian theologians such as Saint Augustine of Hippo developed the just war theory.

Thus, from the time of Constantine forward Christian thinkers defended fighting defensive wars (though of course they unfortunately were not the only wars waged). In the medieval West when there no longer existed any fragment of the *Pax Romana* of the Roman Empire (especially after the disintegration of the Carolingian Empire in the ninth century), the Catholic Church launched two efforts at promoting nonviolence, the *Pax Dei*, or "Peace of God," and the *Treuga Dei*, or "Truce of God." In the Peace of God, launched in 989 CE, the church declared that peasants and church properties were protected from violence. The Truce of God began in 1027 CE, mandating that certain days and seasons—e.g., Sundays and holy days (of which there were many), Fridays, and the liturgical season of Lent—were off limits as far as fighting was concerned. They both were more or less successful.

Some Christians did, and some still do, argue that Yeshua was a complete pacifist—that is, he insisted on no physical violence for any reason. They refer to his statements such as, "If anyone strikes you on one cheek, turn the other" (Matt 5:29); and, "But I tell you, love your enemies and pray for those who persecute you" (Matt 5:44). However, critics of this viewpoint highlight other statements and actions of Yeshua—statements such as, "Think not that I have come to bring peace on earth; I came not to bring peace, but a sword" (Matt 10:34); and, "From the days of John the Baptist until now the kingdom of heaven suffers violence, and the violent take it by force" (Matt 11:12); and, "He said to them, '. . . the one who has no sword must sell his cloak and buy one'" (Luke 22:36). Those who oppose labeling Jesus a complete pacifist point to his angry action when he "went into the temple of God, and cast out all them that sold and bought in the temple, and overthrew the tables of the money changers, and the seats of them that sold doves" (Matt 21:12).

Given the pull between militarism on the one hand and pacifism on the other, Christian theologians, particularly following the lead of Saint Augustine in his monumental work *Civitas Dei* (*The City of God*), developed the just war theory. In brief that theory runs as follows:

There are two sets of criteria, one for the right to go to war, the *jus ad bellum*, and second, the right way to conduct war, the *jus in bello*.

The criteria of the *jus ad bellum* are:

(1) there must be a just cause for a war;

(2) there must be a probability of success; and

(3) war must be taken up only as a last resort.

The criteria of the *jus in bello* are:

(1) distinction must be made between the guilty and innocent of the opposing country, between combatants and civilians; the former may be attacked, but not the latter;

(2) the force used must be proportional to the wrong to be righted; and

(3) minimal force must be used to accomplish the goal.

Probably the vast majority of Christians would follow the just war theory rather than strict pacifism, but nevertheless in the past and still today many individual Christians espouse pacifism, but so too do certain Christian denominations, particularly the so-called peace churches: Church of the Brethren, Mennonites, and Religious Society of Friends (Quakers).

Even as the just war theory, Christian pacifism, and peace churches must be mentioned, many other Christian peace organizations must be noted: these may not espouse strict pacifism, but they nevertheless systematically and in organized ways work to foster peace. These include the Catholic Peace Fellowship, the Fellowship of Reconciliation, and many others. Many Christians, including, Father Max Metzger,[2] have given their lives working for peace.

Thus, let me repeat here what I wrote above: It is clear that Yeshua was aiming at changing *this world*, and that the path to that goal was through an interior transformation. However, he did not naively think that we were all atoms who operated in isolated fashion, as some very conservative Christians argue. Rather this *basileia* was necessarily *entos hymon*, that is, both *within* and *among us*—in accordance with the dual meaning of *entos*. That meant that the change *within* us *must* find expression in the relations *among* us, and thanks to a nonideological liberation theology, we now know that includes the *structures* of society, which also need changing.

Whatever one in the end thinks Yeshua advocated—strict passivism or not (I think not)—it appears to me that there are times and situations where one cannot avoid violence, when not to act with violence unavoidably brings about greater violence. At times in real life a choice comes before us not between good and evil, but only between greater and lesser evil—and not to choose is to choose. It will not do to argue that "I will not engage in active violence, even if it is necessary to prevent greater violence." The Golden Rule points in the other direction.

Example: If the only way to prevent U.S. Army Lieutenant William Calley—were he my unit commander at My Lai, Vietnam—from "wasting" more than a hundred innocent Vietnamese women and children, I would have had to arrest, or perhaps even shoot him, many would argue that, according to the Golden Rule, the murdered children would want me to shoot him—hence, I would be *morally bound* to shoot him. (For those not old enough to remember the Vietnam War, the massacre at My Lai was an actual incident. None of the enlisted men had the courage to shoot Lieutenant Calley, but they shot the village children instead!) Perhaps it is morally permissible to refuse to defend one's own life with violence, but it surely is not morally permissible to sacrifice the lives of other innocents on the

---

2. See Swidler, *Bloodwitness*. Father Max Metzger was an extraordinarily active and courageous German Catholic priest. He, like most everyone on all sides of World War I, enthusiastically joined his nation's call to arms in 1914. However, no sooner was he mustered out with a medical discharge in 1915—this very time of year exactly one hundred years ago as I sit and write these words—than he founded a Catholic peace organization. Between the wars he promoted the cause of peace (along with many other causes, such as nonalcoholic restaurants, Esperanto, ecumenism, smuggling Jews to safety) even to the point of sending on its way in the wake of the German defeat at Stalingrad during World War II a peace plan to the English bishops through a Swedish bishop—only to be caught by a Gestapo spy, incarcerated for nine months, and at Easter 1944, beheaded.

grounds of preserving one's commitment to nonviolence in order to keep one's conscience pristine at the cost of innocent children's lives. In real life, one may be morally required to dip one's hands in blood in order to prevent others from swimming in their own blood. Is a pristine conscience more valuable than the lives of innocent children? I think that Yeshua's answer would be no. Of those who would even simply "lead astray a little one," he said simply, "it would be better for him to be thrown into the sea with a millstone around his neck" (Luke 17:23): this is pretty strong language. Is it meant only metaphorically?

However, these are usually extreme situations (and yet, too present to ignore). They are not the major focus of Christians, or indeed of all people, should be. Rather, the followers of Yeshua (whether formally Christians or not) should center on his core teaching, taught not just by his profound wisdom and words but most of all by his awesome living, and dying: While hanging in death throes, Yehsua managed to rasp, "Forgive them Father, for they know not what they do" (Luke 23:24) In this profound sense, *Yeshua was a deep pacifist.*

Most recently major elements in the Catholic Church from around the world gathered to request that Pope Francis (whose very choice of papal name prominently reflects his commitment to nonviolence, to pacifism) "to share with the world an encyclical on nonviolence and Just Peace."[3] It is interesting, and important, to note a tendency to use the terms *nonviolence* and *peacebuilding* rather than *pacifism*. Perhaps this is because many committed persons are reluctant to commit to a total "negative" Pacifism in the abstract, but increasingly prefer practical positive efforts to effect change on the ground and in consciousness expressed in the terms and the concrete efforts of Nonviolence and Peacebuilding.

---

3. Conference. Nonviolence and Just Peace: Contributing to the Catholic Understanding of and Commitment to Nonviolence, held in Rome between April 11 and 13, 2016.

3

Yeshua Was a Feminist

GOSPEL SETTINGS

Definition and Argument

PERHAPS TODAY IS THE *kairos* (New Testament Greek for "the key moment") when what is the last rampart of human oppression will finally for Christians yield to the power of the model of Yeshua's feminism and the grace of the moment, the contemporary ongoing secular movement toward a full, equal human development of women: *feminism*. What is the model of Yeshua's encounter with women? If we look at the Gospels not with the eyes of male chauvinism or the "eternal feminine," we will see that the model Yeshua presents is that of a feminist: Yeshua was a feminist.

A feminist is a person who promotes the equality of women with men, who advocates and practices treating women primarily as human persons, and contravenes social customs in so acting. This definition of feminism is the one that I used in 1971, reflecting then-current usage. Subsequently many women became scholars of the social sciences, as well of other fields, and focused their thought and research in depth on what it means to be a woman, often thereby creating another reality—women's studies—which also began to be called feminism by some. Obviously this later meaning is not what I meant and mean by naming Yeshua, and myself, among other males, as feminists. Rather, as stated, what is meant is the initial, and still valid, description of commitment to equality for women.

To prove the thesis "Yeshua was a feminist," it must be demonstrated that, so far as we can tell, Yeshua neither said nor did anything to indicate that he advocated treating women as intrinsically inferior to men, but that on the contrary he said and did things that indicated he thought of women as the equals of men, and that in the process he willingly violated pertinent social mores.

The negative portion of the argument can be documented quite simply by reading through the four Gospels. Nowhere does Yeshua treat women as inferior beings. In fact, it is apparent that Yeshua understood himself to be especially sent to the typical classes of so-called inferior beings, such as poor people, people with disabilities, sinners, children, and women—to call them all to the freedom and equality of the *basileia tou Theou*, the "*reign* of God." (As I noted above, I use the term "reign of God" and its euphemistic equivalent "reign of heaven" instead of the traditional "kingdom of God": for the original idea is about God's *torah*—Hebrew for "teaching"—*ruling* in one's life.) But two factors raise this negative result—of using "kingdom" rather than "reign"—exponentially in its significance: (1) the status of women in Palestine at the time of Yeshua, and (2) the nature of the Gospels. Both need to be recalled here in some detail, particularly the former.

The Status of Women in Palestine

The status of women in Palestine during the time of Yeshua was that of inferiors (and everywhere else as well!). Despite the fact that there were several heroines recorded in the Hebrew Scriptures, according to most rabbinic customs[1] of Yeshua's time—and long after—women were not allowed to study the Scriptures (Torah). One first-century rabbi, Eliezer, put the point sharply: "Rather should the words of the Torah be burned than entrusted

---

1. In rabbinic writings, including the Mishnah (codified 200 CE), the Tosephta (codified just afterwards), the Palestinian Talmud (400 CE), and the Babylonian Talmud (500 CE), there are many references to persons and things as far back as 200 BCE. Thus, in many matters we can know what the rabbis of the time of Yeshua taught, even though caution must be exercised since later codifiers might have adjusted texts for their own purposes. Nevertheless, until cogent arguments and evidence are brought forth that substantial revision did occur in the pertinent passages, good scholarship dictates that the available texts be utilized with due care. For a broad treatment of this subject, see Swidler, *The Status of Women*; and Swidler, *Biblical Affirmations of Woman*.

to a woman ... Whoever teaches his daughter the Torah is like one who teaches her lasciviousness."[2]

In the vitally religious area of prayer, women were so little thought of as not to be given obligations of the same seriousness as men. For example, women, along with children and slaves, were not obliged to recite the Shema, the morning prayer, or prayers at meals.[3] Such customs may in an ancient past have begun to relieve house- and children-burdened wives, but if so, they quickly became tokens of male privilege and power. In fact, the Talmud states, "Let a curse come upon the man who (needs have) his wife or children say grace for him."[4] Moreover, in the daily prayers there was a threefold thanksgiving: "Praised be God that he has not created me a gentile; praised be God that he has not created me a woman; praised be God that he has not created me an ignorant man."[5] (It was clearly a version of this rabbinic prayer that Paul rejected in his letter to the Galatians: "There is neither Jew nor Greek, there is neither slave nor free, there is neither male nor female; for you are all one in Christ Jesus" [Gal 3:28]. Here might be one of a few echoes of Yeshua's feminism in Paul.)

Women were also greatly restricted in public prayer. It was not even possible for them to be counted toward the number necessary for a quorum to form a congregation to worship communally (*minyan*)[6]—they were again classified with children and slaves, who similarly did not qualify. Of course this was already far earlier the case in the Ten Commandments given to Moses on Mount Sinai wherein in the last commandment about not coveting, wives are grouped along with a man's other possessions, including his slaves, ox, donkey, and so forth There is also an interesting parallel in canon 93 of the 1917 Roman Catholic canon law: *Codex Juris Canonici*, CIC—valid in the Catholic Church until 1983—which grouped married women, minors, and the insane.) In the great temple at Jerusalem women were limited to one outer portion, the women's court, which was five steps below the court for the men.[7] In the synagogues the women were also separated from the men, and were not allowed to read aloud or take

---

2. *Mishnah*, Sota 3:4.
3. *Talmud*, Kid. 33b; *Mishnah*, Ber 3:3.
4. *Talmud*, Ber. 20b.
5. *Tosephta*, Ber. 7:18; *Talmud*, Ber. 13b; Men. 43b.
6. *Mishnah*, Abot 3:6.
7. Josephus, *Antiquities* 15.418-419; Josephus, *Jewish War* 5.5.198-199; *Mishnah*, Middoth 2:5.

any leading function.[8] (The same is still true in many Orthodox synagogues today—canon 1262 of the 1917 *CIC* also stated that "in church the women should be separated from the men.")

Besides the disabilities women suffered in the areas of prayer and worship there were many others in the private and public forums of society. The "Proverbs of the Fathers" contain the injunction:"'Speak not much with a woman.' Since a man's own wife is meant there, how much more does not this apply to the wife of another? The wise men say, 'Who speaks much with a woman draws down misfortune on himself, neglects the words of the law, and finally earns hell.'"[9] If it were merely the too free intercourse of the sexes which was being warned against, this might signify nothing derogatory to women. But since a man may not speak even to his own wife, daughter, or sister in the street,[10] then only male superiority can be the motive, for intercourse with uneducated company is warned against in exactly the same terms: "One is not so much as to greet a woman."[11] In addition, save in the rarest instances, women were not allowed to bear witness in a court of law.[12] Some Jewish thinkers, as for example, Philo, a contemporary of Yeshua, thought women ought not leave their households except to go to the synagogue (and that only at a time when most of the other people would be

---

8. See Sukenik, *Ancient Synagogues*, 47ff. See also Brooten, *Women Leaders*, where the author raises serious questions about how early the physical division of men and women was reflected in the synagogue architecture. By the nature of the issue, she cannot offer positive proof that there was no such architectural separation (which, as we know, definitely existed later, and does still up to the present in some synagogues). She does, however, argue that the claim that an architectural separation between men and women did exist at the time of Yeshua is less than certain. Nevertheless, looking at all the evidence, I am persuaded that it is more likely that women and men were separated in the synagogues at the time of Yeshua.

Dr. Brooten also argues for some modicum of leadership for women in ancient Judaism, albeit as exceptions. Her scholarship is excellent and her case solid. But the exceptions that she adduces, important as they are as "useable history" for women, remain so much just that, the proverbial "exceptions that prove the rule"; the general description of ancient Jewish women as largely officially excluded from leadership roles in my judgment still stands.

9. *Mishnah*, Aboth 1:5.
10. *Talmud*, Ber. 43b.
11. Ibid.
12. *Mishnah*, Shab. 4:1; *Talmud*, B.K. 88a; Josephus, *Antiquities* 4.219.

at home);[13] girls ought not even not cross the threshold that separated the male and female apartments of the household.[14]

In general, the attitude toward women was epitomized in the institutions and customs surrounding marriage. For the most part the function of women was thought of rather exclusively in terms of childbearing and rearing; women were almost always under the tutelage of a man, either the father or husband—or if a widow, the dead husband's brother. Polygamy—in the sense of having several wives, but *not* in the sense of having several husbands—was legal among Jews at the time of Yeshua, although probably not heavily practiced. Moreover, divorce of a wife was very easily obtained by the husband—he merely had to give her a writ of divorce; women in Palestine, on the other hand, were not allowed to divorce their husbands.

Rabbinic sayings also provide an insight into the attitude toward women: "It is well for those whose children are male, but ill for those whose children are female."[15] "At the birth of a boy all are joyful, but at the birth of a girl all are sad."[16] "When a boy comes into the world, peace comes into the world: when a girl comes, nothing comes."[17] "Even the most virtuous of women is a witch."[18] "Our teachers have said: Four qualities are evident in women: They are greedy at their food, eager to gossip, lazy and jealous."[19]

In conclusion, the condition of women in Palestinian Judaism was that of inferiors.

The Nature of the Gospels

The four Gospels—virtually the only sources of information about Yeshua—are not the straight factual reports of eyewitnesses of the events in the life of Yeshua of Nazareth as one might find in the columns of the *New York Times* or the pages of a critical biography. Rather, they are four different faith statements reflecting more than four primitive Christian communities who believed that Yeshua was the Messiah. They were composed from a

13. Philo, *Flaccus* 89; *De specialibus legibus* 3.172.
14. Philo, *De specialibus legibus* 3.169.
15. *Talmud*, Kid. 82b; cf. also Sanh. 100b.
16. *Talmud*, Nid. 31b.
17. Ibid.
18. *Mishnah*, Terum 15; *Palestinian Talmud*, Kid. 4,66b, 32; Soferim 41a in *The Minor Tractates of the Talmud*, 288.
19. Midrash Genesis Rabbah 45:5.

variety of sources, written and oral, over a period of time and in response to certain needs felt in the communities and individuals at the time; consequently, they are many-layered. Since the gospel writers and editors were not twenty-first-century critical historians, they were not particularly intent on recording the "very words of Yeshua," the *ipsissima verba Jesu*; nor were they concerned to winnow out all of their own cultural biases and assumptions. Indeed, it is doubtful that they were particularly conscious of them.

This modern critical understanding (briefly outlined earlier) of the Gospels, of course, does not impugn the historical character of the Gospels; it merely describes the type of historical documents they are so their historical significance can more accurately be evaluated. Its religious value lies in the fact that modern Christians are thereby helped to know much more precisely what Yeshua meant by certain statements and actions as they are reported by the first Christian communities in the Gospels. With this new knowledge of the nature of the Gospels it is easier to make the vital distinction between the religious truth that is to be handed on and the time-conditioned categories and customs involved in expressing it.

Yeshua as Source and as Jew

When the fact that the Gospels express no negative attitudes from Yeshua toward women is set side by side with the relatively recently discerned "communal faith-statement" understanding of the nature of the Gospels, the importance of the former is vastly enhanced. For whatever Yeshua said or did comes to us only through the lens of the recollections of the first Christians. If there were no very special religious significance in a particular concept or custom—like drinking wine or speaking Aramaic—we would expect that current concept or custom to be reflected by Yeshua. The fact that the overwhelmingly negative attitude toward women in Palestine did *not* come through the primitive Christian communal lens showing us Yeshua, by itself underscores the clearly great religious importance Yeshua attached to his positive attitude—his feminist attitude—toward women: Hence, *feminism—that is, personalism extended to women—is a constitutive part of the gospel, the good news, of Yeshua*. It will be seen, however, to be suppressed and even viciously contradicted by the early Christian church just a few decades after Yeshua's death.

It should also be noted here that although in the analysis that follows it is the image of Yeshua as it emerges from the four Gospels that will be dealt with, the feminist character that is found there is ultimately to be attributed to Yeshua himself and not to the primitive Christian church, the evangelists, or their sources. Basically the "principle of dissimilarity" operates here. Recall that principle, devised by twentieth-century New Testament scholars, states that if a saying or action attributed to Yeshua is contrary to the cultural milieu of the time, then it most probably had its origin in Yeshua. In this case the feminism of Yeshua could hardly be attributable to Palestinian Judaism or the primitive Christian church and hence must reflect the attitude and action of Yeshua.

As is seen already in the later New Testament, the early church quickly became not only nonfeminist, but even antiwoman. For example, "The women should keep silence in the churches. For they are not permitted to speak, but should be subordinate, as even the law says";[20] "Let a woman learn in silence with all submissiveness. I permit no woman to teach or to have authority over men; she is to keep silent."[21] The misogynist slide continued after the New Testament: In the second century Tertullian, the "father of theology," said of woman: "You are the devil's gateway";[22] in the next century Origen wrote: "What is seen with the eyes of the creator is masculine, and not feminine, for God does not stoop to look upon what is feminine and of the flesh";[23] in the fourth century Epiphanius said, "The devil seeks to vomit out his disorder through women."[24]

20. 1 Cor 14:34.

21. 1 Tim 2:11–12.

22. Addressing all women, Tertullian says, "And do you not know that you are (each) an Eve? The sentence of God on this sex of yours lives in this age: the guilt must of necessity live too. You are the devil's gateway; you are the unsealer of that (forbidden) tree: you are the first deserter of the divine law: you are she who persuaded him whom the devil was not valiant enough to attack. You destroyed so easily God's image, man. On account of your desert—i.e., death—even the Son of God had to die." *De cultu feminarum* 1.1, in *Disciplinary, Moral, and Ascetical Works*, 117–18. It is interesting that according to Tertullian the serpent (who Tertullian interprets as the devil) did not dare to approach the "stronger mind," that of the Man, but chose that of "the weaker intellect," the Woman's—for one mind could be overcome only by a more powerful one. Amazingly Tertullian did not notice that his line of argument then included the necessary inference that the Woman's mind was more powerful than that of the Man, for after eating the forbidden fruit, "the Woman gave the fruit to her Man, and [and simply] he ate!" (Gen 3:6).

23. Origen, *Selecta in Exodus* XVIII.17, Migne, *Patrologia Graeca*, 12:cols. 296–97.

24. Epiphanius wrote: "For the female sex is easily seduced, weak, and without much understanding. The devil seeks to vomit out his disorder through women . . . We wish to

Three Jesus Certitudes

In Jewish culture, women were held to be, as the first-century Jewish historian Josephus put it, "in all things inferior to the man."[25] Since it was out of that milieu that the evangelists were writing and from which they drew their sources, neither the male evangelists nor their male sources could have been the source of the feminism found in the Yeshua of the Gospels. Its only possible *ultimate* source was Yeshua himself. In fact, given the misogynist tendency exhibited both in the Judaism of Yeshua's time and in the early Christian church, there is every likelihood that the strong feminism of Yeshua has been muted, even played down in the Gospels, as can be seen for example by the fact that—as we saw above—the story of the woman taken in adultery and not condemned by Yeshua[26] is absent from the earliest Greek manuscripts and almost did not make it into the canon of the New Testament.[27]

A further word of caution is needed here. Jewish culture of Yeshua's time treated women as inferior to men, as did also the surrounding cultures, and in this matter Yeshua ran counter to that culture. In the case of women, as in that of other marginalized groups, Yeshua raised a powerful prophetic protest. But it needs to be remembered that raising a prophetic voice was precisely a Jewish thing to do; in this Yeshua was not acting in a non-Jewish manner but in a specifically Jewish tradition. Moreover, after the first enthusiastic response of the women followers Yeshua's liberating feminist move, the newly forming Christian church quickly sank back into a nonfeminist, even misogynist, morass until our time—where the great majority of it still continues.

Hence, there is no ground here for Christians to claim superiority over Jews, but rather just the opposite. Christians claim to be followers of Yeshua, whereas Jews do not. Christians therefore had far more reason to be, like Yeshua, feminists. But they—we—failed, and continue to fail, miserably!

---

apply masculine reasoning and destroy the folly of these women." *Adversus Collyridianos*, in Migne, *Patrologia Graeca*, 42: cols. 740–41.

25. Josephus states: "The woman, says the law, is in all things inferior to the man" *Against Apion* 2.201.

26 John 8:2–11.

27 For a discussion of this "wandering" story of Yeshua and the adulteress see Swidler, *Biblical Affirmations of Woman*, 185–86., 250–51, and 275–76, where the evidence for its having first been recorded by a woman "evangelist" is discussed, as well as in Swidler, *Jesus Was a Feminist*.

Further, there are also no grounds for us twenty-first-century humans to feel greatly superior vis à vis the past. We are only now becoming increasingly aware of how deep and pervasive the problem of the abuse of women by men is. For a tiny yet deeply disturbing set of examples of contemporary ongoing abuse of women, see www.womenundersiegeproject.org/.

This whole point of this portion of these reflections is to attempt to present evidence that Yeshua ha-Notzri, Jesus of Nazareth, is a model of how to relate to women in a positive, *feminist*, way—already two thousand years ago!

In this regard it is interesting to note that at least two early New Testament textual variants directly accuse Yeshua of being a feminist, of running counter to the culture, and "leading women astray." A variant manuscript reading of Luke 23:5 attested to by the fourth-century Palestinian-born church father Epiphanius: The chief priests said to Pilate concerning Yeshua, "He is inflaming the people with his teaching all over Judea; it has come all the way from Galilee, where he started, down to here"—to which Epiphanius's attested text added, "and he has turned our children and wives away from us for they are not bathed as we are, nor do they purify themselves."[28] The second text is even earlier, from the first half of the second century, when some of the New Testament was still being written. It is attested to by Marcion (d. 160 CE) and is in Luke 23:2: "They began their accusation by saying, 'We found this man inciting our people to a revolt, opposing payment of the tribute to Caesar'"—to which Marcion's attested text adds, "leading astray the women and the children."[29]

WOMEN FOLLOW YESHUA

Women Disciples of Yeshua

One of the first things noticed in the Gospels about Yeshua's attitude toward women is that he taught them the gospel, the meaning of the Scriptures, and religious truths in general. When it is recalled that in Judaism it was considered improper, and "obscene," to teach women the Scriptures, this action of Yeshua was an extraordinary, deliberate decision to break with a

---

28. *Et filios nostros et uxores avertit a nobis, non enim baptizantur sicut nos nec se mundant.*

29. *Kai apostrephonta tas gynaikas kai ta tekna.* For these variant texts and references see Nestle, ed., *Novum Testamentum Graece et Latine*, 221; and Gryson, *Ministry of Women in the Early Church*, 126.

custom invidious to women. Moreover, women became disciples of Yeshua not only in the sense of learning from him but also in the sense of following him in his travels and ministering to him.[30] A number of women, married and unmarried, were regular followers of Yeshua. In Luke 8:1ff. several are mentioned by name in the same sentence with the Twelve: "He made his way through towns and villages preaching and proclaiming the good news of the reign of God. With him went the Twelve as well as certain women ... who ministered to (*diekonoun*) them out of their own resources."[31] The significance of this phenomenon of women following Yeshua about, learning from, and ministering to him, can be properly appreciated only when it is recalled that not only were women not to study the Scriptures, but in the more observant settings they were not even to leave their households, whether as a daughter, a wife, or a member of a harem.

Women and Resurrection from the Dead

Within this context of women being disciples and ministers, Yeshua quite deliberately broke another custom disadvantageous to women. It concerns the claims of resurrection. Regardless of what a twenty-first-century person might think about such claims, they were critical in the minds of many Jews of Yeshua's time, as well as throughout the New Testament. Hence, the New Testament claims made about them warrant serious attention. In addition, it should be recalled that women we often considered as "impure" as corpses.

According to the Gospels, Yeshua's first appearance after his resurrection to any of his followers was to a woman (or women), who was (or were) then commissioned by him to bear witness of the risen Yeshua to

---

30. For a brief discussion of the implications of the Greek word used for "ministering," *diakoneo*, see Swidler, *Biblical Affirmations of Woman*, 194–95. There is also a reference in the Acts of the Apostles to a woman by name as a disciple of Yeshua: "At Jaffa there was a woman disciple (*mathetria*) called Tabitha, or Dorcas in Greek" (Acts 9:36).

31. Cf. also Mark 15:40–41 and Matt 27:55–56, where the women are also reported to have "ministered" (*diekonoun*) to Yeshua. A fascinating second-century gnostic document refers to the seven holy women named in the Gospels as disciples on a par with the twelve apostles: "After he had risen from the dead, when they came, the twelve disciples (*mathetes*) and seven women who had followed him as disciples (*matheteuein*), into Galilee, ... there appeared to them the Redeemer." *Sophia Jesu Christi*, in Hennecke and Schneemelcher, eds., *New Testament Apocrypha*, 1:246. See Swidler, *Biblical Affirmations of Woman*, 195–96. for further similar texts.

the Eleven.[32] In typical male Palestinian style, they refused to believe the women since according to Judaic law, women were not allowed to bear legal witness. Clearly this was a dramatic linking of a very definite rejection of the second-class status of women with a central element of the Gospel: the resurrection. The effort to connect these two points is so obvious—an effort clearly not attributable to the male disciples/evangelists—that it is an overwhelming tribute to male intellectual myopia not to have discerned it in two thousand years. In this case the source obviously was the *women followers of Yeshua.*

The intimate connection of women with resurrection from the dead is not limited in the Gospels to the resurrection of Yeshua. Accounts of three other resurrections are found the Gospels—all closely involving a woman. The most obvious connection of a woman with a resurrection account is that of the raising of a woman, Jairus's daughter.[33] A second resurrection Yeshua performed was that of the only son of the widow of Nain: "And when the Lord saw her, he had compassion on her and he said to her, 'Do not weep.'"[34] The third resurrection Yeshua performed was Lazarus's, at the request of his sisters, Martha and Mary.[35]

From the first it was Martha and Mary who sent for Yeshua because of Lazarus's illness. But when Yeshua finally came, Lazarus was four days dead. Martha met Yeshua and pleaded for his resurrection: "Lord, if you had been there, my brother would not have died. And even now I know that whatever you ask from God, God will give you." Then followed Yeshua's raising of Lazarus from the dead. Thus, Yeshua raised one woman from the dead, and raised two other persons largely because of women.

Two more details must be noted in these three resurrection stories. The first is that only in the case of Jairus's daughter did Yeshua touch the corpse—which made him ritually unclean. In the cases of the raising of two men, Yeshua did not touch them but merely said, "Young man, I say to you, arise," or, "Lazarus, come out." One must at least wonder why it was noted that Yeshua chose to violate the laws for ritual purity in order to help a woman, but not a man. The second detail is in Yeshua's conversation with Martha after she pleaded for the resurrection of Lazarus. Yeshua declared himself to be the resurrection ("I am the resurrection and the life."),

---

32. Matt 28:9–10; Mark 16:9ff; John 20:11ff.
33. Matt 9:18ff.; Mark 5:22ff.; Luke 8:41ff.
34. Cf. Luke 7:11ff.
35. Cf. John 11.

the only time he did so that is recorded in the Gospels. Yeshua here again revealed a central element in the Gospel—the resurrection—to a woman.

Women as Sex Objects

Of course numerous occasions are recorded in the Gospels when women are treated by various men as second-class citizens. There are also situations where women are treated by others not at all as persons but as sex objects, and it Yeshua was expected to treat women in this way. These expectations were disappointed. One such occasion occurred when Yeshua was invited to dinner at the house of a skeptical Pharisee,[36] and a woman of ill repute entered and washed Yeshua's feet with her tears, wiped them with her hair, and anointed them. The Pharisee saw this woman solely as an evil sexual creature: "The Pharisee . . . said to himself, 'If this man were a prophet, he would know who this woman is who is touching him and what a bad name she has.'" But Yeshua deliberately rejected this approach to the woman as a sex object. He rebuked the Pharisee and spoke solely of the woman's human spiritual actions; he spoke of her love, her unlove (i.e., her sins), her being forgiven, and her faith. Yeshua then addressed her as a human person: "Your sins are forgiven . . . Your faith has saved you; go in peace." (It was not proper to speak to women in public, especially to so-called improper women.)

A similar situation occurred when the scribes and Pharisees used a woman reduced entirely to a sex object to set a legal trap for Yeshua.[37] It is difficult to imagine a more callous use of a human person than what the "adulterous" woman was put to by Yeshua's enemies. First, she was surprised in the intimate act of sexual intercourse (quite possibly a trap was set up ahead of time by the suspicious husband or fiancé), and then she was dragged before the scribes and Pharisees, and then she was taken by them before an even larger crowd that Yeshua was instructing and was made to "stand in full view of everybody." Yeshua's opponents said to him that she had been caught in the very act of committing adultery and that Moses had commanded that such women be stoned to death.[38] "What have you to say?" The trap was partly that if Yeshua said yes to the stoning, he would be violating the Roman law, which restricted capital punishment.

36. Luke 7:36ff.
37. John 8:2–11.
38. Deut 22:22ff.

(The Romans retained the *Jus gladii*), and if he said no to the stoning, Yeshua would appear to contravene Mosaic law. It is clear that the enemies of Yeshua would not have thought of this case as presenting Yeshua with some kind of trap if he did not already have a reputation among them as a champion of women. There apparently was no question but that the woman was guilty of the "crime" of adultery, since she was caught *in delicto flagrante*, and therefore was subject to the Mosaic punishment of death. The question was, would Yeshua retain his reputation as the great rabbi, the teacher of the Torah, or would he retain his reputation as the champion of women?

Yeshua of course eluded their snares by refusing to become entangled in legalisms and abstractions. Rather, he dealt with both the accusers and the accused directly as spiritual, ethical human persons. He spoke directly to the accusers in the context of their own personal ethical conduct: "If there is one of you who has not sinned, let him be the first to throw a stone at her." To the accused woman he likewise spoke directly with compassion, but without approving her conduct: "'Woman, where are they? Has no one condemned you?' She said, 'No one, Lord.' And Yeshua said, 'Neither do I condemn you; go, and do not sin again.'"

(One detail of this encounter provides the basis for a short excursus related to the status of women. The Pharisees stated that the woman had been caught in the act of adultery and according to the law of Moses was therefore to be stoned to death. Since the type of execution mentioned was stoning, the woman must have been a "virgin betrothed," as referred to in Deut 22:23–24. There provision is made for the stoning of *both* the man and the woman, although in the gospel story only the woman is brought forward. However, the reason given for why the man ought to be stoned was not because he had violated the woman, or God's law, but "because he had violated the wife of his neighbor." It was the injury of the man through the misuse of his property—his wife—that was the great evil.)

This story of Yeshua and the woman taken in adultery is worthy of further analysis here. It is found in the Fourth Gospel, although, as I noted earlier, scholars agree that it was not originally located there. It is not found in the earliest Greek manuscripts and comes into the canonical Scriptures through the manuscripts of the Western church, although the third-century *Didascalia*, of Syrian origin, references the story. Although the report of Yeshua's encounter with the woman seized in the act of adultery is usually located in the Fourth Gospel,[39] it is the scholarly consensus that the Fourth

---

39. John 7:53—8:11.

Gospel evangelist certainly did not write it. In fact, it has many characteristics akin to the style of the Synoptic Gospels (Matthew, Mark, and Luke). Rather, there is manuscript evidence that it originally might well have been located in Luke after 21:38.

Why the long resistance to this story? Probably partly because Yeshua was totally forgiving of adultery, and much of early Christianity took a severe stance against sexual offenses. At the same time, while Yeshua's treating of the woman in the story as a person rather than simply as a creature of sex probably called forth resistance from certain elements in the church, other elements (most probably women) persisted in retaining the story, and ultimately succeeded.

Healing of Women by Yeshua

Unlike other rabbis about whom stories of miraculous healing and raising the dead are recorded, Yeshua does heal women. They are seen by him first as persons with both physical needs and spiritual strengths (faith), the two of which call forth his healing action. Perhaps the reason there is no recorded instance of a Jewish woman ever asking Yeshua for a cure is that Jewish women were conditioned by their culture to assume they would not be recognized by a public religious figure.

It is significant that Yeshua's first recorded healing in the oldest gospel, Mark (and followed in this by Luke 4:38–39 but not Matt 8:14–15), at the very beginning of Yeshua's public life, was the healing of a woman, Simon Peter's mother-in-law.

> On leaving the synagogue, he went with James and John straight to the house of Simon and Andrew. Now Simon's mother-in-law had gone to bed with fever, and they told him about her straight-away. He went to her, took her by the hand, and helped her up. And the fever left her and she began to wait on them.[40]

Healing on the Sabbath

Luke/Luka, whose gospel, as we have seen, shows the greatest sympathy for women by the relatively large number of events and stories involving women that he includes, reports three healings on the Sabbath—which

40. Matt 8:14–15; Mark 1:29–30; Luke 4:38–39.

caused Yeshua difficulties. Two were healings of men; the other was the healing of a woman. The Fourth Gospel also records the healing of two men on the Sabbath,[41] whereas both Mark[42] and Matthew[43] report only the healing of one man; none of these three report the healing of any women on the Sabbath. Given that the Hellenistic world experienced an extended "women's liberation" movement after Yeshua's career, perhaps Luke's Hellenistic background and intended audience encouraged him to emphasize Yeshua's feminism—particularly by drawing upon a (possibly) female source—an evangelist I call Luka. It should also be noted that in Luke/Luka's story Yeshua not only healed the woman on the Sabbath, but he also spoke to her in public, an unseemly thing for any man in that culture to do, especially a rabbi. He also referred to her as a "daughter of Abraham," an almost unheard-of honorific, although "son of Abraham" is a standard phrase used throughout Hebrew and Jewish literature as well as by Yeshua (e.g., Luke 19:9) as a way of referring to a (male) member of the chosen people. For Yeshua, women were full-fledged participants within the people and covenant of God.

One Sabbath day Yeshua was teaching in one of the synagogues, and a woman was there who for eighteen years had been possessed by a spirit that left her enfeebled; she was bent double and quite unable to stand upright. When Yeshua saw her he called her over and said, "Woman, you are rid of your infirmity," and he laid his hands on her. And at once she straightened up, and she glorified God.

> But the synagogue official was indignant because Yeshua had healed on the Sabbath, and he addressed the people present. "There are six days," he said "when work is to be done. Come and be healed on one of those days and not on the Sabbath." But the Lord answered him. "Hypocrites!" he said. "Is there one of you who does not untie his ox or his donkey from the manger on the Sabbath and take it out for watering? And this woman, a daughter of Abraham whom Satan has held bound these eighteen years—was it not right to untie her bonds on the Sabbath day?" When he said this, all his adversaries were covered with confusion, and all the people were overjoyed at all the wonders he worked.[44]

---

41. John 5:10; 9:14–17.
42. Mark 3:1–6.
43. Matt 12:9–14.
44. Luke 13:10–17. Cf. Luke 6:6–11; 14:1–6.

Yeshua's Rejection of the Blood Taboo

All three of the Synoptic Gospels insert into the middle of the account of Jesus raising Jairus's daughter from the dead the story of curing the woman who had an issue of blood for twelve years.[45] What is especially touching about this story is that the affected woman was so reluctant to project herself into public attention that she, "said to herself, 'If I only touch his garment, I shall be made well.'" Her shyness was not because she came from the lower classes, for Mark pointed out that over the twelve years she had been to many physicians—with no success—on whom she had spent all her money. Her shyness probably emerged from the fact that for twelve years, as a woman with a flow of blood, she was constantly unclean,[46] which, not only made her incapable of participating in any cultic action and made her in some sense "displeasing to God," but also rendered anyone and anything she touched (or anyone who touched what she had touched!) similarly unclean. (Here was the basis for the Catholic Church's not allowing women in the sanctuary during Mass until after Vatican II: she might be menstruating, and hence unclean.) The sense of self-degradation and contagion that her "womanly weakness" worked upon her over the twelve years doubtless was oppressive in the extreme. This would have been especially so when a religious teacher, a rabbi, was involved. But not only does Yeshua's power heal her, in one of his many acts of compassion on the downtrodden and afflicted, including women, but Yeshua also makes a great to-do about the event, calling extraordinary attention to the publicity-shy woman:

> Yeshua, perceiving in himself that power had gone forth from him, immediately turned about in the crowd, and said, "Who touched my garments?" And his disciples said to him, "You see the crowd pressing around you, and yet you say, 'Who touched me?'" And he looked around to see who had done it. But the woman, knowing what had been done to her, came in fear and trembling and fell down before him and told him the whole truth. And he said to her, "Daughter, your faith has made you well; go in peace, and be healed of your disease."

It seems clear that Yeshua wanted to call attention to the fact that he did not shrink from the ritual uncleanness incurred by being touched by the "unclean" woman (on several occasions Yeshua rejected the notion of

---

45. Matt 9:20ff.; Mark 5:25ff.; Luke 8:43ff.
46. Lev 15:19ff.

ritual uncleanness) and by immediate implication rejected the uncleanness of a woman who had a flow of blood, menstruous or continual. Yeshua apparently placed a greater importance on dramatically making this point, both to the afflicted woman herself and the crowd, than he did on avoiding the temporary psychological discomfort of the embarrassed woman, which in light of Yeshua's extraordinary concern to alleviate the pain of the afflicted, meant he placed a great weight on teaching this lesson about the dignity of women.

Yeshua's Concern for Widows

As I already remarked, Yeshua felt himself especially sent to the poor and oppressed, and that clearly included in a preeminent way the largest class of that group, women. However, if women were a more oppressed class among the oppressed, the most oppressed of women were widows, for they had almost no means of livelihood or standing before the law, nor anyone to provide for them. Yeshua was clearly most concerned about these most oppressed of the most oppressed class of the oppressed, and his concern was translated into action. It should be noted that all of the eight following accounts concerning Yeshua and widows, save the final one, are recorded in Luke, again reflecting Luke's sensitivity to this dimension of Yeshua's mission.

(1) Luke records that almost at the beginning of his life Yeshua was prophesied over by a widow.

> There was a *woman prophet* also, Anna the daughter of Phanuel, of the tribe of Asher. She was well on in years. Her days of girlhood over, she had been married for seven years before becoming a *widow*. She was now eighty-four years old and never left the Temple, serving God night and day with fasting and prayer. She came by just at that moment and began to praise Cod; and she spoke of the child to all who looked forward to the deliverance of Jerusalem.[47]

(2) Yeshua set before his disciples the example of a widow's minute contribution as being greater than the largesse of the rich.[48]

(3) Yeshua publicly and vigorously condemned the scribes (part of the male establishment) for their oppression of widows—thereby earning

47. Luke 2:36–38.
48. Luke 21:1–4.

himself many enemies. In his teaching he said, "Beware of the scribes who like to walk about in long robes, to be greeted obsequiously in the market squares, to take the front seats in the synagogues and the places of honor at banquets; these are the men who swallow the property of widows, while making a show of lengthy prayers. The more severe will be the sentence they receive."[49]

(4) In his teaching Yeshua used the image of widows when illustrating how a prophet is not accepted in his own country.

> There were many widows in Israel, I can assure you, in Elijah's day, when heaven remained shut for three years and six months and a great famine raged throughout the land, but Elijah was not sent to any one of these: he was sent to a widow at Zarephath, a Sidonian town. And in the prophet Elisha's time there were many lepers in Israel, but none of these was cured, except the Syrian, Naaman.[50]

(5) Also in his teaching Yeshua used the image of a widow as one in the weakest and most hopeless of positions to illustrate the need for perseverance in prayer.[51]

(6) Luke also records Yeshua's curing of a widow, Simon Peter's mother-in-law. The fact that she was living at Peter's house is a clear indication that she was widowed.[52]

(7) As seen above, the most moving action of Yeshua for the sake of a widow was his raising to life the only son of the widow of Nain; she, unlike Peter's mother-in-law, had no one to provide for and protect her. Yeshua was "moved with pity" for her "and said to her, 'Do not cry.'"

> Soon afterward he went to a town called Nain, and his disciples and a large crowd accompanied him. As he approached the gate of the town a dead man was being carried out, the only son of a widowed mother. A considerable crowd of townsfolk were with her. The Lord was moved with pity upon seeing her and said to her "Do not cry." Then he stepped forward and touched the litter; at this, the bearers halted. He said, "Young man, I bid you get up." The dead man sat up and began to speak. Then Yeshua gave him back to his mother. Fear seized them all and they began to praise God. "A great prophet has risen among us," they said; and, "God

---

49. Mark 12:38–40; cf. Luke 20:45–47.
50. Luke 4:25–27.
51. Luke 18:1–8; see above, p. [X-ref].
52. Luke 4:38–39; cf. Matt 8:14–15; Mark 1:29–31.

has visited his people." This was the report that spread about him throughout Judea and the surrounding country.[53]

(8) Just as there was a widow (Anna) and his mother at the beginning of his life,[54] so also at the end of Yeshua's life there was a widow and his mother—and the two were one. According to the Fourth Gospel, even in his death agony Yeshua looked to the welfare of his beloved, most oppressed, widows; he provided his mother's future home with his "beloved disciple."

> Near the cross of Yeshua stood his mother and his mother's sister Mary the wife of Clopas, and Mary of Magdala. Seeing his mother and the disciple he loved standing near her, Yeshua said to his mother "Woman, this is your son." Then to the disciple he said, "This is your mother." And from that moment the disciple made a place for her in his home.[55]

YESHUA AND THE SAMARITAN WOMAN

On another occasion Yeshua again deliberately violated the then-common code concerning men's relationship to women. It is recorded in the story of the Samaritan woman at the well of Jacob.[56] Yeshua was waiting at the well outside the village while his disciples were getting food. A Samaritan woman approached the well to draw water. The fact that the woman came to the well alone makes it clear that she was ostracized by the rest of the reputable women in the town. We cannot know, but one can imagine a scene wherein Yeshua overheard several of the women of the town who were at the well remark about the scandalous woman who was approaching, and then scurried off, leaving Yeshua with the necessary information with which to speak to the woman "with the scarlet letter." The woman was not just any ordinary woman but must have been something of a scandal, since the man she was living with was her fifth man! Hence, by talking with her in such a public place Yeshua was also putting his reputation on the line.

Normally a Jew would not address a Samaritan, as the woman pointed out: "Jews, in fact, do not associate with Samaritans." But also normally

---

53. Luke 7:11–17.
54. Luke 2:36–38.
55. John 19:25–27.
56. John 4:5ff.

Three Jesus Certitudes

a man would not speak to a woman in public (doubly so in the case of a rabbi). However, Yeshua startled the woman by initiating a conversation. The woman was aware on both counts—her being a Samaritan and being a woman—that Yeshua's action was out of the ordinary, for she replied, "How is it that you, a Jew, ask a drink of me, a woman of Samaria?"

Here Yeshua was building further his reputation for gathering the marginalized of society: As hated as the Samaritans were by the Jews, it is nevertheless clear that Yeshua's speaking with a woman was considered a much more flagrant breach of conduct than his speaking with a Samaritan, for the Fourth Gospel relates, "His disciples returned, and were surprised to find him speaking to a *woman*, though none of them asked, 'What do you want from her?' or, 'Why are you talking to her?'" However, Yeshua's bridging of the gap of inequality between men and women continued further, for in the conversation with the woman, according to the gospel writer, Jesus revealed himself in a straightforward fashion as the Messiah for the first time: "The woman said to him, 'I know that the Messiah is coming' . . . Yeshua said to her, 'I who speak to you am he.'"

Just as when Yeshua revealed himself to Martha as "the resurrection," and to Mary Magdalene as the "risen one" and bade her to bear witness to the disciples, Yeshua here also revealed himself in one of his key roles, as Messiah, to a woman. (All these instances are recorded only in the Fourth Gospel—which is one of the reasons why I argued elsewhere, as well in this volume, that the penultimate version of the Fourth Gospel was written by a woman, and most likely by Mary Magdalene.[57]) The woman to whom Jesus reveals himself in the Gospel of John immediately *bore witness* of the fact to her fellow villagers. It is interesting to note that apparently the testimony of women carried greater weight among the Samaritans than among the Jews, for the villagers came out to see Yeshua: "Many Samaritans of that town believed in him on the strength of the woman's testimony" (vv. 25-26) It would seem that Fourth Gospel writer deliberately highlighted this contrast in the way she wrote about this event, and also that she clearly wished thereby to reinforce Yeshua's stress on the equal dignity of women.

This stress on the witness role for the Samaritan woman is further underscored by the Fourth Evangelist's language. The evangelist says the villagers "believed . . . because of the woman's word" (*episteusan dia ton*

---

57. As I noted earlier, I make the argument that the Fourth Gospel, or rather the penultimate version, was written by a woman evangelist, namely Mary Magdalene: Swidler, *Jesus Was a Feminist*.

logon [John 4:29]); she records almost the identical words in Yeshua's so-called priestly prayer at the Last Supper when Yeshua prays not only for his disciples "but also for those who believe in me through their word" (. . . *pisteuontōn dia tou logou*).[58] As Raymond E. Brown notes, "the Evangelist can describe both a woman and the (presumably male) disciples at the Last Supper as bearing witness to [Yeshua] through preaching and thus bringing people to believe in him on the strength of their word."[59]

One other point should be noted in connection with this story. As the crowd of Samaritans was walking out to see Yeshua, he was speaking to his disciples about the fields being ready for the harvest and how he was sending them to reap what others had sown. He was clearly speaking of the souls of humans, and most probably was referring directly to the approaching Samaritans. Such exegesis is standard. It is also standard to refer (e.g., in the *Jerusalem Bible*) to "others" in general and only to Yeshua in particular as having been the sowers whose harvest the apostles were about to reap But it would seem that the evangelist also meant specifically to include the Samaritan woman among those sowers, for immediately after she records Yeshua's statement to the disciples about their reaping what others had sown, the evangelist added the above-mentioned verse: "Many Samaritans of that town had believed on the strength of the woman's testimony." The Samaritan woman preached the good news, the *evangelion*, of Yeshua: that is, she was an evangelist.

Yeshua and the Penitent Woman

Scholars have always found Luke's story of Yeshua and the penitent woman difficult to understand and translate (especially the key portion, Luke 7: 47). Joachim Jeremias provides perhaps the most helpful suggestion when he supposes that Yeshua had just delivered a powerful sermon that moved the Pharisee Simon to see Yeshua as a prophet and the sinful woman to confess and repent of her sins and be filled with gratitude for the forgiveness she received in the sermon. Several things should be recalled here in the relationship between the woman and Yeshua. First, in that culture one did not publicly speak even to one's own wife, let alone to a strange woman, indeed a known "sinner," probably a prostitute! Yeshua not only spoke with her but let her touch him and kiss him. Further, a woman was never to let

---

58. John 17:20.
59. Brown, "Roles of Women in the Fourth Gospel," 691.

Three Jesus Certitudes

her hair be uncovered, and to loose it in public was grounds for mandatory divorce; this woman uncovered her hair, loosed it, and wiped Yeshua's feet with it, without thereby scandalizing Yeshua—although Simon was clearly scandalized. Yeshua rebuked the Pharisee and treated the woman not as a sexual creature but as a person; he spoke of her human and spiritual actions, her love, her unlove (her sins), her being forgiven, and her faith.

> One of the Pharisees invited him to a meal. When he arrived at the Pharisee's house and took his place at table, a woman came in, who had a bad name (*ēn hamartōlos*, "was a sinner") in the town. She had heard he was dining with the Pharisee and had brought with her an alabaster jar of ointment. She waited behind him at his feet, weeping, and her tears fell on his feet, and she wiped them away with her hair; then she covered his feet with kisses and anointed them with the ointment.
>
> When the Pharisee who had invited him saw this, he said to himself, "If this man were a prophet, he would know who this woman is that is touching him and what a bad name she has." Then Yeshua took him up and said him "Simon, I have something to say to you." "Speak, Master," was the reply. "There was once a creditor who had two men in his debt; one owed him five hundred denarii, the other fifty. They were unable to pay, so he pardoned them both. Which of them will love him more?" "The one who was pardoned more, I suppose," answered Simon. Yeshua said, "You are right."
>
> Then he turned to the woman. "Simon," he said, "you see this woman? I came into your house, and you poured no water over my feet, but she has poured out her tears over my feet and wiped them away with her hair. You gave me no kiss, but she has been covering my feet with kisses ever since I came in. You did not anoint my head with oil, but she has anointed my feet with ointment. For this reason, I tell you that her sins, her many sins, must have been forgiven her, or she would not have shown such great love. It is the person who is forgiven little who shows little love." Then he said to her, "Your sins are forgiven." Those who were with him at table began to say to themselves, "Who is this man, that he even forgives sins?" But he said to the woman, "Your faith has saved you; go in peace."[60]

---

60. Luke 7:36–50.

Prostitutes and the Reign of God

On at least one other occasion Yeshua reached out to despised women, in this case in his teaching concerning the most despised of human creatures, prostitutes—often serially murdered to this very day by maniacal, cowardly men. Yeshua made it clear in both his words and actions that he understood his mission to preach in word and deed the good news, the coming of the reign of God, to the poor and oppressed. In a debate with the chief priests and the elders of the people, Yeshua named two of the most unlikely classes of these oppressed as entering into the reign of God ahead of the chief priests and elders, namely, tax collectors and prostitutes—the two most despised groups of that society. A sexual parallelism should be noted here: the male tax collector and the female prostitute. It is difficult to believe that such a sexual balance was not struck deliberately by Yeshua, for the Synoptic Gospels usually connect tax collectors and *sinners* (a much broader term than *prostitutes*) with Yeshua ten different times, and only on this occasion are tax collectors and *prostitutes* mentioned. In fact (except in the parable of the Prodigal Son), this is the only time the term "prostitute" is used in any of the Gospels. The source for the term "prostitutes" in this connection could then, almost certainly, only be Yeshua.

As I reflect on this, I find it really quite extraordinary that Yeshua would picture prostitutes as under the reign of God, as being saved. Clearly for him a woman reduced completely to a sex object is seen as the object, not of disdain, but rather of exploitation, who nevertheless is a *person*, one among those who can "make their way to the reign of God."

> He had gone into the Temple and was teaching, when the chief priests and the elders of the people came to him . . . Yeshua said to them, "I tell you solemnly, tax collectors and prostitutes are making their way into the reign of God before you. For John came to you, a pattern of true righteousness, but you did not believe him, and yet the tax collectors and prostitutes did."[61]

Marriage and the Dignity of Women—Cana

In the Fourth Gospel, the first of the public signs of Yeshua was worked by him at the (at least indirect) bidding of a woman, his mother. Yeshua's

---

61. Matt 21:23, 31–32.

presence and support at the wedding at Cana confirms his affirmation of marriage and rejection of hyperasceticism. Perhaps the evangelist (a woman, perhaps Mary Magdalene) had this especially in mind when deciding to include this account, as a counterweight to the encratic, gnostic elements springing up at the time of the composition of this gospel, for those movements tended to be antimarriage, antisex, or both.

Also to be noted in this account is Yeshua's coupling respect for his mother with care to distance himself from her—part of his attempt to loosen the often oppressive cultural bonds of family. Yeshua addresses his mother as "Woman," a polite enough public usage with other women, but according to contemporary literature, surely not usual with one's mother. This distancing move is reinforced by his remark, "How does this concern of yours involve me?" (John 2:1–11)

Marcus Borg sets the Cana scene well:

> It is the opening scene, the inaugural story, of Jesus' public activity in the Gospel of John [Magdalene]. Inaugural stories are important in the Gospels. In each, the opening scene of Jesus' public activity discloses what the story of Jesus, the Gospel, is most centrally about. As John's [Magdalene's] inaugural story, the wedding at Cana functions as his [her] way of saying what the story of Jesus is about, what constitutes the good news.
>
> The first few words of the story are wonderfully evocative: "On the third day..." Big things happen in the Bible "on the third day," most notably the resurrection of Jesus. Thus at the beginning of his [her] Gospel, John [Magdalene] anticipates its climax. The next words, "there was a wedding," are equally evocative. Marriage was a rich religious metaphor in Judaism and early Christianity: the marriage of God and Israel, the wedding of heaven and earth, the mystical marriage between an individual and God, the church as the bride of Christ... These associations help us to understand the power of John's [Magdalene's] inaugural scene: the story of Jesus is about a wedding. And more: it is a wedding at which the wine never runs out. More: it is a wedding at which the best wine is saved for last. All of this flows from a more-than-literal reading, from hearing the story as a metaphorical narrative, from a parabolic reading of it... A literal reading risks missing the story's metaphorical meaning.[62]

---

62. Borg, *Jesus*, 58.

Yeshua Affirms Parents

Yeshua affirmed parenthood. Luke notes that Yeshua "lived under the authority" of his mother and father (Luke 2:51). And Yeshua reiterated the traditional affirmation of parenthood in his own words on one occasion when he accused his opponents of avoiding their obligations to their mothers and fathers. However, in this support of parents Yeshua in no way set the father's prerogatives above those of the mother.

> Pharisees and scribes from Jerusalem then came to Yeshua and said, "Why do your disciples break away from the tradition of the elders? They do not wash their hands when they eat food." "And why do you," he answered, "break away from the commandment of God for the sake of your tradition? For God said: Do your duty to your father and mother, and: Anyone who curses father or mother must be put to death. But you say, 'If anyone says to his father or mother: Anything I have that I might have used to help you is dedicated to God,' he is rid of his duty to father or mother. In this way you have made God's word null and void by means of your tradition. Hypocrites!" (Matt 15:1-7; cf. Mark 7:1–13)

Yeshua's Problems with His Family

Despite Yeshua's affirmation of marriage and parenthood, he had severe problems with his family. Early in his public life they tried to pack him off because they thought he was insane. More than that, he was rejected by his home community simply because they knew his family. His family not only tried to lock him in, but their very existence also tended to lock the community out.

> He went home again, and once more such a crowd collected that they could not even have a meal. When his family heard of this, they set out to take charge of him, convinced he was out of his mind. (Mark 3:20–21)
>
> Going from that district, he went to his home town and his disciples accompanied him. With the coming of the Sabbath he began teaching in the synagogue and most of them were astonished when they heard him. They said, "Where did the man get all this? What is this wisdom that has been granted him, and these miracles that are worked through him? This is the carpenter, surely, the son of Mary, the brother of James and Joset and Jude and Simon? His

sisters, too, are they not here with us?" And they would not accept him. And Yeshua said to them, "A prophet is only despised in his own country, among his own relations and in his own house"; and he could work no miracle there, though he cured a few sick people by laying his hands on them. He was amazed at their lack of faith. (Mark 6:1–6; cf. Matt 13:53–58; Luke 4:16–30)

Spiritual Bonds above Blood Bonds

In Near Eastern society, despite positive qualities, the demands of the patriarchal family relationships were at times overwhelming, often crushing individual personal growth, and most especially was this so for women. Almost any rule could be bent or broken, but not the obligations to family. Yeshua, having experienced family repression himself, clearly and often fought this social form of oppression, which weighed most often and most heavily on women. He insisted on personal, spiritual bonds as being more important than blood bonds.

> He was still speaking to the crowds when his mother and his brothers appeared; they were standing outside and were anxious to have a word with him. But to the man who told him this Yeshua replied "Who is my mother? Who are my brothers?" And stretching out his hand towards his disciples he said, "Here are my mother and my brothers. Anyone who does the will of my Father in heaven, he is my brother and sister and mother." (Matt 12:46–50, cf. Mark 3:31-35; Luke 8:19-21; 11:27-28)

Yeshua Dismantles Restrictive Family Bonds

A number of sayings of Yeshua stress following him as rising above the bonds of family obligations so vigorously as to be clearly hyperbolic in tone at times—as, for example, "hating" one's parents (in Aramaic "hating" really has the meaning of "loving less"). What is apparent is Yeshua's setting himself the task of dismantling the awesomely powerful restrictive forces of the patriarchal family, whose most obvious victims were women.

> (1) Peter took this up. "What about us?" he asked him. "We have left everything and followed you." Yeshua said, "I tell you solemnly, there is no one who has left house, brothers, sisters, father, children

or land for my sake and for the sake of the gospel who will not be repaid a hundred times over, houses, brothers, sisters, mothers, children and land—not without persecutions now in this present time, and in the world to come eternal life." (Mark 10:28–30)

(2) "Do not suppose that I have come to bring peace to the earth: it is not peace I have come to bring, but a sword. For I have come to set a man against his father, a daughter against her mother, a daughter-in-law against her mother-in-law. A man's enemies will be those of his household." (Matt 10:34–36)

(3) "Anyone who prefers father or mother to me is not worthy of me. Anyone who prefers son or daughter to me is not worthy of me." (Matt 10:37–38)

(4) "And everyone who has left houses, brothers, sisters, father, mother, children or land for the sake of my name will be repaid a hundred times over, and also inherit eternal life." (Matt 19:29)

(5) "Do you suppose that I am here to bring peace on earth? No, I tell you, but rather division. For from now on a household of five will be divided: three against two and two against three; the father divided against the son, son against father, mother against daughter, daughter against mother, mother-in-law against daughter-in-law, daughter-in-law against mother-in-law." (Luke 12:51–53)

(6) "If anyone comes to me without hating his father, mother, wife, children, brothers, sisters, yes and his own life too, he cannot be my disciple." (Luke 14:26)

(7) Then Peter said, "What about us? We left all we had to follow you." He said to them, "I tell you solemnly, there is no one who has left house, wife, brothers, parents or children for the sake of the reign of God who will not be given repayment many times over in this present time and, in the world to come, eternal life." (Luke 18:28-30)

YESHUA SAYS YES! ON DIVORCE

One of the most important stands of Yeshua in relation to the dignity of women was his position on marriage. His unpopular attitude toward marriage[63] presupposed a feminist view of women; they had rights and respon-

---

63. Cf. Matt 19:10: "His disciples said to him, 'If such is the case of a man with his wife, it is not expedient to marry.'"

sibilities equal to those of men. It was quite possible in Jewish law for men to have more than one wife, though the reverse was not possible. Divorce also was a simple matter, to be initiated only by the man. In both situations women were basically chattel to be collected or dismissed as the man was able and wished to; the double moral standard was flagrantly apparent.

Yeshua rejected both by insisting on monogamy and restricting divorce in general; both the man and the woman were to have the same rights and responsibilities in their relationship toward each other.[64]

It is interesting to note here the remarks of a modern Jewish scholar when commenting on the theme of divorce in Matt 5:31–32.

> In these verses the originality of Jesus is made manifest. So far, in the Sermon on the Mount, we have found nothing which goes beyond Rabbinic religion and Rabbinic morality, or which greatly differs from them. Here we do. The attitude of Jesus towards women is very striking. He breaks through oriental limitations in more directions than one. For (1) he associates with, and is much looked after by, women in a manner which was unusual; (2) he is more strict about divorce; (3) he is also more merciful and *compassionate*. He is a great champion of womanhood, and in this combination of freedom and pity, as well as in his strict attitude to divorce, he makes a new departure of enormous significance and importance. If he had done no more than this, he might justly be regarded as one of the great teachers of the world.[65]

The key to properly understanding Yeshua's position on divorce lies in a rabbinic dispute at the time that raged between the school of Shammai, who said a wife can be divorced only for adultery (Yeshua here agreed with Shammai), and the school of Hillel, who said a wife can be divorced "for any reason" (here Yeshua disagreed with Hillel); Hillel's view became the accepted position in subsequent Judaism.[66]

In the Mishnah (written around the year 200 CE) we find the following:

> The School of Shammai say: "A man may not divorce his wife unless he has found something unseemly in her, for it is written, 'Because he hath found in her *indecency* in anything.' And the School

---

64. Cf. Matt 19:3ff; Mark 10:2ff.

65. Montefiore, *Rabbinic Literature and Gospel Teaching*, 217–18.

66. One should remember that Yeshua might well have had both Hillel and Shammai as his teachers in Galilee and most of the time agreed with the school of Hillel; see Swidler, *Yeshua*. Also, the school of Shammai was dominant until the destruction of Jerusalem in 70 CE, after which the school of Hillel became dominant into to the present.

of Hillel say "(He may divorce her) even if she spoiled a dish for him, for it is written, 'Because he hath found in her indecency in *anything*.'" Rabbi Akiba says: "Even if he found another more beautiful than she, for it is written, 'And it be if she find no favour in his eyes.'"[67]

The recent work done by Ann Nyland, professor of Greek and other ancient languages in Australia, is extremely enlightening here. She has published a new translation of the New Testament based on the recent publication of thousands of first-century Greek papyri and inscriptions, which clarified many previous puzzles. Her work about divorce merits lengthy quotation here:

> In Matthew 19:3, the Pharisees asked Jesus, "Is it legal for a person to divorce his wife on the grounds of "Any Matter" [*pasan aitian*]? The Rabbis were asking Jesus about his interpretation of Deuteronomy 24:1 ["If a man marries a woman who becomes displeasing to him because he finds something indecent about her . . ."]. The "Any Matter" is a technical term from Jewish divorce law, a form of divorce introduced by Rabbi Hillel. The other type of divorce, on the grounds of "General Sexual Immorality" was available to both men and women, both of whom were able to divorce the partner on the specific grounds based on Exodus 21:10–11 ["If a man marries another woman, he must provide. If he does not provide her with these three things, she is to go free.] This traditional divorce was becoming rarer by the start of the first century, being replaced by the "Any Matter" divorce, which was for men only, and popular as no grounds had to be shown and there was no court case. For an "Any Matter" divorce, the man simply had to write out a certificate of divorce and give it to his wife. By Jesus' time, the "Any Matter" was the more popular form of divorce, but the rabbis were still arguing about the legalities of it. The disciples of Shammai were particularly opposed to it. See Josephus, *AJ* 4.253: "He who desires to be divorced from his wife who is living with him on the grounds of 'Any Matter' must certify in writing . . ." Philo, *Special Laws* 3.30: "if a woman is parting from her husband on the grounds of 'Any Matter'"; see also the Rabbinic *Commentary Sifre/Deuteronomy* 269.
>
> Jesus replied that divorce on the grounds of "Any Matter" was not legal, that whoever divorces his wife, unless it's on the grounds of "General Sexual Immorality" [*epi porneiai*] and marries

---

67 *Mishnah*, Git. 9:10; for full discussion see Swidler, *Women in Judaism*; and Swidler, *The Status of Women*, 198.

someone else, commits adultery. Jesus is simply saying that if someone divorces by a form other than the grounds of "General Sexual Immorality" form of divorce, they are not properly divorced and thus not free to remarry, and thus are committing adultery if they do so. He is continuing his statement that he disagrees with the "Any Matter" form of divorce.

It is most important to note the significance of the above. The way the passage has traditionally been (mis)translated implies that Jesus was asked the question, "Is it ever legal to divorce?" and he answered, "No, except on the grounds of sexual immorality." This is not the case. Jesus was asked if it was legal to divorce on the grounds of "Any Matter" and he answered, "No, only on the grounds of "General Sexual Immorality." In other words, he was disagreeing with the "Any Matter" form of divorce. He certainly was not saying that at that time, or in the time to come, people were never to divorce except for sexual immorality.[68]

This misunderstanding of Yeshua's stance was one that was rather thoroughly assimilated by the Christian church with disastrous effect. It was applied in an overly rigid way concerning divorce in Western Catholic Christianity, where divorce eventually was almost never allowed, even in the case permitted by Yeshua according to Matt 19:9: "Whoever divorces his wife, except for unchastity"—*mē epi porneiai*.[69] Fortunately, the overrigid position of Western Catholic Christianity was not taken by Eastern Orthodox Christianity, where divorce continues to be allowed.

If someone could lay before a courageous pope this clarification of the obviously egregious misunderstanding and mistranslation by the traditional Catholic interpretation of gospel material on divorce, millions of personal tragedies could be avoided—though past billions cannot be undone.

See below for the discussion of why Mark has a version of Yeshua's discussion whose brevity has led to such a catastrophe in Western Christianity.

Anointment of Yeshua by Mary of Bethany—A Time Warp

It was customary that women did not eat with men when guests were present, nor indeed did they even enter the dining area. Above I mentioned my experience in Israel and Palestine during which females were out of sight during the meals. I had read during my year's research on the status

68. Nyland, *Source*, 192–93.
69. Cf. also Matt 5:28.

of women during the early rabbinic period that women indeed did all the cooking, but they could not even serve it when guests were present, but that boys had to do that. I experienced precisely that in 1972 in the small Arab village of Deir Semit in the West Bank. I had met an Arab Muslim shop owner, Hajj Omar, in Jerusalem through my American friend of the University of Tübingen days, John Landgraf. We both were invited for the weekend to Hajj Omar's house in his home village, Deir Semit, where John had previously spent a year working alone on an archeological site, and hence was well known and loved by all in the village.

It happened that when we arrived on a rickety bus in the village, the primary school was just letting out. When the first children spotted John, they all began to jump up and down and shout "John! John!" When the rest of the children poured out of the school, they began to shout in Arabic "Wain John? Wain John? [Arabic: "Where's John? Where's John?"]" What popped into my head was that they had it backward; it should be, "John Wayne! John Wayne!" A silly thought.

While at the village I was introduced to all the important men—I tried to find the women doing all the cooking to say thanks, but to no avail. That evening John, I, the schoolteacher, the *muktar* (village head man), and Hajj Omar all had a sumptuous meal on the roof of the muktar's home. All the food was served to us by a young boy—nary a female in sight!

To return to Yeshua's time (since which nothing seemed to have changed), nevertheless when a woman (Mary of Bethany, according to John 12:3) entered the room where Yeshua was dining and anointed him, he neither resisted nor rebuked her. To be sure, others showed unhappiness at her intrusion, expressed especially at her "wasting" the expensive ointment. But, as in the Martha and Mary story in Luke 10:38–42, Yeshua defended Mary's act of special discipleship to him.

Yeshua was at Bethany in the house of Simon the leper; he was at dinner when a woman came in with an alabaster jar of very costly ointment, pure nard. She broke the jar and poured the ointment on his head. Some who were there said to one another indignantly, "Why this waste of ointment? Ointment like this could have been sold for over three hundred denarii and the money given to the poor"; and they were angry with her. But Yeshua said, "Leave her alone. Why are you upsetting her? What she has done for me is one of the good works. You have the poor with you always, and you can be kind to them whenever you wish, but you will not always have me. She has done what was in her power to do: she has anointed my body beforehand for its burial. I tell you solemnly, wherever throughout all the world the Good News is proclaimed, what she has done will be told also, in remembrance of her."[70]

Anointment of Yeshua by Mary of Bethany—Again

The Fourth Gospel's account of the anointment of Yeshua by Mary confirms the all-male character of the banquet, in accordance with the custom of the day, for it states that Lazarus (brother of Martha and Mary) was at table, and that Martha, as usual, served.[71] Also as usual, Mary did not serve but related to Yeshua in a very special way both poignantly personal and "transcendent," apparently oblivious of, or disregarding, her intrusion into a male sanctum, probably because she knew from experience that Yeshua would support her—which he did.

It should also be noted that both Mark and Matthew report this story, but with the variance that Mary poured the ointment on Yeshua's head, not his feet, wiping them with her hair, as the Fourth Gospel reports. Luke does not report this story but recalls the one about the "penitent woman" who in the house of a Pharisee washed the feet of Yeshua with her tears and wiped them with her hair—hence the subsequent confusion in the Christian tradition, which often lumped together Mary of Bethany, the prostitute who washed Yeshua's feet with her tears and wiped them with her hair, and Mary Magdalene.

The confusion was confirmed in the West by Pope Saint Gregory I the Great (590–604) when he wrote:

> It is clear, that the woman previously used the unguent to perfume her flesh in forbidden acts. What she therefore displayed more scandalously, she was now offering to God in a more praiseworthy manner. She had coveted with earthly eyes, but now through penitence these are consumed with tears. She displayed her hair to set off her face, but now her hair dries her tears. She had spoken proud things with her mouth, but in kissing the Lord's feet, she now planted her mouth on the Redeemer's feet. For every delight, therefore, she had had in herself, she now immolated herself. She turned the mass of her crimes to virtues, in order to serve God entirely in penance. (*Homily XXXIII*)

---

70. Matt 26:6–13; Mark 14:3–9; cf. John 12:1–8.

71. See Swidler, *Biblical Affirmations of Woman*, 194–95, for an analysis of the significance of the word "served," *diēkonei*, used here.

It is clear today that Mary of Bethany, Mary of Magdala, and the "prostitute" were three separate persons. The mutual influence of the Gospel writers and their various sources is still not completely clarified, nor is it ever likely to be!

> Six days before the Passover, Yeshua went to Bethany, where Lazarus was, whom he had raised from the dead. They gave a dinner for him there; Martha waited on them and Lazarus was among those at table. Mary brought in a pound of very costly ointment, pure nard, and with it anointed the feet of Yeshua, wiping them with her hair; the house was full of the scent of the ointment. Then Judas Iscariot—one of the disciples, the man who was to betray him—said, "Why wasn't this ointment sold for three hundred denarii, and the money given to the poor?" He said this, not because he cared about the poor, but because he was a thief; he was in charge of the common fund and used to help himself to the contributions. So Yeshua said, "Leave her alone; she had to keep this scent for the day of my burial. You have the poor with always, you will not always have me."[72]

Women in Yeshua's Language

One of the places where Yeshua's commitment has been extremely evident—for those who have eyes to see it!—is in the very language attributed to Yeshua in the Gospels.

First, Yeshua often used women in his stories and sayings, something most unusual for his culture.

Second, the images of women Yeshua used were never negative, but rather always positive—in dramatic contrast to his predecessors and contemporaries, as we saw in the rabbinic material cited above.

Third, these positive images of women were often exalted, at times being associated with the reign of heaven, likened to the chosen people, and even to God herself!

Fourth, Yeshua often taught a point by telling two similar stories or using two images, one of which featured a man and one a woman. This balance, among other things, indicated that Yeshua wanted it to be abundantly clear that his teaching, unlike that of other rabbis, was intended for both women and men—and he obviously wanted this to be clear to the men as

---

72. John 12:1–8; cf. Matt 26:6–13; Mark 14:39–47.

well as the women, since he told these stories to all his disciples and at times even to crowds.

Fifth, these parallel stories and images also confirm the presence of women among his hearers; they were used to bring home the point of a teaching in an image familiar to the women.

Yeshua's parallel stories and images range from very brief pairings to lengthy parables. Their frequency in the Synoptic Gospels is impressive: there are nine of them. For example, the reign of heaven is likened to a mustard seed, which a man sowed, and to leaven, which a woman put in her dough; or, in the final days one man of two in the field and one woman of two grinding corn will be taken. However, the ultimate parallel story that Yeshua told depicted God as a woman who found a lost coin (Luke 15:8–10). It is important to be aware of these parallel stories, for they tell us much positively about Yeshua's attitude toward women. Analyzed below is the significance of recorded story variations and what the variations tell us about the attitude toward women of the several evangelists and their sources.

The Intellectual Life for Women

Perhaps Yeshua's strongest and clearest affirmation that the intellectual and spiritual life was just as proper to women as to men is recorded in Luke's Gospel in the description of a visit of Yeshua to the house of his friends Martha and Mary.[73] The first thing to be noted is that Yeshua allowed himself to be served by a woman, which was contrary to strict custom, although it might have been somewhat mitigated because it took place in the less rigid village area. This may seem strange today. But,

> There is an interesting corollary to the restrictions on conversing with women within the household, which, among other things, limited their role as a "serving being," albeit with a somewhat demeaning motivation. First, women did not eat with the men whenever there was a guest. This is made clear in two stories about Rabbi Nahman (third century CE), who, when at meal with a guest, asked him to send greetings to his (Nahman's) wife Yaltha. One story is as follows: "Ulla was once at the house of Rabbi Nahman. They had a meal and he said grace, and he handed the cup of benediction to Rabbi Nahman. Rabbi Nahman said to him:

---

73. Luke 10:38ff.

Please send the cup of benediction to Yaltha" (bBer. 51b), but Ulla refused to do so.

At this point Billerbeck comments: "Women normally did not partake at a meal for guests; in order to honor them, the cup of benediction with some left over wine was sent to them."[74] The same custom persists in the villages of Palestine today. While in Israel in 1972, I was in a number of houses of Arabs, Christians, Druze and Muslims, for meals, and never met the wives, or any other women; my friends had many similar experiences.

The separation of women, or rather, females, from the meals of the men was carried even further; the men were not even to be served by women. When the same Rabbi Nahman wanted to have his daughter, who was only a child, serve him and his guest a drink, he was rebuked with the clear quotation of the earlier Rabbi Samuel: "One must not be served by a woman." When Nahman argued that she was only a child, he was told: "Samuel said distinctly, that one must not be served by a woman at all, whether adult or child."

Again, a similar custom persists among contemporary Palestinians; at all the meals I was at, we were never served by girls or women. The women did all the work of preparing the food and usually brought it as far as the door of the dining area, whether it was a room or house roof or whatever, and there it was taken by the youngest males and brought to the guests.[75]

Yeshua here clearly rejected the prevalent notion that the only proper place for women was "in the home." Martha took the woman's typical role and "was distracted with much serving." Mary, however, took the supposedly male role: she "sat at the Lord's feet and listened to his teaching." "To sit at (someone's) feet" is a rabbinic phrase synonymous with "to study with (that person)." (It should be noted that this is a *terminus technicus* for being a disciple—which is even reflected in contemporary English speech when we say, I sat at the master's feet.) That phrase, coupled with the second half, "listened to his teaching," makes it abundantly clear that Mary was acting like a disciple of a teacher, a rabbi. Martha apparently thought Mary was out of place in choosing the role of the intellectual, for Martha complained to Yeshua. But Yeshua's response was a refusal to force all women into the

---

74. Strack and Billerbeck, *Kommentar zum Neuen Testament aus Talmud und Midrasch*, 1:882. Paul Billerbeck is the scholar who did this massive research; H. L. Strack just had the connections to get it published.

75. The entire quotation is taken from Swidler, *Women in Judaism*, 125.

stereotype; he treated Mary first of all as a person (whose highest faculty is the intellect, the spirit) who was allowed to set her own priorities, and who in this instance had "chosen the better part." And Yeshua applauded her: "It is not to be taken from her." Again, when one recalls the Palestinian restriction on women studying the Scriptures or studying with rabbis (that is, engaging in the intellectual life or acquiring any religious authority), it is difficult to imagine how Yeshua could possibly have been clearer in his insistence that women were called to the intellectual and the spiritual life just as were men.

This text of the Lucan Yeshua also suggest strongly that Mary of Bethany might well be Luka.

> In the course of their journey he came to a village, and a woman named Martha welcomed him into her house. She had a sister called Mary, who sat down at the Lord's feet and listened to him speaking. Now Martha who was distracted with all the serving said, "Lord, do you not care that my sister is leaving me to do the serving all by myself? Please tell her to help me." But the Lord answered: "Martha, Martha," he said, "you worry and fret about so many things, and yet few are needed, indeed only one. It is Mary who has chosen the better part; it is not to be taken from her."[76]

In at least one other instance in the Gospels Yeshua clearly taught that the intellectual and spiritual life was definitely for women. One day as Yeshua was preaching, a woman from the crowd apparently was very deeply impressed and, perhaps imagining how happy she would be to have such a son, raised her voice to pay Yeshua a compliment. She did so by referring to his mother, and did so in a way that was probably not atypical at that time and place. But her image of a woman was sexually reductionist in the extreme (one that largely persists to the present)—emphasizing female genitals and breasts: "Blessed is the womb that bore you, and the breasts that you sucked!" Although this was obviously meant as a compliment, and although it was even uttered by a woman, Yeshua clearly felt it necessary to reject this "baby machine" image of women and insist again on the personhood, the intellectual and moral faculties, being primary for all: "But he said, 'Blessed rather are those who hear the word of God and keep it!'"[77]

It is difficult to see how the primary point of this text could be anything substantially other than this. Luke (or rather, "Luka" behind him, as

---

76. Luke 10:38–42.
77. Luke 11:27–28.

I argue elsewhere[78] and below) and the sources he depended on must also have been quite clear about the sexual significance of this event. Otherwise, why would he (and they) have kept and included such a small event from all the years of Yeshua's public life? It was not retained *merely* because Yeshua said that those who hear and keep God's word are blessed, for Luke had already recorded that statement of Yeshua in 8:21.[79] Rather, it was probably retained because Yeshua stressed keeping God's word as being primary in comparison to a woman's sexuality. Luke (Luka) seems to have had a discernment here, as well as elsewhere, concerning what Yeshua was about in his approach to the question of women's status—a discernment that has not been shared by subsequent Christians (and that perhaps was not shared by many of Luke's fellow Christians); for in the explanation of this passage, Christians for two thousand years apparently have not seen its plain meaning—doubtless because of unconscious presuppositions about the status of women inculcated by their cultural and religious milieu.

> Now as he was speaking, a woman in the crowd raised her voice and said, "Happy the womb that bore you and the breasts you sucked!" But he replied, "Blessed rather are those who hear the word of God and keep it!"[80]

God as a Woman

Yeshua strove in many ways to communicate the notion of the equal dignity of women. In one sense that effort was capped by his parable of the woman who found the lost coin,[81] for here Yeshua projected God in the image of a woman. This was extraordinary in the Jewish culture of Yeshua's time. Luke (Luka) recorded that the despised tax collectors and sinners were gathering around Yeshua, and consequently the Pharisees and scribes complained. Yeshua, therefore, related three parables in a row, all of which depicted God's being deeply concerned for that which was lost. The first story was of the shepherd who left the ninety-nine sheep to seek the one lost—the shepherd is God. The third parable is of the prodigal son—the father is God. The second story is of the woman who sought the lost coin—the woman

---

78. Swidler, *Jesus Was a Feminist*.
79. Cf. Matt 12:46–50 and Mark 3:31–35.
80. Luke 11:27–28.
81. Luke 15:8ff.

is God! Yeshua did not shrink from the notion of God as feminine. In fact, it would appear that Luke's (Luka's) Yeshua included this womanly image of God quite deliberately at this point, for the scribes and Pharisees were among those who most of all denigrated women—just as they did the "tax-collectors and sinners." (It should be noted that although Matthew has the story about the lost sheep,[82] only Luke [Luka] has the stories of the prodigal son and the woman whom God is like.)

Perhaps readers have begun to notice by now that Luke's (Luka's) Gospel appears to favor women in an unusually strong way. That impression will only strengthen as this book continues. That pileup of facts earlier led me to investigate the matter more thoroughly. After much intense research, I came to the conclusion that Proto-Luke (which had been discerned by New Testament scholars decades ago as the core of Luke's Gospel as we now have it) was written by a woman—to whom I have given the symbolic name Luka. But that is a story for another whole book by some younger scholar, the basis of which can be found in my 2007 work, *Jesus Was a Feminist* and in this volume.

Interim Conclusion

A great number of further texts from the Gospels deal with women but have not yet been analyzed here. I will cover a significant number of them below when I look at each of the four Gospels for the attitude of the authors and their sources toward women. I have in fact analyzed all of them in greater detail elsewhere,[83] and have found that they completely reinforce the conclusion that the evidence already presented here unavoidably leads to—namely, it is strikingly clear that Yeshua vigorously promoted the dignity and equality of women in the midst of a very male-dominated society—that is, *Yeshua was a feminist*, and a very radical one.

---

82. Matt 18:12–14.

83 See Swidler, *Biblical Affirmations of Woman*; Swidler, *Jesus Was a Feminist*.

Excursus I

A Leap Ahead to a Feminine Holy Spirit

THIS BRIEF EXCURSUS DOES not deal with Yeshua directly, but it figures in Christian feminism, and this seems to be a fitting place to bring it up.

At some points in Christian history the Holy Spirit has been associated with a feminine character: for example, in the third-century Syrian *Didascalia* where in speaking of church offices it says, "The Deaconess however should be honored by you as the image of the Holy Spirit."

It would make an interesting investigation to see if these threefold Lukan images of God (as the father of the prodigal son, as the shepherd of the lost sheep, and as the woman searching for a lost coin) were ever interpreted in a Trinitarian manner—thereby giving the Holy Spirit a feminine image. A negative result in the investigation would be as significant as a positive one, for this Lukan passage would seem to be particularly apt for a later Christian Trinitarian interpretation: The prodigal son's father is *God the Father* (this interpretation has in fact been quite common in Christian history); since Yeshua elsewhere identified himself as the good shepherd (John 10:11, 14), the shepherd seeking the lost sheep is Yeshua, *God the Son* (this usual interpretation is reflected in, among other things, the often-seen picture of Yeshua carrying the lost sheep on his shoulders); the woman who sought the lost coin should logically be God the Holy Spirit.

Statue in the Eggfelden, Bavaria, parish church from the first half of the fifteenth century—the Trinity crowning Mary queen of heaven. The Holy Spirit is depicted as a woman because in Hebrew (and other Semitic languages) the word for "Spirit" (*Ruach*) is feminine. Photo by Wolfgang Schreiner

Fresco of the Trinity in the parish church of Prien bei Chiemsee in Bavaria, by an unknown artist in the first half of the fifteenth century. The woman figure in the center is the Holy Spirit. The Holy Spirit is depicted as a woman because in Hebrew (and other Semitic languages) the word for "Spirit" (*Ruach*) is feminine. Photo by Leonard Swidler.

Should such lack of logic be attributed to the general cultural denigration of women, or Christian abhorrence of pagan goddesses? If the latter, why did Christian abhorrence of pagan gods not also result in a rejection of a male image of God? The only answer can be an underlying and widespread negative attitude toward women that blinded most Christian theologians and commentators to the strong feminism of Jesus in the Gospels:

> The tax collectors and the sinners, meanwhile, were all seeking his company to hear what he had to say, and the Pharisees and the scribes complained. "This man," they said, "welcomes sinners and eats with them." So he spoke this parable to them:
>
> (1) "What person among you with a hundred sheep, losing one, would not leave the ninety-nine in the wilderness and go after the missing one till he found it? . . .

A Leap Ahead to a Feminine Holy Spirit

(2) "Or again, what woman with ten drachmas would not, if she lost one, light a lamp and sweep out the house and search thoroughly till she found it? And then, when she had found it, call together her friends and neighbors? 'Rejoice with me,' she would say, 'I have found the drachma I lost.' In the same way, I tell you, there is rejoicing among the angels of God over one repentant sinner."

(3) He also said, "A man had two sons. The younger said to his father, 'Father, let me have the share of the estate that would come to me.'..."[1]

As evidence of a positive depiction of the third person of the Trinity, the Holy Spirit, consider the following: In the very beginning of the Bible, Genesis 1:2, it says that the spirit (*ruach*) of God hovered over the abyss, and a little later it says that God took a little earth (*'adamah*) and breathed his spirit (*ruach*) into it and created *ha-'adam* (literally "the earthling"). The earthling has no gender yet; that comes a little later in the chapter. It is interesting to note that the Hebrew word *ruach* is feminine in grammatical gender in Hebrew. That fact leads later to the Holy Spirit in Christian tradition being linked with the dove, an ancient symbol of the goddess of love, starting with the Gospel stories of the "Spirit of God" descending on Yeshua at his baptism in the river Jordan. This female face of the Holy Spirit continued beyond the Jewish tradition deep into Christian tradition, producing, among many manifestations, the above two fifteenth-century expressions of the Holy Spirit as a woman.

---

1. Luke 15:1–5, 8, 12

Excursus II

Whence Evil? And, Is Woman Superior to Man?

YESHUA WAS SPIRITUALLY NOURISHED by the Torah, as were all Jews. The beginning of the Torah begins with the Beginning! These first three chapters of Genesis at the beginning of the Bible are an amazing repository of wisdom about the meaning of life, which for centuries has been fundamentally distorted in ways that have had disastrous results to the present—and will continue to have into the future. I am not talking first of all about the fundamentalist distortion that naively assumes that the Genesis account is the historical report of some mythical precreation *Paradise Times* reporter describing what happened *ab initio*, from the beginning. Today one can perhaps only sigh at such a claim. Rather, I am talking about the distortions that had real effects in human life, such as that the story is about *the fall* of humanity into the state of being a sin-sotted soul, or that the man was created superior to the woman.

The first distortion relates to the Western Christian doctrine of original sin, which is not present in Judaism and hence is the source of a potentially creative dialogue between Judaism and Christianity. The second, about the relationship between women and men, as laid out in Gen 1–3, provides a very enlightening and creative dialogue possibility concerning that relationship for both Judaism and Christianity—and, indeed, for Islam and the rest of the world.

I wish, then, to reflect briefly on these two distortions and offer what I believe are more plausible understandings.

THE ORIGIN OF GOOD AND EVIL

All the cultures and civilizations of the ancient world had their various explanations of reality and, especially, whence evil came. Basically, their answers were that good things came from good gods or spirits, and evil things from evil gods or spirits. It was not so with the ancient Israelites. They came up with a breakthrough theory, namely, that everything was created by one God, and this one God created everything good (*tov* in Hebrew). In the first book of the Hebrew Bible, Genesis, the first chapter describes the creation of the various parts of the universe as taking place in six phases ("days"), and at the end of each day it states that God saw that what God had done was *tov* ("good"). At the end of the last day of creation, what God had done was *mod tov* ("very good").

Now, this story set up a problem, one that my then-three-year-old daughter, Carmel, posed very starkly. She was then speaking only German, having been born and raised in Germany till then. We were out for a walk after a very warm rain, and the sidewalk was covered with earthworms, *Regenwürme*, which for her were definitely icky, "evil." She very seriously asked: *Ist Gott gut* (Is God good)? I responded, *Ja*. She then asked, *Hat Gott alles gemacht* (Did God make everything)? I, now becoming somewhat wary, answered, *Ja*. Then she sprang the trap: *Wer dann hat die Regenwürme gemacht* (Who then made the earthworms?): the problem of evil! Well, the ancient Israelites were also aware of that problem and had their answer: the "domino theory."

During the Cold War a domino theory concerning the fall of countries into the camp of Communism was frequently used to justify political or even military intervention. For example, if Vietnam fell to Communism, then Cambodia would fall next, and Laos after that, and then Burma, and so forth, like a row of dominos stood on end next to each other, knocking each other over one after another. Perhaps the first version of the domino theory was developed in Gen 3. As seen in the first chapter of Genesis, everything that God made was *tov*, and hence everything was acting according to its good *nature* (Latin: *natus*, "born")—that is, everything was *tov*, good, as it was created by God. However, when the acme of God's creation, women and men, disobeyed and no longer acted according to their good *nature*, they stepped out of the good relationship with their creator: The first domino fell, and consequently everything else fell out of its originally good relationship to humanity. Hence, the various "curses" in Gen

3, wherein weeds grow amidst the plants, childbirth is painful, and wives become subordinate to husbands (more on this below).

Often the way early Christian thinkers posed the question of moral evil to themselves was to juxtapose the All-Powerful God on the one hand and the radically free human on the other. The Irish theologian Pelagius favored humanity's free will, whereas Saint Augustine (who is credited with "inventing" the doctrine of original sin)—and largely the Western Christian church after him—favored the omnipotence of God. After breaking my head over the question for many years, I decided that the problem was not primarily with the irrational answers given by Augustine, Luther, Calvin, and others, eliminating human free will and blasphemously describing God as creating the majority of humans just in order to cast them into hell for all eternity. Rather, the problem was in the silly forming of the question. We were here dealing with two unknowns. (We, of course, cannot understand or explain the infinite God; nor can we understand or explain radical freedom.) So we were then asking the silly question of what the relationship was between the two unknowns. It reminded me of my boyhood smart-aleck question: What happens when an irresistible force meets an immovable object? Clever answer: An inconceivable reaction. As mathematics teaches us, one cannot rationally expect to answer the question of the relationship between two unknowns.

If we humans are not able rationally to explain to ourselves the antinomy between an omnipotent Creator and a radically free human, if we cannot rationally explain the looming contradiction between *Evil and the God of Love*,[1] as John Hick titled his 1966 book, we can nevertheless find a less pessimistic, dark direction of a response that was offered in earlier Christian thought, as well as in traditional Orthodox Christianity. Hick has laid out that approach in great detail in the above-named book and, subsequently, almost forty years later in his 2004 book, *The Fifth Dimension*.[2] Hick found a more positive interpretation of this dilemma several centuries before Saint Augustine, first of all in Saint Irenaeus of Lyon (130–202 CE)—who, despite being designated by a city of present-day France, Lyon, where he eventually served as bishop, was originally from the East and was Greek-speaking.

Rather than understanding the Genesis story of the first woman and man as a fall into evil from which all subsequent humans cannot escape and

1. Hick, *Evil and the God of Love*.
2. Hick, *The Fifth Dimension*.

are consequently punished—as did Augustine and almost all later Christian thinkers—Irenaeus saw the situation much more the way a modern evolutionary thinker does. Hick noted that Irenaeus

> suggests that man was created as an imperfect, immature creature who was to undergo moral development and growth and finally be brought to the perfection intended for him by his Maker . . . instead of the Augustinian view of life's trials as a divine punishment for Adam's sin, Irenaeus sees our world of mingled good and evil as a divinely appointed environment for man's development towards the perfection that represents the fulfillment of God's good purpose for him.[3]

Irenaeus used an exegesis of Gen 1:26 that no modern Scripture scholar would accept, but it was a way for him to find a biblical basis for his understanding of human life. He asked what the biblical author intended by saying that humanity was made in God's "image and likeness." Why two synonyms, *imago* and *similitudo* in the Latin Vulgate, and *eikon* and *homoiosis* in the Septuagint Greek translations? The answer according to Greek Orthodox scholar P. Bratsiotis was

> The *eikon* is related, according to these Church Fathers [he is referring first to Irenaeus, then to Clement of Alexandria, Origen, Methodius, and Saint Gregory Nanzianus], to man's spiritual nature as a rational and free being. But the *homoiosis* means, according to the same Church Fathers, man's longing and positive striving toward God, and at the same time man's destiny, which is to come into the likeness of God.[4]

This, of course, is the famous Orthodox Christian doctrine of *theosis*. One must be careful to note that the Greek term does not mean "becoming God," as in pantheism, but "becoming God-like"—hence, not "deification" but, more accurately, "divinization."

Hick referred to this Irenaean "evolutionary" understanding of human life as "soul-making." "This world must be a place of soul-making. And its value is to be judged, not primarily by the quantity of pleasure and pain occurring in it at any particular moment, but by its fitness for its primary purpose, the purpose of soul-making."[5]

---

3. Hick, *Evil and the God of Love*, 220–21.

4. Bratsiotis, "Das Menschenverständnis in der griechisch-orthodoxen Kirche," 378; quoted in ibid., 217n3.

5. Hick, *Evil and the God of Love*, 295. He noted that the term "soul-making"

Three Jesus Certitudes

NOT THE FALL OF MAN BUT THE RISE OF HOMO SAPIENS

In Gen 3 the serpent tells Eve that if she eats the forbidden fruit of the tree of the knowledge of good and evil, she will not suffer some dire consequences as predicted by God but will in fact become "like God, knowing good and evil" (Gen 3:5).

According to the Bible, the serpent was not lying, for Eve saw that the fruit "was good for wisdom" (Gen 3:6) and that after she ate it her "eyes were opened" (3:7), and she and Adam learned to know the difference between good and evil. Further, even God says of Eve and Adam, "look, they have become like one of us, *knowing good and evil*" (3:22). Since earlier in the text it is stated that humans were "made in God's image" (1:27), it appears that "becoming like God," as the serpent promises, means "knowing good and evil."

Hence, here is a story that shows that the difference between humans and animals is to be found in humans' knowledge and free choice or love. Further, the text tells in story fashion how this came about. Our Western technical term for humans, *Homo sapiens*, gives us a clue of this development. *Sapiens*, which in Latin means wisdom, comes from *sapere*, "to taste." Hence, wisdom is not theoretical knowledge but the kind of knowledge that a person gains from experience, from "tasting" life. Thus, in the Genesis story, how do Eve and Adam become "wise"? How do they come to know good and evil (that is, come to be human, to be *Homo sapiens*)? By "tasting" (*sapiens*) the fruit of the tree of the knoweledge of good and evil.

They are different from the animals, which operate only on instinct, whereas humans can, and should, operate by learning what is good and what is evil and then choosing, loving, the good. It is not a result of eating the fruit of the tree of the knowledge of good and evil that we humans are now going to die. We were *always* going to die. However, now we humans *know* that we are going to die whereas as animals we did not know. Thus, both my dog and I are going to die; the difference between us in this regard is that I know that I am going to die, but my dog does not know. Again, the difference between animals and humans is knowledge, though, perhaps

---

comes from John Keats in a letter to his brother and sister in 1819: "Call the world if you Please 'The vale of Soul-making' ... Do you not see how necessary a World of Pains and troubles is to school an Intelligence and make it a Soul?" (Forman, ed., *The Letters of John Keats*, 334–35, as cited in Hick, *Evil and the God of Love*, 295n3).

unfortunately, here there is no question of choosing not to die but of choosing how to deal with that fact.

Hence, the Genesis story is not the story of the fall of humanity but of the rise of *Homo sapiens*, the human knowing (*sapiens*) the difference between good and evil, and thus being able freely to choose, to love.

MAN NOT CREATED SUPERIOR TO WOMAN: PERHAPS THE CONVERSE

To begin with, it must be noted that there are two creation stories, one in Gen 1 and a second less full one in Gen 2. The latter, written by the so-called Yahwist writer, probably in the tenth century BCE, doubtless existed far earlier in oral form. The Gen 1 creation story was written by the so-called Priestly writer, probably in the fifth century BCE.

In Gen 1 it is clear that humanity was created female and male simultaneously from the beginning: "And God created humanity, female and male he created them" (1:27). There is no priority of time of creation. What about the much older Yahwist, Gen 2 story of the creation of humanity? Is it not clear that the man is created first and then is put into a deep sleep and the woman is created from the rib of the man? No, that is definitely *not* what the text says; the deutero-Pauline's later, faulty exegesis notwithstanding (1 Tim. 2:13–15).

The Yahwist story of human creation is in Gen 2:6, which, as I noted earlier, states that "God Yahweh took a bit of earth [*'adamah*] and formed the human [*ha-'adam*—literally "the earthling"]." (*Ha* is the definite article, "the" in Hebrew, so that in conjunction with it, *ha-'adam* is not a proper name, "Adam," but "the earthling.") Gen 2:6 continues: "and breathed the 'breath' [Hebrew, *ruach*; *spiritus* in Latin] of life into it." In the Yahwist story the first human being is as yet ungendered, neither female nor male. Perhaps the Yahwist wished to stress that while the human being was from the earth, it was God who was the source of its life. Whatever the reason, it is clear that the Yahwist does *not* say that the male was created first. Rather an initially sexually undifferentiated "earthling" (*ha-'adam*) is taken from the earth (*'adamah*).

But, then, how do we account for the fact that there are men and women? In answering this question with an "etiological" story (*etios* [Greek: "origin"]), the Yahwist takes a wide detour by having God first create the garden of Eden (including with many geographical specifics, such as the names of the Tigris and Euphrates Rivers of present-day Iraq). God then sends the earthling (*ha-'adam*) in to tend it. However, God then says that "It is not good for the earthling [*ha-'adam*] to be alone," and so God creates the animals and brings them to the earthling one by one to be named. Thus, in the Yahwist story God created all the flora and only one fauna, namely, the earthling; only then did God create the rest of the fauna—an odd sequence, but indicative that what the Yahwist writer was after was not to present a kind of primitive evolutionary picture but, rather, a "story with a point," that is, an *etio*logical story to explain the *origin* of something, in this case, of gender.

Next, God sees that all the various animals are good in themselves, but they are not a "like" partner (2:18) for the earthling. It is important to note two things at this point. One is that the partner God sought for the earthling was a *like* one, and, hence, the other animals would not do. The second is that the Hebrew term here, *'ezer*, is most often translated "helper" and thereby is often assumed to mean *less* than the earthling—which assumption, of course, the additional use of "like" invalidates. Moreover, *'ezer* is also used elsewhere in the Bible to describe God as humanity's "helper"; hence, *'ezer* clearly does not denote an inferior.

God then places the earthling in a deep sleep and takes out a rib and forms it into a woman and brings this "cloned" creature to the earthling, who at the sight of her describes her (in the first word-play of many found in the Bible) "as woman (*'isshah*), for she was taken from the man" (Hebrew for male, *'ish*—2:23).

Thus, the Yahwist storyteller states that God first created the earthling, then the woman, at whose sight the earthling was transformed into the (male) man. The Priestly writer, on the other hand, has God creating humanity simultaneously as male and female. In neither case is any inferiority implied. This point is further reinforced by the fact that in Gen 3, as a so-called curse, woman is made subordinate to the man; it could not be a curse if she were created inferior to the man.

I hinted in the heading of this section that perhaps, contrary to the usual patriarchal traditions, at least the *image* of the woman in the garden of Eden story (the Yahwist story) is superior to that of the man.

In Gen 3 the serpent engages the woman in a heavy conversation about good and evil, life and death, being like God. She holds her own in the conversation with one who is said to be "the most cunning" of all the animals created by God. In the end she is persuaded—and, as we saw earlier, correctly so—that eating the fruit of the tree of the knowledge of good and evil would not cause her to die (she was going to die eventually anyway) but in fact would make them "as God," which proves to be the case, as God acknowledges in the same chapter. In fact, five hundred years after the writing of the Yahwist story, the Priestly writer stated it straightforwardly: "God said, let us make humanity (*ha-'adam*) in our image and likeness" (1:26).

Thus, the image of the woman is of someone who (1) engaged in a profound philosophical and theological dialogue about (2) truth and lies, (3) authority and freedom, and (4) life and death. The woman is someone who (5) thought things over, (6) made a decision, and (7) acted on it.

What is the *image* of the man? The Yahwist simply states that the woman gave the fruit of the tree of the knowledge of good and evil to her man, "and he ate" (3:6). No heavy dialogue with a cunning partner, no reflection, no executive decision—just, "he ate," as if he were just appetite and stomach. The next time the man appears, God is walking in the garden in the cool of the evening and asks him whether he had eaten of the forbidden fruit: "And the man said, 'The woman whom you gave to be with me gave me of the tree, and I ate.'" My four-year-old grandchild would probably have characterized his brave stand as that of a wimp and buck-passer!

The two different images of the man and the woman *in the text* stand out very clearly, not in need of any profound analysis to discern. Why then has the Christian tradition almost overwhelmingly, until most recently, not only *not* seen the seemingly obvious but indeed insisted on some sort of inverted distortion whereby the man is the superior—because he was created first? Psychological projection? Internalizing of the patriarchal myth and code? Nietzsche's *Wille zur Macht* (Will to Power)? Whatever the reasons, when it comes to this text's common, centuries-old interpretation, today more and more Christians are hearing the voice of the little child saying that the "emperor has no clothes."

4

Yeshua's Women Followers Created Christianity

IN THIS SECTION, I reverse the focus used up until now. Instead of looking at the Gospel texts to learn how Yeshua treated women, I look at the gospel texts to ask where they came from, who bothered to record them and transmit them. The evidence will show, I am convinced, that (1) underlying Mark's Gospel, the earliest written gospel we have, is a gospel written in Aramaic (now lost), traditionally said to have been written by the apostle Matthew—referred to by scholars as Aramaic Matthew; (2) the second gospel written is the expanded Greek translation of Aramaic Matthew, referred to as Greek Matthew, which is so strongly prowoman that one should say that it is, if not written, then sourced, by a "Matthea"; (3) a "feminist" Proto-Luke (written or sourced by, I suggest, a "Luka") underlies the Gospel of Luke; 4) the Fourth Gospel in its penultimate version was written by a woman, most probably Mary Magdalene.

Hence, if one were to take away all the information about Yeshua that is sourced by women, and erase the promoting efforts of women followers of Yeshua in the early centuries of the Common Era, there would, at most, have arisen only a very anemic tradition about Yeshua. There would have been the communities shaped by Saul/Paul and fellow preachers about *Christos*, though judging from Paul's letters and the descriptions of the early post–crucifixion/resurrection communities found in Luke's Acts of the Apostles, they seemed to have precious little knowledge about the teaching/healing Rabbi Yeshua. Consequently, any subsequent religious institution based on Rabbi Yeshua would have been, at best, weak and ephemeral, passing from the human scene in a few short centuries at most, just as did, e.g., Mithraism and Gnosticism.

In brief, *Christianity historically was given birth by the women followers of Yeshua!* In fact, one could slightly paraphrase the Latin translation of Yeshua's statement inscribed in Saint Peter's Basilica in Rome mentioned above: *Tu es Femina, et super hanc feminam aedificabo ecclesiam meam!* "You are woman, and upon this woman I will build my church"!

ATTITUDE TOWARD WOMEN OF GOSPEL WRITERS AND SOURCES

As outlined earlier, one of the contributions of modem scriptural scholarship is the idea that the Gospels are not simple accounts of the words and actions of Yeshua as related by several different eyewitnesses. The fact that they are many-layered faith statements brought together from several sources, written and oral, and put into their present four forms by at least four different Gospel writers means that they will tell us something not only of the attitude of Yeshua toward women but also of the attitudes of the evangelists and their sources. At times, in certain accounts, it is difficult to determine whether it is Yeshua's or the evangelists' or their sources' attitudes that are reflected, but for the most part those passages which clearly reveal Yeshua's own attitude have been treated above. However, many passages that in some way deal with women have not been treated here, though I have treated them elsewhere.[1] Only those will be listed below by Gospel and analyzed where pertinent for any additional light they cast on the attitude toward women expressed by the Gospel writer and his/her sources. (Often this will be traced in some form ultimately back to Yeshua.)

By presenting the material systematically according to each Gospel, I anticipate that a picture of the attitude toward women from each evangelist and his/her sources will emerge. The attitude of each can be compared to those of the others, and to that of Yeshua insofar as his attitude can be distilled out and seen separately from those of the evangelists and their sources.

---

1. Swidler, *Biblical Affirmations of Woman*; Swidler, *Jesus Was a Feminist*.

THREE JESUS CERTITUDES

THE GOSPEL ACCORDING TO MARK

The first Gospel to be presented will be Mark's since it is thought by most scholars to be the oldest. However, even earlier were the oral traditions, "sayings," of Yeshua, which are referred to as "Q," from the German word *Quelle*, meaning "source." Over the first decades after Yeshua's death around 30 CE, these "sayings," were passed on at first in their original Aramaic, and then also gradually in Greek translation. They ended up being assimilated in our current Gospels according to Matthew and Luke. Further complicating matters, the first attempt at writing a coherent story about Yeshua's teaching and life, a Gospel, was—as mentioned above—what many scholars refer to as Aramaic Matthew: that is, a Gospel that can be seen underlying the current Gospel according to Matthew, which is written in Greek and hence referred to as Greek Matthew. It seems that the writer of the Gospel according of Mark had at his disposal Aramaic Matthew, plus other sources.

Then will come Matthew's Gospel because it is the second gospel written; it also happens to contain second-largest number of women passages. Then will follow Luke's Gospel, which has the highest number of women passages and was the third gospel to be written. These three gospels—Mark, Matthew, and Luke—are referred to as the Synoptic Gospels because they treat many of the same events and teachings of Yeshua (*syn-optic*, Greek: "seen together"). The Fourth Gospel will be treated last because it was the last to be written, and because it has by far the smallest number of accounts that deal with women; moreover, they are almost totally unrelated to the material in the three Synoptic Gospels, outside the final section of all the Gospels, which treats the passion and resurrection of Yeshua.

Mark, as I said, is thought by most scholars to be the earliest of the four gospels. It is also the shortest, being about 62 percent of the length of Luke. (Matthew is about 92 percent of Luke's length, and the Fourth Gospel 75 percent.) Of the three Synoptic Gospels, Mark has by far the least to say about women. In Mark, there are twenty passages for a total of 114 verses that deal with one or more women, of with the feminine.

The Holy Spirit Shares a Symbol with the Goddess of Love

Mark began his Gospel by telling of John the Baptist, who baptized Yeshua in the Jordan river. As Yeshua came out of the water, Mark reported, a voice from heaven said "You are my beloved son in whom I am well pleased," and the Spirit descended on him in the form of a dove. As a consequence of that Markan report and similar ones from the other three gospels, the dove has for two thousand years been the most frequent symbol of the Holy Spirit (which after the fourth century became known also as the third person of the Blessed Trinity). Most Christians, however, do not realize that for centuries before, and after, the dove was the universal symbol of the goddess of love, under many names, including the *Mater Magna*, the "Great Mother"!

However, the connection of the Goddess of Love with the Holy Spirit is in many ways quite apt. To begin with, the very idea and language of the Holy Spirit as somehow a manifestation of God came from the Hebrew Bible, and therefore in the Hebrew language, wherein the Spirit (*Ruach*) is feminine in gender, and hence in poetic imagery.

> However, since the most ancient times the dove is the holy animal not only of the Cyprian Aphrodite, but also of almost all the Goddesses of Fertility and Love of the Near East. Already in neolithic times the "Great Mother" who was venerated in Crete was represented with dove and lily. The Greek word for dove, *peristera*, means "bird of Istar," the Assyrian-Babylonian Goddess of Love, but also of the Underworld and Death. Istar had many names: Astarte (Ashtoreth) and Hathor, Inanna and Nut, Cybele and Isis, and many others. However, as also with the Greek Aphrodite and the Roman Venus, the dove was always holy to them. Often they themselves appeared winged, like a great dove brooding over the world, as in Knossos and Mycenae, in Sicily and Carthage, on the Euphrates and on Cyprus, and even in India. Doves were cultically protected; great towers were built for them in which they could nest; they were called *columbaria* (*columba* is the Latin word for dove). *Columbaria*, dove houses, were also known in ancient Rome, however, as grave chambers with niches for urns.
>
> The dove is the only symbol for the Holy Spirit permitted by the Church. Thus the dove in the cupolas or over the high altars of Diessen, Dietramszell, Vierzehnheiligen, Ottobeuren, Weingarten, Ettal, and the Wieskirche also point to the "Great Mother" just as much as does the fact that the cathedrals of Hagia Sophia in Constantinople, Kiev, and many other Orthodox cities are consecrated to heavenly Wisdom, which is presented in feminine form.[2]

---

2. Kaltenbrunner, "Ist der Heilige Geist weiblich?" 275–76.

Woman Holy Spirit in Christian Art

Following the Hebrew tradition of the Holy Spirit (*Ruach ha-qadosh*) being feminine, some Christian artists have depicted the Holy Spirit as a woman. I offer two striking examples that I saw in Bavaria. Both come from the first half of the fifteenth century (that is, from the late Middle Ages). In the one, a three-dimensional figure, the Trinity, crowns Mary as queen of heaven. The third person of the Trinity is clearly a woman. The second image is a fresco in a vault in a small gothic church; the painting also is from the first half of the fifteenth century—before the Protestant Reformation—and in it the Trinity is depicted as having one body in the lower half and three torsos and heads above. Again, there is a male with a white beard, God the Father, then a second male with a dark beard, God the Son, and finally a clean-faced woman, God the Holy Spirit. The photos are on previous pages (in excursus 2).

Jairus's Daughter and the Woman with a Flow of Blood

See above for an analysis of these two spliced accounts of cures of women—one from death! Here we should simply focus on the fact that Mark has placed this spliced account of the cures of women next to the account of a cure of a man—the cleansing of a man of an "unclean spirit." These are the only cures recorded by Mark in this portion of his gospel; both preceding and following them are other kinds of matters: a series of parables by Yeshua, accounts of Yeshua's traveling, and the beheading of John the Baptist. Though we cannot be certain, it seems likely that Mark placed these accounts of cures side by side because they showed Yeshua curing both women and men. (Perhaps the arrangement of the materials is as he found them in his written or oral sources.) Because this set so very closely parallels the earlier cures of, first, a man possessed of an "unclean spirit" in Capernaum (Mark 1:21-28), and, second, Peter's mother-in-law (Mark 1:29-31), it again seems most likely that Mark placed these accounts of cures side by side because they likewise showed Yeshua curing both women and men. It is possible that here, and in the earlier set, Mark found these accounts already so arranged in his written or oral sources. We cannot know, but if it was so, it would simply be *evidence that an awareness of Yeshua's sexual egalitarianism preceded the composition of the Gospel of Mark*, and that Mark affirmed it and handed it on.

Also as in the earlier parallel set of cures Luke in copying Mark here likewise follows Mark's structure, thereby also handing on this evidence of Yeshua's egalitarian attitude toward the sexes and confirming it with his own. Matthew again rearranged Mark's structure here for other purposes (Mark 5:1–2, 21–43; cf. Matt 8:28–34; 9:18–26; Luke 8:26–39, 40–56).

Herodias, Salome, John the Baptist

This is the only story in Mark not in some way about Yeshua; Mark tells it because he saw John the Baptist as the prophet Elijah returning (Mark 9:11–13) as a precursor to the Messiah, Yeshua. It projects a very evil picture of women: Herodias indirectly asked for the head of John the Baptist, and Salome her daughter asked for it directly. It is from Josephus, the first-century Jewish historian, that we learn Salome's name (*Antiquities* 18.136). Josephus also records a different description of the execution of John the Baptist—ordered by Herod for political reasons (*Antiquities* 18.5.1–2). Mark parallels Queen Jezebel, who wished to kill Elijah (1 Kgs 21) with Herodias, who "was furious with him [John the Baptist—'Elijah returned'] and wanted to kill him" (Mark 6:19). Mark also was influenced by the story of Esther, with the woman called to "perform" before a crowd of tipsy courtiers, the king's promise of half his kingdom (cf. Esth 5:6), and the woman's beauty leading to the death of her enemy.[3]

Thus we have projected one of the few negative images of women in all the Gospels, but it is in a story that is not even about Yeshua. The fact, however, that it is recorded in Mark is simply a reflection of the culturally pervasive negative attitude toward women, perhaps indicating that Yeshua's positive attitude was not completely shared by Mark, or perhaps reflecting also the tradition Mark represented.

Matthew summarized Mark's twenty-seven-verse account in twelve verses: he in fact often shortened Mark's accounts (some scholars speculate that these short Matthean accounts were really the residues of the earlier Aramaic-language Matthew, which Mark later expanded). In doing so, he placed the desire to kill the Baptist not in Herodias but Herod, thereby very slightly mollifying the image of women that is projected; perhaps he too knew of the tradition of Herod's political motivation for killing John that Josephus mentioned. Luke, however, simply referred to John's criticism of Herod "for his relations with his brother's wife Herodias" (Luke 3:19),

---

3. See Swidler, *Biblical Affirmations of Woman*, 115–18, where this story is analyzed.

and later said that Herod had John beheaded (Luke 9:7–9)—no negative image of women. It seems that in this instance Yeshua's positive attitude toward women was not persuasive enough to persuade Mark or Matthew not to write the story of Herodias and Salome, but it did convince Luke/Luka not to include it. Matthew, however, did partly shift the guilt from the women alone and shortened the account by about 40 percent. Apparently Luke/Luka's sensitivity about women led him/her to find the vicious popular story about Herodias and Salome offensive, or at least irrelevant to the gospel of Yeshua as s/he understood it.

> It was this same Herod who had sent to have John arrested, and had him chained up in prison because of Herodias, his brother Philip's wife whom he had married. For John had told Herod, "it is against the law for you to have your brother's wife." As for Herodias, she was furious with him and wanted to kill him; but she was not able to, because Herod was afraid of John, knowing him to be a good and holy man, and gave him his protection. When he had heard him speak he was greatly perplexed, and yet he liked to listen to him.
>
> An opportunity came on Herod's birthday when he gave a banquet for the nobles of his court, for his army officers and for the leading figures in Galilee. When the daughter of this same Herodias came in and danced, she delighted Herod and his guests; so the king said to the girl, "Ask me anything you like and I will give it you." And he swore her an oath, "I will give you anything you ask, even half my kingdom." She went out and said to her mother, "What shall I ask for?" She replied, "The head of John the Baptist." The girl hurried straight back to the king and made her request, I want you to give me John the Baptist's head, here and now, on a dish." The king was deeply distressed but, thinking of the oaths be had sworn and of his guests, he was reluctant to break his word to her. So the king at once sent one of the bodyguards with orders to bring John's head. The man went off and beheaded him in prison; then he brought the head on a dish and gave it to the girl, and the girl gave it to her mother. When John's disciples heard about this, they came and took his body and laid it in a tomb. (Mark 6:17–29; cf. Matt 14:3–12; Luke 3:19–20; 9:7–9)

Yeshua's Mission to Non-Jews through a Woman

Mark was writing for a Gentile readership, and, according to a number of scholars, wished to develop a section on Yeshua's mission to Gentiles. Mark wrote in chapter 7, verse 24, "He set out for the [Gentile] territory of Tyre," and then told the story of the cure of the daughter of the Gentile woman (Mark 7:24–30). But then immediately Mark recorded Yeshua's trip farther north to Sidon (also a largely Gentile area) and back to the shores of the Sea of Galilee, a Jewish area: "Returning from the district of Tyre, he went by way of Sidon towards the Sea of Galilee, right through the Decapolis region" (Mark 7:31).

Thus, the only evidence Mark could find in the tradition for Yeshua's missionary tour of Gentile territory was this trip to Tyre and Sidon and back. The really interesting fact is that this trip produced nothing remembered other than the encounter with the Syro-Phoenician woman whose daughter Yeshua cured at her insistence. Was it because the status of women in the Roman world, for whom Mark wrote, was much higher than in Jewish society that Mark chose this story to show Yeshua reaching out to the Gentiles? Or was it that Mark simply found no other story in the tradition he knew that exemplified Yeshua's mission tour of pagan areas?

Given Mark's readership, most likely he would have included other such stories from Yeshua's trip if there were any, and so the second explanation is the more likely. But the first should not be ruled out as at least a contributing motive as well. It would seem that Mark thought that Yeshua conceived of his mission in pagan country as being directed only to his fellow Jews living there, for Mark says that "he [Yeshua] did not want it known, but it was not possible," and thus a Greek Syro-Phoenician woman came and asked Yeshua to cure her daughter

Then follows the first recorded instance of Yeshua helping Gentiles. (Mark's Gospel is unlike Matthew's, in which Jesus states directly, "I was sent to the lost sheep of the house of Israel" [Matt 15:24].) Mark, writing his gospel for Gentiles, does not record the remark of Matthew's Yeshua about his being sent only to Jews. Jesus's first recorded healing of a Gentile was to heal a female, at the persistent insistence of another woman: the daughter's mother. It was the mother's human quality, her "faith," that Yeshua perceived and that moved him to extend himself; she was not treated as an inferior category, a woman, but as a person, who had "great faith."

It is also interesting to note that this is the only recorded instance wherein Yeshua was bested in a verbal exchange—and it was by a pagan, and a woman!

> He left that place and set out for the territory of Tyre. There he went into a house and did not want anyone to know he was there, but he could not pass unrecognized. A woman whose little daughter had an unclean spirit heard about him straightaway and came and fell at his feet. Now the woman was a pagan, by birth a Syro-Phoenician, and she begged him to cast the devil was out of her daughter. And he said to her "The children should be fed first, because it is not fair to take the children's food and throw it to the house-dogs." But she spoke up: "Ah yes, sir," she replied, "but the house-dogs under the table can eat the children's scraps." And he said to her, "Woman, you have great faith. Let your wish be granted." And from that moment her daughter was well again. (Mark 7:24–30; cf. Matt 15:11–28)

No Divorce . . . Except

We have already seen above that in Matthew's Gospel Yeshua was asked by the Pharisees whether he agreed with the Hillelites or Shammaites among them, that is, whether a man may divorce his wife "for any matter" (*pasan aitian*—the Hillelite position), or "for unchastity" (*epi pornei*, the Shammaite position, citing Exod 21:10–11). Yeshua's answer was to reject the Hillelite position and affirm the traditional Shammaite position of allowing divorce on the grounds of unchastity.

Rabbi Solomon Schechter has written, "In the Mishnaic period the theory of the law that the husband could divorce his wife at will was challenged by the school of Shammai. It interpreted the text of Deut xxiv. 1 in such a manner as to reach the conclusion that the husband could not divorce his wife except for cause, and that the cause must be sexual immorality (Giṭ. ix. 10; Yer. Soṭah i. 1, 16b). The school of Hillel, however, held that the husband need not assign any reason whatever; that any act on her part which displeased him entitled him to give her a bill of divorce (Giṭ. ib.). The opinion of the school of Hillel prevailed."[4]

Rabbi Schechter then confirmed Matthew's description of Yeshua's position on divorce, namely, that "Jesus seems to have held the view of the

---

4. Schechter and Amram, "Divorce."

school of Shammai (Matt. xix.3–9)." However, in Mark's Gospel none of those distinctions are present. Mark's Yeshua simply says that if anyone divorces and remarries, s/he is guilty of adultery—seemingly rejecting the Torah, which allowed divorce for unchastity. Yeshua also spoke about a woman divorcing her husband, apparently already an impossibility in the then-Hillite-developed Jewish law (although possible according to Exod 21:10–11 and the Shammaite understanding of it, and as well in Hellenistic and Roman law of the time)—in that culture a revolutionary egalitarianism—but the parallel accounts in Matthew and Luke do not describe the husband as capable of adultery. Perhaps to underscore the newness of this teaching, Mark's version includes "against her" *(ep' autēn).* "He said to them, 'The man who divorces his wife and marries another is guilty of adultery against her. And if a woman divorces her husband and marries another she is guilty of adultery too.'"[5] Thus, according to Mark, Yeshua flatly contradicted the Jewish law and custom of his time by saying that a husband could be *moikatai ep' auten*, "guilty of adultery against her [his wife]." According to the Torah, as the ninth of the Ten Commandments makes clear, the "sin" is even coveting the neighbor's property—donkey, wife, servants, or what have you.

Of course, divorcing women were known in Palestine around the time of Yeshua, and he may have meant to include them in his remarks. Therefore it is not necessary to suggest that Mark—perhaps writing in Rome—was responsible for adding that phrase. On the other hand, if the Roman Mark included it because of his Gentile readership, then why did the Hellenistic Luke not include such phrasing, since he had Mark's Gospel in front of him? In any case, Yeshua's sexual egalitarianism in marriage comes through here very strongly, albeit only in a negative way. That is, Mark's Yeshua evenhandedly rejects divorce for both the woman and the man—not a particularly helpful egalitarianism. The really important question here, however, is, how could Mark's Yeshua seem to be unaware of the Pharisaic debate about which method of divorce was acceptable—not whether divorce was allowable at all or not? After all, Yeshua clearly was a rabbi learned in Torah matters, and very probably had been a student of both Hillel and Shammai.

For a long time, Western scholars and church leaders judged that Mark's version was most likely the closest to Yeshua's original words, and certainly faithful to the early tradition that Yeshua set forth a new teaching

---

5. Mark 10:11–12; cf. Matt 19:9; Luke 16:18.

clearly in favor of putting women on the same level as men in the crucial matter of marriage fidelity. In Jewish law, adultery could be committed *only* against a husband: that is, sex between a husband and an unmarried woman was *not* adultery against his wife, but sex between a wife and any man other than her husband was adultery against her husband (deserving the death penalty). But here in Mark's Gospel Yeshua speaks of a husband "being guilty of adultery against *her* [his wife]."

Still, it seems extraordinary that a rabbi would simply dismiss a clear Torah statute. When one looks at the parallel passage in Matthew, the matter is dramatically different—and appears much more likely authentic, for there Rabbi Yeshua is very aware of the split between his two teachers, and chooses to side with Shammai and Moses, against his favorite more liberal teacher, Hillel!

Given that Matthew's Gospel clearly is the one that is most thoroughly Jewish in a whole range of ways, it is more likely to have gotten the intra-rabbinic debate right than Mark, who most probably was writing with a Roman readership in mind. Given that Yeshua everywhere took positions favorable to equality for women—and everything that Mark records reinforces this—it would seem that Mark recorded only Yehsua's evenhanded male-female position (that a wife equally with the husband could not divorce); Mark's Yeshua did not comment about the possibility of divorce. Mark either did not know about the rabbinic debate or dropped it, perhaps because he thought it would be either confusing or displeasing to his intended pagan readership. Through his missionary travels, he would have been aware that the Gentile *theophobeis* ("God-fearers") Luke describes in the Acts of the Apostles were ubiquitous in the Roman Empire's synagogues.

It is probable that the nuanced posing of the question to Yeshua and his answer recorded in Greek Matthew were also present in the prior Aramaic Matthew since it concerned a specifically Jewish, rabbinic debate. However, it is also possible that the much more prowoman Greek Matthew ("Matthea"?) made sure Mark's truncated and oppressive version was corrected by recording the distinguishing terms of the rabbinic debate, with Yeshua confirming the Shammaite/Mosaic position that divorce was possible because of adultery. As Rabbi Solomon Schechter has stated, Yeshua "held the view of the school of Shammai."

Yeshua's Concern for Women's Welfare

There have been many scholarly suggestions for the real sources of the apocalyptic-sounding predictions of the end of the world found in all three of the Synoptic Gospels; these suggestions include solidly represented arguments that a prophetic statement of Yeshua is the source—just as the Gospels represent. General agreement exists that the evangelists made some editorial adaptation, but scholars usually disagree on exactly what was adapted. No one, however, denies that the statement, "Alas for those with child, or with babies at the breast, when those days come!" was in the original version. Since there is no reason Yeshua could not have made the original prophetic statement, however it may have been differently adapted by the evangelists, and since the documents claim that he did, it is logical to conclude that it is at least probable that he did. In that case Yeshua would be the utterer of the cry of concern for women.

There is a certain sexual parallelism in Jesus's teaching: references to a man on the housetop and a man in the fields are balanced by references to expectant mothers and nursing mothers. The desolation described is so sudden and devastating that only immediate flight offers some chance of safety; hence relatively immobilized mothers are at a severe disadvantage, and Yeshua expressed great concern for them—about no one else did he so express his concern.

Matthew and Luke used basically the same words concerning the women as did Mark.

> When you see the disastrous abomination set up where it ought not to be (let the reader understand), then those in Judaea must escape to the mountains; if a man is on the housetop, he must not come down to go into the house to collect any of his belongings; if a man is in the fields, he must not turn back to fetch his cloak. Alas for those with child, or with babies at the breast, when those days come! Pray that this may not be in winter. For in those days there will be such distress as, until now, has not been equaled since the beginning when God created the world, nor ever will be again. And if the Lord had not shortened that time, no one would have survived; but he did shorten the time, for the sake of the elect whom he chose. (Mark 13:14–20; cf. Matt 24:15–25; Luke 21:20–24)

Women in Yeshua's Passion and Resurrection

Women followers of Yeshua were extraordinarily supportive of him in his passion, death, and burial; in their presence at the empty tomb; in their seeing the risen Yeshua; and in their reporting to the rest of the disciples. Almost all these elements are reported by each of the four Gospels—an extraordinary near unanimity.

- Only women remain by Yeshua through his death (Mark 15:40–41; cf. Matt 27:55–56; Luke 23:49; John 19:25)
- Women witness the burial of Yeshua (Mark 15:47; cf. Matt 27:61; Luke 23:55)
- Women first witnesses to the empty tomb (Mark 16:1–8; cf. Matt 28:1–8; Luke 24:1–8; John 20:1–10)
- Women testify about resurrection to male disciples (Mark 16:7, 11; cf. Matt 28:8; Luke 24:9–11; John 20:18)
- The risen Yeshua appears to women first (Mark 16:9; cf. Matt 28:9-10; John 20:11–17)

Conclusion

To recall, Mark's Gospel is the earliest of the four canonical Gospels that we have, being written about the year 70. However, it was based on an earlier Aramaic gospel that has since been lost, usually referred to as Aramaic Matthew (to whom it was traditionally attributed), plus other oral and perhaps written sources. Mark's Gospel has the least number of passages dealing with women of the three Synoptic Gospels (20 to Matthew's 36 and Luke's 42) and the smallest number of verses concerning women of all four Gospels (114 to the Fourth Gospel's 119, Matthew's 180, and Luke's 220). Of course it is the shortest gospel in overall size, but proportionately nevertheless has the least emphasis on women of the three Synoptics, but still more than the Fourth Gospel's in terms of proportionate quantity.

Because it is the earliest extant gospel, it apparently was available to both Greek Matthew and Luke, and consequently almost all of it reappears in one form or another in either Matthew or Luke or both, and that includes all the passages dealing with women. Hence in comparison to the other two Synoptics, Mark seems much less pro-woman in terms of the number of accounts dealing with women that are recorded. Still, the important fact that nothing negative about women is recorded (with the exception of the non-Yeshua story of the beheading of John the Baptist, discussed above) and the significant number of positive accounts about women that Mark does record lead to the conclusion that Mark's Gospel is pro-woman in its stance, though not nearly as much as the Gospels of Matthew and Luke, or even the Fourth Gospel.

THE GOSPEL ACCORDING TO MATTHEW

It is clear that no negative statements, attitudes, or actions concerning women by Yeshua appear in the Gospel of Mark. That in itself has a great significance. And while Mark provides a smaller amount of positive evidence of Yeshua's attitude toward women in comparison to the other two Synoptic Gospels, Matthew and Luke, this evidence nevertheless does indeed support a claim that Yeshua was a champion of women—though in comparison to the other three Gospels, only modestly so.

However, the situation is quite different when we come to the next two Synoptic Gospels, Matthew and Luke. Not only in neither of them is there any negative attitude toward women expressed by Yeshua, but also every one of the above accounts in Mark dealing with women is, as noted just above, found in either Matthew or Luke, or in both, and sometimes even in the Fourth Gospel as well.

Furthermore, Matthew records eighteen additional accounts significantly concerned with women that Mark does not mention—making a total of thirty-six accounts in Matthew dealing with women. Of these non-Markan accounts, ten are peculiar to Matthew; eight of them Luke also records along with Matthew. (The Fourth Gospel records none of these eighteen accounts.) The ten passages peculiar to Matthew plus the four it has in common with Mark that Luke does not have make fourteen accounts concerning women that Matthew records and that Luke does not.

Clearly what had happened is that the relatively brief Aramaic Matthew, which was the basis for Mark's Gospel, has been greatly expanded in Greek Matthew (the version we possess) partly because a large number had been added of the Sayings of Yeshua (known together as Q), which had been circulating since Yeshua's lifetime, as well as additional material from other sources. Tradition suggests the apostle Matthew as author of both Aramaic Matthew as well as Greek Matthew. However, if Mark was written in 70 and Greek Matthew only in 85, there must have been at least fifteen—or even more—years between the writing of Aramaic Matthew and Greek Matthew, which fact lessens, but does not eliminate, the likelihood that both Aramaic Matthew and Greek Matthew were the same author. In addition, because of the extraordinary quantity and quality of the prowoman, "feminist," material in Greek Matthew—so very much more than in Mark, and hence also even more than in Aramaic Matthew, behind Mark—one might well speculate about an anonymous woman, "Matthea," as a possible author of Greek Matthew, or at least as a major source thereof. However, for now, let us leave the speculation there and look further at the evidence.

Passages Common to Matthew and Luke Alone

The Virginal Conception of Yeshua

Matthew's account of the virginal conception of Yeshua, that is, by the Holy Spirit in the womb of Mary, does perforce focus on the woman Mary. But it focuses still more sharply on the man Joseph. Even though the couple was only betrothed, the legal force of their state was practically as strong as marriage—sexual intercourse by the betrothed woman with any other man would have been considered not fornication but adultery (though not so for the betrothed man if he did the same). Joseph was under obligation to divorce his apparently adulterous betrothed (necessary even though they were only betrothed). He could have subjected her to the humiliating ordeal of *Sotah* (for a description of it, the only trial by ordeal in the Bible, see Num 5:11–31 and the Talmudic tractate *Sotah*), and possibly have had her executed. However, Joseph, "being a man of honor and wanting to spare her publicity, decided to divorce her informally": this was a significant sensitivity toward women enacted at the beginning of Yeshua's life.

Luke's account of the virginal conception of Yeshua was within a different context from Matthew's, namely, the "annunciation" to Mary (Luke 1:18–26), to be discussed below. It should be noted that whereas in Matthew's account Joseph was the main focus of attention and the angel appeared to him, in Luke's account Mary was the center of attention and the angel appeared not to Joseph but to Mary.

> This is how Jesus Christ came to be born. His mother Mary was betrothed to Joseph; but before they came to live together she was found to be with child through the Holy Spirit. Her husband

> Joseph, being a man of honor and wanting to spare her publicity, decided to divorce her informally. He had made up his mind to do this when the angel of the Lord appeared to him in a dream and said, "Joseph son of David, do not be afraid to take Mary home as your wife, because she has conceived what is in her by the Holy Spirit. She will give birth to a son and you must name him Yeshua, because he is the one who is to save his people from their sins." Now all this took place to fulfil the words spoken by the Lord through the prophet: The virgin will conceive and give birth to a son and they will call him Emmanuel, a name which means "God-is-with-us." When Joseph woke up he did what the angel of the Lord had told him to do: he took his wife to his home and, though he had not had intercourse with her, she gave birth to a son; and he named him Yeshua. (Matt 1:18-25; cf. Luke 1:26-38)

Queen of Sheba

One of the most interesting passages treated by both Matthew and Luke is the one referring to the queen of the South, the queen of Sheba. Mark has simply a report of a demand made of Yeshua by the Pharisees for a sign, which Yeshua rejected (Mark 8:11–12), and referred to Jonah in the whale. As I have noted, Mark's Gospel is based on Aramaic Matthew, and that often this earlier layer can be discerned in our present expanded Greek version of Matthew. Here is such an example: Scholars find an instance of the early Aramaic Matthew in our present Greek version of Matt 16:1–4, where a sign was asked of Yeshua, which request he rejected—except for the "sign of Jonah." However, in the second version (that is, the later Greek version of Matthew ["Matthea"?]—Matt 12:38–42), the story is repeated in an *expanded* form that includes a reference not only to Jonah but also to the queen of Sheba. A tradition including additional references to women was obviously known and used by the author of Greek Matthew ("Matthea"?), and of Luke ("Luka"?)—Luke 11:29-32—which was not known to the earlier authors of either Aramaic Matthew or Mark. This strengthens the argument that Greek Matthew was either written by a woman ("Matthea"?) or very heavily sourced by women.

> Then some of the scribes and Pharisees spoke up. "Master," they said, "we should like to see a sign from you." He replied, "It is an evil and unfaithful generation that asks for a sign! The only sign it will be given is the sign of the prophet Jonah. For as Jonah was in

the belly of the sea-monster for three days and three nights, so will the Son of Man be in the heart of the earth for three days and three nights. On judgement day the men of Nineveh will stand up with this generation and condemn it, because when Jonah preached they repented; and there is something greater than Jonah here. On judgment day the queen of the South will rise up with this generation and condemn it, because she came from the ends of the earth to hear the wisdom of Solomon; and there is something greater than Solomon here." (Matt 12:38–42; cf. Matt 16:1–4; Mark 8:11–12; Luke 11:29–32)

The Wedding Feast

Of the eight accounts dealing with women that only Matthew and Luke recorded, the seventh account concerns women only indirectly, and only in Matthew. It is a story of Yeshua's describing what the reign of heaven was like (the "reign of God" in Luke). Matthew describes the reign of heaven as a wedding feast, whereas Luke has it simply as a feast. Furthermore, in the story Luke makes getting married an excuse for not going to the banquet. In Matthew's account, getting married is not offered as an excuse. Hence, in this case, compared to Luke, Matthew is more sympathetic, if not to women, at least to marriage, on two points—one positive (imaging the reign of God as a wedding feast) and one negative (not offering marriage as an excuse to keep from entering God's reign).

The Genealogy of Yeshua

The eighth and last common account that Matthew and Luke have is like the seventh in that only Matthew's version deals with women. The account in each gospel concerns Yeshua's genealogy. At the beginning of Matthew's Gospel is a very interesting genealogy of Yeshua, which is supposed to establish him as the Messiah, as a son of David, and a son of Abraham. It is clearly intended to be artificial in that there are three sections to the genealogy with fourteen names each (two times the holy number of fullness, 7), though to make the structure symmetrical some generations listed in the Hebrew Bible were omitted by Matthew. It is, however, of interest here to note that the names of five women are included in the genealogy, an oddity since paternity alone was the source of legal rights. Moreover, each of the women had a "moral flaw" connected with sex: Tamar played a harlot and seduced Judah, her father-in-law; Rahab was a prostitute; Ruth sneaked into Boaz's bed and seduced him to marry her; Bathsheba, Uriah's wife, committed adultery with David, and Mary was found with child before her marriage. Christians claimed Yeshua's virginal conception, and doubtless therefore detracting stories circulated about his "immoral," extramarital origin: how could such a one be the Messiah? Matthew/Matthea's response was a messianic genealogy that listed four sexually "immoral" women (other women, such as the very popular "matriarchs" Sarah, Rebecca, and Rachel, are not mentioned) at key points in the Davidic line: Tamar was associated with the founding fathers of the twelve tribes of Israel, namely, "Judah and his brothers"; Rahab played a role in the gaining of the promised land; Ruth was remembered as founding mother of the house of David (see Ruth 4:17–22); Bathsheba was the wife of David, the first real king of Israel, and the mother of its greatest king, Solomon. Matthew/Matthea obviously saw this pattern of sexually irregular women playing crucial roles at turning points in the history of the chosen people. This history reached its climax in Mary, the mother of the Messiah. It is perhaps an indication of the relatively high status of women among the primitive Christian communities in Palestine—where (probably) and for whom Matthew/Matthea's gospel was written—that such a proud claim could be made to such women in Yeshua's ancestry.

A genealogy of Yeshua Christ, son of David, son of Abraham:

1.
Abraham was the father of Isaac,
Isaac the father of Jacob,
Jacob the father of Judah and his brothers,
Judah the father of Perez and Zerah, *Tamar being their mother,*
Perez was the father of Hezron,
Hezron the father of Ram,
Ram was the father of Amminadab,
Amminadab the father of Nahshon,
Nahshon the father of Salmon,
Salmon was the father of Boaz, *Rahab being his mother,*
Boaz was the father of Obed, *Ruth being his mother,*
Obed was the father of Jesse;
and Jesse was the father of King David.

2.
David father of Solomon, *whose mother had been Uriah's wife,*

Solomon was the father of Rehoboam,
Rehoboam the father of Abijah,
Abijah the father of Asa,
Asa was the father of Jehoshaphat,
Jehoshaphat the father of Joram,
Joram the father of Azariah,
Azariah was the father of Jotham,
Jotham the father of Ahaz,
Ahaz the father of Hezekiah,
Hezekiah was the father of Manasseh,
Manasseh the father of Amon,
Amon the father of Josiah,
and Josiah was the father of Jechoniah and his brothers.

3.
Then the deportation to Babylon took place.
After the deportation to Babylon;
Jechoniah was the father of Shealtiel,
Shealtiel the father of Zerubbabel,
Zerubbabel was the father of Abiud,
Abiud the father of Eliakim,
Eliakim the father of Azor,
Azor was the father of Zadok,
Zadok the father of Achim,
Achim the father of Eliud,
Eliud was the father of Eleazar,
Eleazar the father of Matthan,
Matthan the father of Jacob;
and Jacob was the father of Joseph the husband of *Mary;*
of her was born Yeshua who is called Christ.

The sum of generations is therefore: fourteen from Abraham to David; fourteen from David to the Babylonian deportation; and fourteen from the Babylonian deportation to Christ. (Matt 1:1–17)

Compare this genealogy in Matthew with the one in Luke—3:23–38—which is almost completely different and mentions no women.

Passages Special to Matthew

As I noted above, ten passages deal with women in Matthew alone. Of these, three really reflect nothing as far as the attitude toward women is concerned.

Yeshua's Women Followers Created Christianity

Infancy Narratives

Three accounts surrounding the infancy of Yeshua that deal with women are peculiar to Matthew. The woman mainly involved was Mary the mother of Yeshua. The first account was about the coming of the magi. Matthew records that when the magi found the house, they went in and "they saw the child with his mother Mary" (Matt 2:11). Later Joseph was told by an angel in a dream to "take the child and his mother" (2:13) into Egypt; he did so (2:14). After Herod's death Joseph was again told by an angel in a dream to "take the child and his mother" (2:20) back to Israel; and he did so (2:21). Following the pattern established in the earlier portion about the virginal conception of Yeshua, Matthew, in contrast to Luke, continued to make Joseph the lead character in the story, with the angel always appearing to him. Mary appears only as "his mother," who was either with Yeshua when the Magi found him or was taken to or from Egypt by her husband. These passages reflect nothing of Yeshua's attitude toward women, and certainly indicate nothing positive on the part of Matthew.

> (1) After Yeshua had been born at Bethlehem in Judaea during the reign of King Herod, some wise men came to Jerusalem from the east. "Where is the infant king of the Jews?" they asked. "We saw his star as it rose and have come to do him homage." The sight of the star filled them with delight, and going into the house they saw the child with his mother Mary, and falling to their knees they did him homage. (Mt 2:1-2, 10-11)
>
> (2) After they had left, the angel of the Lord appeared to Joseph in a dream and said, "Get up, take the child and his mother with you, and escape into Egypt, and stay there until I tell you, because Herod intends to search for the child and do away with him." So Joseph got up and, taking the child and his mother with him, left that night for Egypt, where he stayed until Herod was dead. (Matt 2:13-15)
>
> (3) After Herod's death, the angel of the Lord appeared in a dream to Joseph in Egypt and said, "Get up, take the child and his mother with you and go back to the land of Israel, for those who wanted to kill the child are dead." So Joseph got up and, taking the child and his mother with him, went back to the land of Israel. But when he learnt that Archelaus had succeeded his father Herod as ruler of Judaea he was afraid to go there, and being warned in a dream he left for the region of Galilee. There he settled in a town called Nazareth. (Matt 2:19-23)

THREE JESUS CERTITUDES

Adultery of the Heart

The saying attributed to Yeshua that the man who lusts after a woman commits adultery with her in his heart does not reflect a great deal about Yeshua's or Matthew's attitudes toward women. The primary point seems to be that moral evil lies in the will—even if the fulfillment of the act were not carried out. In this, Yeshua was not teaching something new, even concerning sexual morality. The sixth (or seventh) commandment says, you shall not commit adultery, and the ninth (tenth) goes on to the evil in the heart when it says, you shall not covet your neighbor's wife. Yeshua's teaching was clearly traditional.[6] The absence of any parallel statements in the Decalogue, in Job, in the Testaments of the Twelve Patriarchs, or here in Matthew forbidding the woman to covet the man does reflect patriarchal assumptions. Is this male bias by omission to be attributed to Yeshua or Matthew and/or his sources? We cannot of course be certain, but given the many other sexually parallel statements, stories, and images used by Yeshua, there is a stronger likelihood the imbalance comes from Matthew and/or his sources.

> You have learnt how it was said: You must not commit adultery. But I say this to you: if a man looks at a woman lustfully, he has already committed adultery with her in his heart. (Matt 5:27–28)

The Mother of the Sons of Zebedee

In Matthew's Gospel, Salome, the wife of Zebedee and the mother of the apostles James and John, asked Yeshua for places of honor for her sons; in Mark's earlier version the brothers asked for themselves (Mark 10:35–40). Matthew's account (Matt 20:20–23) is a bit awkward, for in verses 20 and 21 the exchange is between Yeshua and the mother (the verbs are singular),

---

6. See also Job 31:1, and the Testaments of the Twelve Patriarchs, written around 106 BCE: "Do ye, therefore, my children, flee evildoing and cleave to goodness. For he that hath it looketh not on a woman with a view to fornication, and he beholdeth no defilement"—Testament of Benjamin 8:1-2; "I never committed fornication by the uplifting of my eyes"—Testament of Issachar 7:2; Charles, *The Testaments of the Twelve Patriarchs*, "The Testament of Issachar," http://www.earlychristianwritings.com/text/patriarchs-charles.html/.

but in 22 and 23, without any indication of a change in the conversation partners, Yeshua addressed the brothers (the verbs are now plural). Is this because in changing the Markan account Matthew neglected to add a phrase something like, "and turning to the brothers, Yeshua said . . ."?

Why does Matthew's tradition make the mother ask rather than the sons? If it is because it reflects the historical fact, it would indicate that at least this woman wielded a strong influence with two apostles and presumably also with Yeshua. She obviously did not approach Yeshua unbeknownst to her sons; they were there and collaborated. It would seem she was the mediator because she was thought to have greater influence with Yeshua than her two apostle sons—all the more extraordinary since these two men were not shy, being nicknamed by Yeshua "sons of thunder," and along with Peter were regularly the inner circle of the apostles, being chosen to view the Transfiguration, to go apart with Yeshua at the Garden of Gethsemane, and so forth. The apostles' mother's standing with Yeshua must have been considerable! In return she remained by Yeshua to the crushing end—and the resurrection: she stood by the cross (Matt 27:56; Mark 15:40), and was at the empty tomb (Mark 16:1).

> Then the mother of Zebedee's sons came with her sons to make a request of him, and bowed low; and he said to her, "What is it you want?" She said to him, "Promise that these two sons of mine may sit one at our right hand and the other at your left in your kingdom." "You do not know what you are asking," Yeshua answered. "Can you drink the cup that I am going to drink?" They replied, "We can." "Very well," he said, you shall drink my cup, but as for seats at my right hand and my left, these are not mine to grant; they belong to those to whom they have been allotted by my Father." (Matt 20:20–23; cf. Mark 10:35–40)

The Multiplication of Loaves

All four of the Gospels include the account of the multiplication of the loaves and fishes by Yeshua to feed a multitude in the desert. Two of them, Mark and Matthew, recorded two such events; many scholars argue that these are simply two forms of the same account. However that may be, what should be especially noted here about Matthew's account is that it alone speaks of women; all the other Gospel writers spoke of five thousand *men* (*andres*) being fed. Matthew in both his accounts says there were

Three Jesus Certitudes

"five [or four] thousand men (*andres*), besides women (*gynaikôn*) and children." From what we know from elsewhere in the Gospels there were many women among Yeshua's listeners. Yet women are not mentioned in any version of this episode except Matthew's. All the evangelists must have known that women would have been present at this teaching and miracle as well as men. But apparently the primitive form of the story of the five thousand that the earliest Gospel, Mark, has (and Aramaic Matthew behind it?—Mark 6:31-44)—which referred only to men—was accepted by Luke and the Fourth Gospel writer without their reflecting that certainly women would also have been present; or if they did reflect, without their thinking it important enough to allude to. (Mark's other account, of the feeding of four thousand—Mark 8:1-10—referred to the "crowd," and not to men or women.)

For Matthew either there was additional information available about the presence of women, or there were some insistent voices in his sources that made it important to allude to the women and children, or Matthew (or "Matthea"?) decided it was important enough that they should be explicitly mentioned. Perhaps the desire to enhance the magnitude of the miracle influenced Matthew to mention the women. But besides the fact that the women and children were doubtless present, and the fact that mentioning them would magnify the miracle, it is also true that having compassion on the women and children fit perfectly with Yeshua's extremely positive attitude toward both groups. This would seem to be a clear indication that Matthew/Matthea was sensitive to the "feminism" of Yeshua.

> When Yeshua received this news he withdrew by boat to a lonely place where they could be by themselves. But the people heard of this and, leaving the towns, went after him on foot. So as he stepped ashore he saw a large crowd; and he took pity on them and healed their sick.
>
> When evening came, the disciples went to him and said, "This is a lonely place, and the time has slipped by; so send the people away, and they can go to the villages to buy themselves some food." Yeshua replied, "There is no need for them to go: give them something to eat yourselves." But they answered, "All we have with us is five loaves and two fish." "Bring them here to me," he said. He gave orders that the people were to sit down on the grass; then he took the five loaves and the two fish, raised his eyes to heaven and said the blessing. And breaking the loaves he handed them to his disciples who gave them to the crowds. They all ate as much as they wanted, and they collected the scraps remaining, twelve

baskets full. Those who ate numbered about five thousand men, to say nothing of women and children. (Matt 14:13–21; cf. Mark 6:31–44; Luke 9:10–17; John 6:1–13)

Yeshua went on from there and reached the shores of the Sea of Galilee, and he went up into the hills. He sat there, and large crowds came to him bringing the lame, the crippled, the blind, the dumb and many others; these they put down at his feet, and he cured them. The crowds were astonished to see the dumb speaking, the cripples whole again, the lame walking and the blind with their sight, and they praised the God of Israel.

But Yeshua called his disciples to him and said, "I feel sorry for all these people; they have been with me for three days now and have nothing to eat. I do not want to send them off hungry, they might collapse on the way." The disciples said to him, "Where could we get enough bread in this deserted place to feed such a crowd?" Yeshua said to them, "How many loaves have you?" "Seven," they said, "and a few small fish." Then he instructed the crowd to sit down on the ground, and he took the seven loaves and the fish, and he gave thanks and broke them and handed them to the disciples who gave them to the crowds. They all ate as much as they wanted, and they collected what was left of the scraps, seven baskets full. Now four thousand men had eaten, to say nothing of women and children. (Matt 15:29–38; cf. Mark 8:1–10)

Prostitutes and the Reign of God

As noted on page 55, it is very unlikely that Matthew can be credited in 21:31–32 with substituting the term "prostitutes" (*pornai*) for "sinners" as a pair with "tax collectors" (the latter two are connected ten times with Yeshua in the Gospels; this is the only time "prostitute" is mentioned in the Gospels other than in a parable); Yeshua himself must have used the term deliberately, with all its pro-woman implications. Still, either the term and story were retained only in Matthew's special sources, or if they were also known by Mark or Luke, they either were not used by them or were used and later suppressed. This scenario is possible only with Luke (or rather with Luka, as I will discuss below), given Luca's sympathy for women, given Luka's unique recording of the story of the sinful woman (probably a prostitute—Luke 7:38–50), and given the strong likelihood that this story (now found in John 8:2–11) was excised from after Luke 21:38 (where some manuscripts locate it). This scenario is plausible because the language of John 8:2–11 is quite Lucan and certainly does not fit the style of the Fourth Gospel. However, in view of the lack of any positive manuscript evidence that Luke had used the term *prostitute* in this connection, the most likely conclusion is that this story was known only to Matthew's special source. That Matthew did not leave the story aside or substitute the word "sinners" for "prostitutes," not only indicates Yeshua as the ultimate source of the story and term, but also indicates that here again Matthew's sources favorable to women were at work in the tradition peculiar to Matthew/Matthea, which retained this story: Matthew himself was also sufficiently influenced by the pro-woman attitude of Yeshua and the tradition that transmitted the evidence for it as to include this story and term here. (Matt 21:23, 31–32)

Pilate's Wife

We know nothing of Pilate's wife except that she sent a message to her husband in support of Yeshua during his trial. As the wife of a Roman procurator of Judea, she doubtless was not Jewish but rather a pagan. We have no reason to doubt the historicity of her intervention; in fact, elsewhere in the contemporary world there are recorded instances of similar interventions by women. She apparently was so upset by the attempt to destroy Yeshua that she had a bad dream about him. Bad dreams were taken very seriously by most if not all people then, the vast majority of whom inclined toward superstition. Such a disturbing dream, bringing her to the point of intervening in a public proceeding of the most serious and formal kind ("as he was seated in the Chair of Judgment"), and of interrupting a husband who was known for his vicious and brutal temper, tells us something about Pilate's wife and Yeshua.

Yeshua obviously was known to her, and most probably not simply by general, or even detailed, reputation. She may well have been in one or more of the crowds that followed Yeshua's teaching. For her to have become so disturbed as to attempt to interfere in Yeshua's behalf when such a tumult was being raised would make it most likely that she had personally been deeply impressed by Yeshua. She would not have been the only woman whom Yeshua deeply affected, nor the only pagan—nor indeed the only "Roman"[7]—nor the only pagan woman.[8]

One wonders, of course, how the writer of Matthew's Gospel came to know about this private conversation. Presumably Pilate's wife was the ultimate source (that is, she told others that she spoke to her husband about Yeshua), though conceivably someone could have overheard her conversation with Pilate and passed on the information. We can only speculate, but the former seems most likely.

Only Matthew records the story of Pilate's wife speaking to Pilate in behalf of Yeshua. This is another example of the pro-woman element in Matthew's sources and his sympathizing with it enough to put it in his Gospel. Since the story showed at least this presumably Roman woman in a light sympathetic to Yeshua, one might have expected to find it in Mark's Gospel since he presumably was writing in Rome for Gentiles. Its absence in Mark, then, can mean only that Mark's sources did not contain it, again highlighting the strongly pro-woman element in Matthew/Matthea's special sources.

> Now as he was seated in the chair of judgment, his wife sent him a message, "Have nothing to do with that man; I have been upset all day by a dream I had about him."[9]

Sexually Parallel Stories and Images in the Synoptics

Several sexually parallel stories and images are found in the Gospels. These are either sets of stories or images that focus on a man and on a woman in parallel fashion. Note should be taken here of their relationship to the several Gospel writers and the implications of those relationships. It is especially interesting that with a single possible exception they all are recorded in either Matthew or Luke or in both; none are to be found in the Fourth Gospel, and perhaps only one is found in Mark. Both Matthew and Luke record the same three of the parallel sets; one set is peculiar to Matthew; four are peculiar to Luke. Did one simply copy the idea and three common sets from the other and then go on to put together another one or four

---

7. Cf. the centurion from Capernaum, Matt 8:5; and the centurion under the cross, Matt 27:54.
8. Matt 27:19.
9. Matt 27:19.

pairs on his own? But then why did Luke not copy all four of Matthew's sets instead of just three—or, even more, why did Matthew not copy all seven of Luke's sets instead of just three? These omissions, among other evidence elsewhere, would argue against copying happening in either direction.

Moreover, scholars are not at all agreed on what the relationship in general is between Matthew and Luke. First, as I noted above, both Matthew and Luke had Mark's Gospel before them. Further, Greek Matthew had Aramaic Matthew, which he expanded. In addition, there are 230 verses that Matthew and Luke have in common but that are not found in Mark (or in the Fourth Gospel). As I noted above, most scholars postulate a third document prior to both Matthew or Luke, now lost (called Q—German *Quelle*, "source"), which both Matthew and Luke had separately. Matthew and Luke each also had sources completely peculiar to themselves. Some scholars also suggest that not only prior common and independent written documents but also prior common and independent oral traditions are necessary to account for all the similarities and dissimilarities in the Gospels. It would seem that this latter combination is the most likely solution of this Synoptic problem, though precisely what the documents and oral traditions were and their relationships to one another has by no means been satisfactorily explained to date—if indeed it is completely possible at all.

In this matter of the sexually parallel images and stories it is clear that forces were at work in the sources of both Matthew and Luke which discerned a strongly affirming attitude toward women by Yeshua, an attitude that saw women as equal to men. The images and stories about women were there in the sources of Matthew and Luke, whether written or oral. Hence a balancing of images and stories about women and men could not be attributed to either Matthew or Luke but probably would have to be attributed to Yeshua himself. However, it should be noted that (*a*) Mark records almost none of these female images or stories individually, let alone in sexually parallel pairs, and (*b*) all of the female images and stories used by Yeshua (save the one where Yeshua likens himself to a hen) are found only in these parallel sets in Matthew and Luke. This strongly suggests that these particular close pairings would have to be attributed to the sources of Matthew and Luke, whether written, oral, or both. Yeshua himself, however, may well have juxtaposed one or more of our present sets of sexually parallel images or stories. Since Yeshua obviously told the original stories and used the images, at least in some form if not always exactly as we have them recorded in the Gospels, and hence must have consciously balanced male images and stories with female ones, it seems likely that he also paired some of the stories, though which ones we cannot easily know. In any case, the presence of these eight sexually parallel images and stories in Matthew and Luke is a clear indication that forces sympathetic to women were strongly at work in the sources of both Matthew and Luke.

Further, from evidence elsewhere in both Matthew and Luke it is clear that this positive attitude toward women not only was in the sources prior to the Gospels of Matthew and Luke but was also picked up by the Gospel writers themselves. I will argue below when dealing with Luke's Gospel that a woman evangelist—a "Luka"—was responsible for producing a prior document known as Proto-Luke. I have already suggested that the number and quality of the prowoman passages in Greek Matthew (the Gospel of Matthew that we have) automatically raise the question whether the author of Greek Matthew might in fact be more accurately designated "Matthea" than Matthew. Then, one is also moved to ask about the sources of Q.

Nevertheless, since the pro-woman attitude on the part of Yeshua is expressed, both positively and negatively, in all four of the Gospels, and since we have absolutely no evidence of such a "feminist" movement in Palestinian Judaism of the time (in fact, just the opposite occurred with the development of rabbinic Judaism), this "feminism" would have to be attributed ultimately and powerfully to Yeshua; it was then joyfully embraced and passed on by his women followers, named and unnamed.

In fact, one of the most fundamental criteria that scholars (e.g., Ernst Käsemann and Reginald H. Fuller) used to discover authentic sayings or actions of Yeshua—as seen above in the discussion of the second quest for the historical Jesus—was to discern whether the sayings are distinctive over against his environment. As I noted earlier, a Jewish scholar put the principle into action when he wrote: "The relation of Yeshua to women seems unlike what would have been usual for a Rabbi. He seems to have definitely broken with orientalism in this particular . . . But certainly the relations of Yeshua towards women, and of theirs towards him, seem to strike a new note, and a higher note, and to be off the line of Rabbinic tradition."[10]

The following are the texts involved:

Common to Luke and perhaps Mark

| Luke 8:16–17 | Mark 4:21–22 |

10. Montefiore, *Rabbinic Literature and Gospel Teachings*, 217–18.

Common to Matthew and Luke

Matt 24:29–31	Luke 17:34–37
Matt 12:38–42	Luke 11:29–32
Matt 13:33	Luke 13:20–21

Special to Luke

Luke 4:24–27
Luke 15:1–3
Luke 18:1–8

Special to Matthew

Matt 25:1–3

Conclusions

As I noted at the beginning of the section, Greek Matthew's Gospel went far beyond Mark's in its pro-woman attitude. This is true in terms of absolute quantity (36 passages dealing with women of 180 verses in length compared to Mark's 20 passages of 114 verses in length), proportion of "women passages" in comparison to overall length (Mark is 67% the length of Matthew, but has only 55% the number of women passages), and the uniquely positive attitude of a significant number of Matthew's passages.

One important point, as seen, is the great intensification of a sensitivity toward women from the earliest written form of a gospel, the Aramaic version of Matthew, of which Papias (100 CE) perhaps spoke when he referred to Matthew's composition of Yeshua's discourses *(logia)* in Aramaic. (Scholars do in fact find something of a flavor of a Greek translation of Aramaic in Yeshua's discourses as recorded in the present Greek version of Matthew, but not in the narrative sections.) As noted, many scholars contend that Mark had this Aramaic Matthew (or a very literal Greek translation of it) at his disposal when composing his Gospel, and that the canonical Greek Matthew Gospel writer in turn had Aramaic Matthew, Mark, Q sayings, and other written and oral sources at his disposal. Thus the chronological order of composition, as seen, would have been as follows: Aramaic Matthew, Mark, Greek Matthew.

When it is recalled that, for example, the later Greek Matthew (Matt 16:1–4) strand of the demand of a sign from Yeshua added the sexually parallel sign of the queen of Sheba—not found in either the earlier Aramaic Matthew strand (Matt 12:38–42) or Mark (Mark 8:11–12)—and that Greek Matthew strongly communicated a pro-woman message in the very structuring of Yeshua's events and discourses—of course not a quality found in the Aramaic Matthew listing of Yeshua's discourses—a movement toward an ever-sharper focus on women in Yeshua's life and Gospel becomes visible.

Besides the pro-woman accounts that Mark recorded (all but two of which Matthew also recorded) and the additional accounts that Matthew had in common with Luke (which at times were even more sympathetic toward women than Luke's), Matthew also recorded a number of unique, pro-women elements: (1) including women in Yeshua's genealogy, (2) likening the reign of heaven to a wedding feast, (3) placing prostitutes in it before priests, (4) listing women among those whom Yeshua fed by the multiplication of loaves and fishes, and (5) mentioning Pontius Pilate's wife among Yeshua's sympathizers.

In sum, the present Gospel of Matthew (Greek Matthew) is very strongly pro-woman in the image of Yeshua it projects—considerably more so than either Aramaic Matthew or Mark or the Fourth Gospel. This plethora of Yeshua stories and actions that are positive toward women must have been experienced by women with not only deep appreciation but also extreme enthusiasm, for clearly no one else with the gravitas of Yeshua had ever treated them in such an egalitarian manner. Hence, of course all Yeshua's stories and actions favorable to women were experienced, remembered, and passed on in the early tradition by women followers. More than this, there is every reason to assume that many if not all of the other stories and actions of Yeshua would have been equally experienced, remembered, and passed on by women as much as by men. Hence, the women followers doubtless were not only the sources of the total of Greek Matthew, but the actual writer of Greek Matthew might well have been a woman, who might tentatively be named "Matthea." We cannot know this, but we can be certain that the sources of large portions of Greek Matthew were women followers of Yeshua.

THE GOSPEL ACCORDING TO LUKE

Where the Fourth Gospel has eight passages dealing with women, Mark twenty, and Matthew thirty-six, Luke has forty-two. It should be noted that the number of passages dealing with women is not contingent on the length of each Gospel. It is true that Luke is the longest Gospel and the one with the most passages and verses dealing with women. However, the number of women passages in each Gospel relative to each Gospel's length is quite irregular. Taking Luke as the standard for Gospel length and number of women passages and verses, the relationships run as follows:

Gospel	Length	Women Passages	Women Verses
Luke	100%	(42) 100%	(220) 100%
Matthew	92%	(36) 85%	(180) 82 %
John	75%	(8) 19%	(119) 54%
Mark	62%	(20) 47%	(114) 52%

As the table above shows, the Fourth Gospel has by far the smallest number of women passages, though it is the third in overall length (four of the passages, however, are very long, so that in total length the Fourth Gospel has more verses of women passages than Mark). Even Mark has dropped from 62 percent of the length of Luke to 47 percent of the number of women passages of Luke (52 percent in terms of verses about women). Matthew and Luke both have a large number of women passages as compared to Mark and to especially the Fourth Gospel; on the basis of the number of women passages, the Gospels of Matthew and Luke could be called strongly prowoman; Mark moderately so, and the Fourth Gospel weakly so—but the Fourth Gospel would have to be designated moderately strong in view of the number of women verses and the uniquely positive quality of some of his material. In comparing Matthew with Luke on the basis of number of its women passages in comparison to overall length it is clear that Luke has pulled ahead of even Matthew in "feminism." Where Matthew was 92 percent of the length of Luke, Matthew dropped to 85 percent in the number of women passages of Luke (82 percent in terms of women verses).

Of Luke's forty-two passages dealing with women or the "feminine," three are common to all four evangelists, and nine more are common to all three Synoptics—Luke, Matthew, and Mark; another five are common to just Luke and Matthew, and two are reported by only Luke and Mark. Luke has far and away the largest number of unique women passages (twenty-three) whereas Matthew has ten special to him, the Fourth Gospel has three, and Mark none. Thus both on the basis of sheer quantity and the very large number of women passages special to Luke, it is clear that Luke exhibits the greatest stress on women by far, followed by Matthew, much farther back by Mark, and least of all by the Fourth Gospel.

The relationship of the forty-two women passages in Luke and the other Gospels is as follows:

Special to Luke	23
Common to Luke and Mark Alone	2
Common to Luke and Matthew Alone	5
Common to Luke, Mark, and Matthew Alone	9
Common to Luke, Mark, Matthew, and John	3

Passages Special to Luke

A Woman Evangelist?

Of the forty-two passages in Luke dealing with women or the feminine, over half, twenty-three, are special to Luke. This compares to ten special to Matthew out of a total of thirty-six, three special to the Fourth Gospel (though these are all quite long) out of a total of eight, and none special to Mark out of a total of twenty. Here is further indication that Luke was most especially open to women in the writing of his Gospel.

It is interesting to note that of the twenty-three women passages special to Luke, sixteen of them occur within the sections of Luke's Gospel that are made up either totally of material special to Luke (1:1—2:52) or of material special to Luke plus material common to Luke and Matthew alone (9:51—18:14). Several scholars point out that although Luke clearly was not a Jew or a Palestinian or an eyewitness of Yeshua, those sections have both such a strong unity and definitely Palestinian Jewish eyewitness character that they must have been either originally written or told by a Palestinian Jewish follower of Yeshua.[11] Given the strong presence of stories about women in this Proto-Gospel within Luke and the strong prejudice against accepting the witness of women ("When the women returned from the tomb they told all this to the Eleven and to all the others . . . But this

---

11. E.g., Rengstorf et al., *Das Neue Testament Deutsch*, Vol. 1, Pt. 3, 10.

story of theirs seemed pure nonsense, and they did not believe them"—Luke 24:9, 11), it is possible that this Proto-Gospel was written or told by a woman disciple of Yeshua and used by Luke without referring to her as his source, lest his Gospel be discredited and disbelieved. A woman Proto-Gospel writer would certainly fit well with the central place women (Elizabeth and Mary) hold in Luke's narrative of events before Jesus's adult life (Luke/Luka 1 and 2), and with the sensitivity with which the inner feelings and thoughts of the women are dealt.

However, what is much easier to sustain than the formal notion of a woman writer of Luke's Proto-Gospel is that one or more women disciples were responsible for the remembrance and handing on, either in oral or written form, of at least most of those passages that pertain in a special way to women. It is not likely that in a male-oriented society men would have been particularly aware of the significance of many of the things Yeshua said and did relating to women, whereas to sensitive women they would have seemed as loud as thunderclaps. These women then, having experienced or noticed these things, would have been the ones to remember them and pass them on and would have been the ultimate sources for the women material in the Proto-Gospel sections of Luke, and the seven other uniquely Lucan women passages. Thus, even if she, or they, might not be proved the proximate evangelist of the Proto-Gospel material of Luke/Luka, they could certainly be called protoevangelists, in the sense of having communicated the good news of Jesus.

Elizabeth Conceives John the Baptist

Immediately after his brief prologue Luke/Luka begins his/her Gospel with the story of a man and a woman who were married but childless. This lack of children was thought to be a great humiliation for the wife, not for the husband. In fact, a little later the rabbis legislated that "if a man took a wife and lived with her for ten years and she bore no child, he shall divorce her" (Talmud bYebamoth 64a; cf. Mishnah Yebamoth 6:6). There is an interesting sort of parity between the man and the woman, Zechariah and Elizabeth, expressed here by Luke's Proto-Gospel source—interesting in the light of the definite inferior social position women held in that society. But Luke's Proto-Gospel source refers to both the woman and the man together and is careful to point out the purity of priestly lineage of Elizabeth as well as of Zechariah. Then the focus on Zechariah that immediately follows (Luke 1:8–22) is balanced by the shift to Elizabeth (Luke 1:23–25, 39–45, 57–66).

The strong resemblance should be noted between, on the one hand, the story of Elizabeth's barrenness and her finally bearing a son who was to become a leading figure in Israel and, on the other hand, similar events with Sarah, who bore Isaac (cf. Gen 17:15ff.); with Samson's mother, whose name we are not told (Judg 13:2–7); and with Hannah, the mother of Samuel (1 Sam 1:5–6). The form of the Elizabeth-Zechariah story strongly suggests that the Proto-Gospel writer was familiar with these earlier stories of the Hebrew Bible, reinforcing the likelihood of the Jewishness of Luke's Proto-Gospel source.

> In the days of King Herod of Judaea there lived a priest called Zechariah who belonged to the Abijab section of the priesthood, and he had a wife, Elizabeth by name, who was a descendant of Aaron. Both were worthy in the sight of God, and scrupulously observed all the commandments and observances of the Lord. But they were childless: Elizabeth was barren and they were both getting on in years.
>
> Now it was the turn of Zechariah's section to serve, and he was exercising his priestly office before God when it fell to him by lot, as the ritual custom was, to enter the Lord's sanctuary and burn incense there. And at the hour of incense the whole congregation was outside, praying.
>
> Then there appeared to him the angel of the Lord, standing on the right of the altar of incense. The sight disturbed Zechariah and he was overcome with fear. But the angel said to him, "Zechariah, do not be afraid, your prayer has been heard. Your wife Elizabeth is to bear you a son and you must name him John. He will be your joy and delight and many will rejoice at his birth, for he will be great in the sight of the Lord; he must drink no wine, no strong drink. Even from his mother's womb he will be filled with the Holy Spirit, and he will bring back many of the sons of Israel to the Lord their God. With the spirit and power of Elijah, he will go before him to turn the hearts of fathers towards their children and the disobedient back to the wisdom that the virtuous have, preparing for the Lord a people fit for him." Zechariah said to the angel, "How can I be sure of this? I am an old man and my wife is getting on in years." The angel replied, "I am Gabriel who stands in God's presence, and I have been sent to speak to you and bring you this good news. Listen! Since you have not believed my words, which will come true at their appointed time, you will be silenced and

have no power of speech until this has happened." Meanwhile the people were waiting for Zechariah and were surprise that he stayed in the sanctuary so long. When he came out he could not speak to them, and they realized that he had received a vision in the sanctuary. But he could only make signs to them, and remained dumb.

When his time of service came to an end he returned home. Some time later his wife Elizabeth conceived, and for five months she kept to herself. "The Lord has done this for me," she said, "now that it has pleased him to take away the humiliation I suffered among people." (Luke 1:5–25)

The Annunciation

There are striking similarities between the announcement of the coming birth of John the Baptist and his kinsman Yeshua: both sons were to be leading figures in Judaism; their conceptions were to be extraordinary—John was conceived in his mother's old age, and his father was told that "even from his mother's womb he will be filled with the Holy Spirit" (Luke 1:15) and Yeshua was conceived without an earthly father—but his mother Mary was told, "the Holy Spirit will come upon you and the power of the Most High will cover you with its shadow" (Luke 1:35); the announcements were delivered by angels. There are also at least two significant differences between the extraordinary stories: Zechariah was somewhat resistant to the announcement and was consequently punished with temporary dumbness, whereas Mary was fully open and hence suffered no punishment; most important, in the case of John the Baptist's birth, the angelic announcement was made to the man whereas in the case of Yeshua's birth, the announcement was made to the woman. The importance of this second difference would not be neutralized simply by noting that any angelic announcement made about the virgin conception of Yeshua would have to be made to the prospective mother because there was no prospective father, for as a matter of fact Matthew's Gospel does do just about that: in Matthew there is a single angelic announcement of the virgin conception recorded, and it is made to Joseph, Mary's betrothed (cf. Matt 1:18–25).

> In the sixth month the angel Gabriel was sent by God to a town in Galilee called Nazareth, to a virgin betrothed to a man named Joseph, of the House of David; and the virgin's name was Mary. He went in and said to her, "Rejoice, so highly favored! The Lord is with you." She was deeply disturbed by these words and asked

herself what this greeting could mean, but the angel said to her, "Mary, do not be afraid; you have won God's favor. Listen! You are to conceive and bear a son, and you must name him Jesus. He will be great and will be called Son of the Most High. The Lord God will give him the throne of his ancestors; he will rule over the House of Jacob forever and his reign will have no end." Mary said to the angel "But how can this come about since I am a virgin." "The Holy Spirit will come upon you," the angel answered, "and the power of the Most High will cover you with its shadow. And so the child will be holy and will be called Son of God. Know this too: your kinswoman Elizabeth has, in her old her age, herself conceived a son, and she whom people called barren is now in her sixth month, for nothing is impossible to God." "I am the handmaid of the Lord," said Mary, "let what you have said be done to me." (Luke 1:26–38)

The Visitation

In this scene Luke describes Mary's visit to her kinswoman Elizabeth. The focus is entirely on the two women, the two expectant mothers of leading figures of Israel. What is especially to be noted here is that according to Luke the first person, besides Mary, to whom Yeshua's messiahship is revealed is a woman, Elizabeth: "Elizabeth was filled with the Holy Spirit . . . and said . . . 'Why should I be honored with a visit from the mother of my Lord [i.e., of Messiah]?'" (Luke 1:41–43). Where Zechariah reacted in a resistant fashion in the face of the divine and was punished, Elizabeth reacted positively and was rewarded by a visit from the Messiah in utero and by being informed that her son was to be named John (cf. Luke 1:60: "But his mother spoke up. 'No,' she said, 'he is to be called John'").

> Mary set out at that time and went as quickly as she could to a town in the hill country of Judah. She went into Zechariah's house and greeted Elizabeth. Now as soon as Elizabeth heard Mary's greeting, the child leapt in her womb and Elizabeth was filled with the Holy Spirit. She gave a loud cry and said, "Of all women you are the most blessed, and blessed is the fruit of your womb. Why should I be honored with a visit from the mother of my Lord? For the moment your greeting reached my ears, the child in my womb leapt for joy. Yes, blessed is she who believed that the promise made her by the Lord would be fulfilled." (Luke 1:39–45)

The Magnificat

The song of joy uttered by Mary when she met Elizabeth starts with the words, "My soul *magnifies* the Lord," in the Western traditional Latin Vulgate, "*Magnificat anima mea Dominum.*" Hence the customary title.

The great majority of early manuscripts state in verse 46 that Mary said the Magnificat, but a few attribute it to Elizabeth. Some scholars[12] follow this minority tradition of attributing the Magnificat to Elizabeth because they are convinced the text makes more sense in Elizabeth's mouth than in Mary's. If that were the case, then the balancing of the focus between Zechariah and Elizabeth would be still more clearly parallel (the Magnificat in Elizabeth's mouth matching the song, the Benedictus—Luke 1:68–79—in Zechariah's), and even tip in Elizabeth's favor (she was believing and rewarded rather than disbelieving and punished).

Whomever the Magnificat is attributed to, it is clear that it very closely resembles the Song of Hannah, the mother of Samuel (1 Sam 2:1–10), mentioned above. In both the Magnificat and the Song of Hannah there is a stress on praising God for lifting up the lowly and the humble, and feeding the hungry. Who are the lowliest of Near Eastern society? Women. Who are the first to go hungry? Widows. There is a clear sense of solidarity, even almost identity, of women with the lowliest and hungriest expressed by placing these two songs in the mouths of women (who were lifted up in the only way possible for women in that society—by bearing a son). Both songs contain cries of joy that the lowly (read: women) were finally raised up. Whoever may have composed the two songs (it is not likely that Mary, or Elizabeth, composed the Magnificat on the spot, given its extraordinary parallels to the Song of Hannah) and in whatever context they were composed, it is apparent that the editor of 1 Samuel and Luke's source for the Magnificat (possibly a woman evangelist) both realized that women—especially those who had not given birth to a son—would be recognized by all as lowly and poor. They expressed this realization simply by attributing these songs, whether composed by women or not, to women.

---

12. For example, Creed, *The Gospel according to St. Luke*; Drury, *Luke*.

Yeshua's Women Followers Created Christianity

Magnificat	Song of Hannah
And Mary said: "My soul proclaims the greatness of the Lord and my spirit exults in God the savior; because he has looked upon his lowly handmaid. Yes, from this day forward all generations will call me blessed, for the Almighty has done great things for me. Holy is his name, and his mercy reaches from age to age for those who fear him. He has shown the power of his arm, he has routed the proud of heart. He has pulled down princes from their thrones and exalted the lowly. The hungry he has filled with good things, the rich sent empty away. He has come to the help of Israel his servant, mindful of his mercy —according to the promise he made to our ancestors— of his mercy to Abraham and to his descendants forever." Mary stayed with Elizabeth about three months and then went back home. (Luke 1:46–56)	Then Hannah said this prayer: "My heart exults in Yahweh my horn is exalted in my God, my mouth derides my foes, for I rejoice in your Power of saving. There is none as holy as Yahweh, (indeed, there is no one but you) no rock like our God. Do not speak and speak with haughty words, let not arrogance come from your mouth. For Yahweh is an all-knowing God and his is the weighing of deeds. The bow of the mighty is broken but the feeble have girded themselves with strength. The sated hire themselves out for bread but the famished cease from labor; the barren woman bears sevenfold, but the mother of many is desolate. Yahweh gives death and life, brings down to Sheol and draws up; Yahweh makes poor and rich, he humbles and also exalts. He raises the poor from the dust, he lifts the needy from the dunghill to give them a place with princes, and to assign them a seat of honor; for to Yahweh the props of the earth belong, on these he has posed the world. He safeguards the steps of his faithful but the wicked vanish in darkness (for it is not by strength that man triumphs). The enemies of Yahweh are shattered, the Most High thunders in the heavens. Yahweh judges the ends of the earth, he endows king with power, he exalts the horn of his Anointed." (1 Sam 2:1–10)

THREE JESUS CERTITUDES

Birth and Circumcision of John the Baptist

In Luke's next scene Elizabeth is the center of focus as the birth of John is briefly related. She is also the center of attention in the first part of Luke's narration of the circumcision and naming of John. It appears that Elizabeth had the name John revealed to her. In typical Palestinian fashion, she was not even going to be consulted—"they were going to call him Zechariah after his father"(Luke 1:59)—but she interposed a no and insisted on John. In typical fashion her authority counted for nothing and the crowd insisted on going to the "real" authority, the man: "they made signs to his father [who was still struck dumb by the angel] to find out what he wanted him called' (Luke 1:62). But Elizabeth's decision was vindicated by Zechariah and, as was to be expected, "they were all astonished." Thus Zechariah supported his wife in the naming of the child John. (There is no indication in the Gospel that the name John came from anyone except through Elizabeth, though it is possible that Zechariah could have written to Elizabeth that the angel said the boy's name was to be John; however, if that were the case, one would have expected that the Gospel might have recorded that Elizabeth said that Zechariah had told her the boy's name was to be John.) Zechariah now received his power of speech again and praised God with his song, the "Benedictus" (from the first word of the Latin Vulgate translation: "Blessed be the Lord, the God of Israel," "*Benedictus Dominus Deus Israel*").

Meanwhile the time came for Elizabeth to have her child, and she gave birth to a son; and when her neighbors and relations heard that the Lord had shown her so great a kindness, they shared her joy.

> Now on the eighth day they came to circumcise the child; they were going to call him Zechariah after his father, but his mother spoke up. No," she said, "he is to be called John." They said to her, "But no one in your family has that name," and made signs to his father to find out what he wanted him called. The father asked for a writing-tablet and wrote, "His name is John." And they were all astonished. At that instant his power of speech returned and he spoke and praised God. (Luke 1:57–64)

The Birth of Yeshua

Only Luke records the birth of Yeshua in any detail. Matthew merely says that Yeshua was "born at Bethlehem in Judaea during the reign of King

Herod" (Matt 2:1). Luke's is the familiar story of Joseph and Mary traveling from Nazareth to Bethlehem to register in a Roman census, and of Jesus' being born there; angels announce the event to shepherds in the area. Of course nothing here indicates anything of Yeshua's attitude toward women, but there are two small hints of Luke's positive attitude in his references to Mary. When recording that the shepherds came to Bethlehem to find the Messiah, Luke mentions Mary first, not a usual order in a patriarchal society: "So they hurried away and found Mary and Joseph, and the baby lying in the manger." Second, Luke then speaks of Mary, not Joseph, keeping and pondering all these things in her heart. This would seem to indicate that Luke had access to Mary, or an intimate tradition stemming from Mary. Joseph apparently had died before Jesus's public life, but Mary lived through it and clearly became an important figure in the early Christian community, although not in the circles Paul traveled in, for he never refers to her. Luke is especially sensitive to Mary—he has twenty references to Mary or Yeshua's mother, as compared to eleven in Matthew, seven in the Fourth Gospel, three in Mark, and none in Paul. This sensitivity in Luke toward Mary parallels his sensitivity toward women in general.

> Now when the angels had gone from them into heaven, the shepherds said to one another, "Let us go to Bethlehem and see this thing that has happened which the Lord has made known to us." So they hurried away and found Mary and Joseph, and the baby lying in the manger. When they saw the child they repeated what they had been told about him, and everyone who heard it was astonished at what the shepherds had to say. As for Mary, she treasured all these things and pondered them in her heart. And the shepherds went back glorifying and praising God for all they had heard and seen; it was exactly as they had been told. (Luke 2:15–20)

PROPHECY OF SIMEON

When Mary and Joseph took the infant Yeshua to the temple at Jerusalem for the ritual redemption of the firstborn son, they were met by a devout man, Simeon, who prophesied concerning Yeshua as the Messiah. Then Simeon addressed not Joseph or both parents, but rather Mary alone, reinforcing the above-discussed pattern of Luke's focusing on Mary. He spoke not only of Yeshua but also of what would happen to Mary because of him: "A sword will pierce your own soul."

> As the child's father and mother stood there wondering at the things that were being said about him, Simeon blessed them and said to Mary his mother, "You see this child: he is destined for the fall and for the rising of many in Israel, destined to be a sign that is rejected—and a sword will pierce your own soul too—so that the secret thoughts of many may be laid bare." (Luke 2:33–35)

Prophecy of Anna

As noted above, we have here another instance of sexually parallel passages. Normally at least two witnesses are required in Jewish law to authenticate something; Luke records both a male and a female witness, indicating again that he understands Yeshua's Gospel, his messiahship, to be for both women and men. Both Simeon and the woman, Anna, are prophets. In fact, only she of the two is explicitly named a prophet (*prophetis*). She too prophesied and spoke publicly of the messianic child. Thus in Luke, for every man playing a significant role in the early and "pre-" life of Yeshua, there is also an equally or more significant woman: Elizabeth and Zechariah, Mary and Joseph, Anna and Simeon.

> There was a woman prophet also, Anna the daughter of Phanuel, of the tribe of Asher. She was well on in years. Her days of girlhood over, she had been married for seven years before becoming a widow. She was now eighty-four years old and never left the Temple, serving God night and day with fasting and prayer. She came by just at that moment and began to praise God; and she spoke of the child to all who looked forward to the deliverance of Jerusalem. (Luke 2:36–38)

Yeshua "Lost" in the Temple

In the sole Gospel account of an event of Yeshua's life between his infancy and his public life, Luke reflects two elements that bear on the status of women. The first is indirect and remote. Elsewhere I pointed out how Yeshua made a strenuous effort to dismantle the restrictive bonds of the family and that this dismantling would have by far the greatest liberating effects on women. Already here, at the preadult age of twelve (Jewish males took on adult responsibility with the rite of *bar mitzvah* at thirteen), Yeshua began his efforts at loosening family bonds. When his parents chide him for going off on his own, he responds that they need not be so overly concerned about him, that he had other matters beyond their scope to attend to—an intimation of much stronger words ahead, coupled, nevertheless, with his obeying his parents after this twelve-year-old foreshadowing experience.

Second, it should also be noted that again in this story Luke focuses not on Joseph, but on Mary. It is her exchange with Yeshua that Luke/Luka records, again pointing to a tradition that goes back to the personal recollections of Mary.

> Every year his parents used to go to Jerusalem for the feast of the Passover. When he was twelve years old, they went up for the feast as usual. When they were on their way home after the feast, the boy Jesus stayed behind in Jerusalem without his parents knowing it. They assumed he was with the caravan, and it was only after a day's journey that they went to look for him among their relations and acquaintances. When they failed to find him they went back to Jerusalem looking for him everywhere
>
> Three days later, they found him in the Temple, sitting among the doctors, listening to them, and asking them questions; and all those who heard him were astounded at his intelligence and his replies. They were overcome when they saw him, and his mother said to him, "My child, why have you done this to us? See how worried your father and I have been, looking for you." "Why were you looking for me?" he replied. "Did you not know that I must be busy with my Father's affairs?" But they did not understand what he meant. (Luke 2:41–50)

Mary's Memoirs

Luke/Luka closes the introductory part of his Gospel by noting that Yeshua obeyed his parents and matured, and that "his mother stored up all these things in her heart," rather pointedly implying that much of the foregoing was based, at least ultimately, on her remembrances. But one is given the impression that the significance of the events was by no means always so clear at the moment, but became so only in Mary's later reflections: "As the child's father and mother stood there wondering at the things that were being said about him" (Luke 2:33); "But they did not understand what they meant" (2:50); "As for Mary, she treasured all these things and pondered them in her heart" (2:19); "His mother stored up all these things in her heart" (2:51). Thus, as no other New Testament writer, Luke/Luka was concerned to gather into his Gospel the tradition of not just Mary's recollections, but her remembrances reflected on—Mary's memoirs.

> He then went down with them and came to Nazareth and lived under their authority. His mother stored up all these things in her heart. And Jesus increased in wisdom, in stature, and in favor with God and humanity. (Luke 2:51–52)

Luke's Introduction—A Woman Evangelist?

In Luke's introductory section, just reviewed, scholars often note the close parallelism and, at the same time, tightly interwoven quality of the John the Baptist and Yeshua stories. But it is equally valid to note the sexual parallelism and, at the same time, the integrated quality of the female and male elements all throughout the introduction. This sexual balance is clearly deliberate on the evangelist's part and reinforces the possibility that this portion of Luke's Gospel, plus Luke 9:51—18:14, originally stemmed from a woman disciple of Yeshua, "Luka," as discussed above.

Yeshua's Concern for Widows

Yeshua's special concern for widows was analyzed above and each of the stories about widows has been treated separately. But here it should again be noted that of the eight stories about widows found in the Gospels, seven of them are found in Luke's Gospel, four of them exclusively so. One is the sexually parallel story of the widow Anna, analyzed just above—as part of Luke's introductory section. The second widow story found in Luke alone is the sexually parallel reference to the widow of Zarephath (Luke 4:25–27). The third, also sexually paired, is the touching story of the widow of Nain (Luke 7:11–17), and the fourth, again sexually paralleled, is Yeshua's story of the widow and the wicked judge (Luke 18:1–8). It is apparent that Yeshua was especially concerned about the plight of widows. But it is also clear that of all the evangelists Luke was by far the most sensitive to Yeshua's concern about the burdens of widows, since he exclusively recorded half the stories about widows, plus three-quarters of the rest. Might this suggest that the possibly female evangelist of the Proto-Gospel, Luka, was herself a widow, or at least closely identified with widows? Since Joseph was no longer alive when Yeshua was active in his public life, his mother Mary was bearing all the burdens of a widow.

Yeshua and the Penitent Woman

See above for a discussion of Yeshua's deliberate breach of several social and religious customs in permitting a woman—of ill repute!—to touch him in public, and in treating her as a full human being, whose primary quality is personhood (Luke 7:36–50).

Women Disciples of Yeshua

See above for an analysis of the report that women also were openly among Yeshua's followers—most extraordinary for that time and place. Was it from among them that Luke's possible woman protoevangelist came? The woman mentioned most often by all the Gospel writers and to whom the risen Yeshua first appeared—Mary Magdalene? Or the committed, intellectual disciple of Yeshua who sat at his feet, Mary of Bethany? Possibly. But we have no documentary means of knowing (Luke 8:1–3).

The Intellectual Life for Women

See above for an analysis of Yeshua's visit to the house of his friends Martha and Mary, of how Yeshua made it abundantly clear that the supposedly exclusively male role of the intellectual, of the theologian, was for women as well as for men, of how he explicitly rejected the housekeeper role as *the* female role. How this story must have buoyed up those Jewish women whose horizons and desires stretched beyond the kitchen threshold! It is, consequently, not at all surprising to find this story in the Proto-Gospel section of Luke (Luke 1:1—2:52; 9:51—18:14) that many scholars attribute originally to a Jewish eyewitness follower of Jesus, who I have suggested might have been a woman disciple. One might ask, who would have particularly noticed or have bothered to remember such a small event as the Martha and Mary story except a woman? It would have meant little to a man, but to a woman it would have been a door to a whole new world.

Hence, it is quite likely that a woman was (or that women were) responsible for the preservation of this episode in Yeshua's life. It also is likely that the woman originally responsible for remembering this event was the one who was there and was deeply impressed by it, namely, Mary of Bethany. Again, the question naturally arises, was this deeply religious intellectual woman disciple of Yeshua the evangelist of Luke's Proto-Gospel? In any case, Luke's sensitivity to women ultimately preserved this *Magna Charta* for women. (Luke 10:38–42)

Rejection of the Baby-Machine Image

See above for an analysis of the brief passage wherein Yeshua explicitly rejected the sexually reductionist baby-machine image of women in favor of a personal, spiritual one. Again, one wonders why this very tiny event was remembered and recorded. And more, who would have even noticed it and striven to preserve it except one to whom it meant a great deal, namely, a woman? This passage too is in the Proto-Gospel (of the woman evangelist?) section of Luke (Luke 11:27–28).

Healing of a Woman on the Sabbath

See above for a discussion of Yeshua's healing on the Sabbath of a woman ill for eighteen years, and the uproar it caused. It should be recalled that the Fourth Gospel recorded no healings by Yeshua on the Sabbath and Matthew and Mark each recorded one healing—of a man—while Luke recorded three Sabbath healings, two of men and one of a woman. This single recollection of the healing of a woman is recorded (by the woman evangelist?) in the Proto-Gospel section of Luke—again reinforcing the likelihood of its originally stemming from a woman. In the passage Yeshua also referred to the cured woman in unheard—of fashion as a *daughter* of Abraham—a detail a woman was much more likely to notice and preserve, since it would mean so much more to her than to a man (Luke 13:10–17).

Yeshua's Dismantling of Restrictive Family Bonds—III

Several times above it has been noted that Yeshua deliberately set about the task of dismantling the restrictive family bonds that often were stifling in that culture, and most especially for women. It was also noted that Mark records one such explicit passage, Matthew two (in common with Luke), and Luke three. It is interesting that two of these passages in Luke occur in the Proto-Gospel section. Though there is a certain sexual asceticism expressed in two of these Lucan passages—or perhaps rather because there is—the fact that two of the three are found in the Proto-Gospel section adds another argument for seeing a woman evangelist as Luke's source here.

> Great crowds accompanied him on his way and he turned and spoke to them. "If any one comes to me without hating his father, mother, wife, children, brothers, sisters, yes and his own life too, he cannot be my disciple." (Luke 14:25-26; cf. Luke 12:51-53; 18:28-30)

God in the Image of a Woman

See above for a discussion of Yeshua's use of a woman as an image of God, a usage vigorously resisted by the Hebrew prophets and other Hebrew devotees of the one true God, Yahweh (e.g., Judg 3:7).[13] As noted above, because of their unique qualities, the three stories about how God is concerned about the "lost" were doubtless told originally by Yeshua. It is also likely that they were told in response to complaints that Yeshua was consorting with sinners; each one makes a most apt reply to such a charge. We cannot, however, be sure that they were all told at one time, as they are recorded in Luke. In fact, since each of them is quite effective in itself, it seems more likely that they were related by Yeshua on similar but different occasions. Still, the inclusion of a story of God's concern for the "lost" which projected God in a female image doubtless must be attributed to Yeshua, along with the rest of the stories and images. Yeshua clearly was concerned to maintain a sexual balance in this category of parables, as in others. This, of course, makes very special sense because the complaint was that Yeshua welcomed "sinners" (*hamartolous*, Luke 15:2), which term included the sort of women who followed Yeshua (e.g., *hamartolos*, Luke 7:37). However, the bringing together of these three stories of Yeshua in one place probably should be attributed to Luke, or perhaps more aptly, Luke's source, where Luke may well have found the three parables already successively arranged. This is particularly likely since the stories are located in the Proto-Gospel section,

---

13. See Patai, *Hebrew Goddess* for details.

which is largely unique to Luke and has an especially cohesive quality. The fact that none of the other Gospels record the story projecting God in a female image—though Matthew does record one of these three stories of God's concern for the lost (Matt 18:12–14)—and that nowhere else in the New Testament is God portrayed in a female image also enhances the likelihood of a female evangelist for this Proto-Gospel section of Luke. A woman would have been especially keen to recall and record such imagery coming from the lips of the Messiah (Luke 15:8–10).

Yeshua in a Female Image

Yeshua did not shrink from applying a female image to himself either; he likened himself to a hen gathering her chicks under her wings. Such an image is interesting because throughout the Hebrew Bible the image of protecting wings is often used in connection with God.[14] But in all these images there is never any intimation of the feminine. In the Hebrew Bible, usually a prayer asks God for shelter under God's wings. One reference is made to birds hovering in protection[15] and one to an eagle "hovering over its young,"[16] but nowhere is reference made to a female bird. The use of that image in the Jewish tradition was left to Yeshua: "Jerusalem, Jerusalem, you that kill the prophets and stone those who are sent to you! How often have I longed to gather your children, as a hen gathers her brood under her wings, and you refused!"[17]

Again, when Yeshua was in the temple on the last day of the Feast of Succoth, at which there was a procession bringing "living" water from the fountain of Shiloh to the temple as a sign of the future messianic salvation, Yeshua uttered a saying that cast him in a female image. He said, "If anyone is thirsty, let him come to me and drink!" The image of drinking from a human being can only be that of a mother.[18]

14. E.g., Pss 17:8; 36:7; 57:1; 61:4; 63:7; 91:4; Ruth 2:12; Isa 31:5; Deut 32:11.
15. Isa 31:5.
16. Isa 31:5.
17. Luke 13:34; cf. Matt 23:37.
18. The fourteenth-century English mystic Dame Julian of Norwich did have a scriptural basis for her vision of Christ the mother. "And thus Jesus our true Mother in kind [nature] of our first making; and he is our true Mother in grace by his taking of our made kind. All the fair working and all the sweet kindly offices of most dear Motherhood are appropriated to the Second Person." Saint Julian of Norwich, *The Revelations of Divine Love*, ch. 59.

Yeshua went on to apply a Scripture paraphrase to himself: "From his *koilia* shall flow fountains of living water." *Koilia* basically means a hollow place and is used to refer to the whole or part of the abdomen. In the context of feeding from within, the reference would be to the upper part of the body cavity, and the word *koilia* could properly be translated "breast." But modern translations generally are fearful of doing the obvious and projecting Yeshua in a maternal image—although Yeshua was not.

> On the last and greatest day of the festival, Yeshua stood there and cried out "If anyone is thirsty, let him come to me! Let him come and drink who believes in me! As Scripture says: 'From his breast *(koilia)* shall flow fountains of living water.'" He was speaking of the Spirit which those who believed in him were to receive; for there was no Spirit as yet because Yeshua had not yet been glorified.[19]

Yeshua and the Adulterous Woman

See above for an analysis of the extraordinary story of the woman caught in the act of adultery being used to set a trap for Yeshua, his avoiding it and his refusing to condemn the woman—which act was probably responsible for the long resistance in early Christian history to receiving the story as authentic. As noted, scholars generally agree on linguistic grounds that the story surely was not written by the Fourth Gospel writer, though it is usually printed there in most Bibles; rather, as a note in the Jerusalem Bible states at Luke 21:38: "The adulterous woman passage of John 7:53—8:11, for the Lucan authorship of which there are many good arguments, would fit into this context admirably." For example, the strong similarity of the wording of Luke 21:37-38 to John 8:1-2 suggests that the latter is simply a modification of the former after the story was cut out of Luke:

> In the daytime he would be in the Temple teaching [1. *didaskon*], but would spend the night on the hill called the Mount of Olives [2. *eis to oros . . . elaion*]. And from early morning all the people [3. *kai pas ho laos*] would gather round him in the Temple [4. *en to hiero*] to listen to him [5. *pros auton*]. (Luke 21:373-8)
>
> And Jesus went to the Mount of Olives [2. *eis to oros ton elaion*]. At daybreak he appeared in the Temple [4. *eis to hieron*] again; and as all the people [3. *kai pas ho laos*] came to him [5. *pros auton*], he sat down and began to teach [1. *edidasken*] them. (John 8:1-2).

19. John 7:37-39.

The story depicts Yeshua as taking an extremely sensitive and courageous stand, but one, as noted in the earlier analysis, which apparently scandalized many early Christians, leading to the story's deletion from all early manuscripts. But it did already have a partial precedent in the other Lucan story of Yeshua and the penitent "prostitute" (Luke 7:36–50). It thus fits well into the strongly prowoman spirit of Luke's Gospel. Because of that general "feminist" kinship, and because of the special kinship of the putatively Lucan story of the adulterous woman with the definitely Lucan story of the penitent "prostitute" (here are represented the amateur and the professional violators of sexual mores), it is quite possible that the wandering story of the adulterous woman also came from the suggested woman evangelist of the "Proto-Gospel" of Luke.

Again, a woman follower of Yeshua would be especially impressed with this event and especially eager to preserve it. Was this unknown woman among those earliest Christians driven into the Syrian Diaspora ("both men and *women*"—Acts 8:3; "men or *women*"—Acts 9:2), where she composed her "Gospel" (*euaggelizomenoi*—Acts 8:4)? Indeed, the solely Lucan passages, i.e., the Proto-Gospel, where this story might earlier have been located, not only betrays an intimate knowledge of Palestinian Judaism but is also clearly aimed at non-Jewish readers. Further, the earliest documentary evidence of the story of the adulterous woman is the reference in the third-century *Didascalia*, which originated in Syria, and which also refers to deaconesses as an image of the Holy Spirit!

Yeshua "Leads Women Astray"

Not only are the Gospels full of incidents wherein Yeshua championed the cause of women and of children (e.g., Luke 9:46–48 and parallels, Luke 18:15–17 and parallels, where Yeshua draws children to himself and says that all must become like them), but his reputation for this behavior was widespread enough that he may well have been denounced to Pilate for having "led women and children astray." As noted earlier, there are at least three variant readings in Luke's Gospel, two of which are very early, that witness to this tradition. The oldest one, stemming from Marcion, who lived in the first half of the second century when some of the canonical New Testament writings were still being written, simply says that Yeshua was accused of "leading astray both the women and the children." The second ancient variant reading comes from the fourth-century Palestinian-born

Yeshua's Women Followers Created Christianity

church father Epiphanius, whose text stated that Yeshua's accusers charged: "and he has turned our children and wives away from us for they are not bathed as we are, nor do they purify themselves."

It is not at all surprising that these very early prowoman traditions turn up in Luke's Gospel, given the strongly prowoman character of that Gospel. They support the notion that Yeshua was a feminist, was widely known to be a feminist, was despised by many for being a feminist, and was politically denounced as a feminist.

It would appear from the second tradition that Yeshua's lesson of the relative unimportance (vis-a-vis the woman's person) of regular female ritual impurity from the issuance of blood, as taught in the episode of the woman with the twelve-year hemorrhage (see Luke 8:43–48), was widely learned and applied. To generate the remembrance of this tradition many women followers of Yeshua must have had a high opinion of their experience of a new attitude toward the purity, or impurity, of their own bodies, and of the fact that so many men perceived Yeshua's teaching as turning their wives away from them. According to these early traditions, this Yeshua teaching so infuriated the men that they publicly denounced Yeshua for it to the Roman governor and demanded that he be executed. These extremely early traditions attached to Luke (were they "suppressed" as was the wandering Lucan story of the adulterous woman?) reflect the notion that Yeshua's feminism was perceived as a capital crime (as were the actions and statements of that other Jewish feminist, Beruria[20]).

As was mentioned above and worth repeating here, the men began their accusation by saying, "We found this man inciting our people to a revolt, opposing payment of the tribute to Caesar, [leading astray the women and the children (*kai apostrephonta tas gynaikas kai ta tekna*)—Marcion], and claiming to be Christ, a king . . . He is inflaming the people with his teaching all over Judaea; it has come all the way from Galilee, where he started, down to here, [and he has turned our children and wives away from us for they are not bathed as we are, nor do they purify themselves (*et filios nostros et uxores avertit a nobis, non enim baptizantur sicut nos nec se mundant*—Epiphanius)]."[21]

---

20. See Swidler, *Women in Judaism*, 84ff.

21. Luke 23:2, 5. For variant texts and references, see Nestle, ed., *Novum Testamentum Graece et Latine*, 221; and Gryson, *Ministry of Women*, 126.

Three Jesus Certitudes

Jerusalem Women on the *Via Dolorosa*

Luke/Luka, again, is the only Gospel writer who mentions the women of Jerusalem meeting Yeshua as he was carrying his cross to the place of execution. S/he recorded that they mourned and cried for him. The Talmud notes that the noble women used to prepare a soothing drink for the condemned, but that is far different from what is described by Luke/Luka. These women clearly must have been devoted followers of Yeshua who were overwhelmed with grief. They are a group distinct from the "large numbers of people" who followed Yeshua; the Greek makes it clear that only the women were said to mourn and lament for Yeshua. They obviously responded with a profound attachment to this Yeshua who had taught them. Nowhere in any of the Gospels is there a similar report of a group of male followers of Yeshua lamenting for him publicly or risking their limbs and lives by meeting and mourning for him in the open. Yeshua's response was typical in that he showed greater concern for them than for himself. Luke/Luka would have him speak with foreknowledge of the coming destruction of Jerusalem (in 70 CE); hence most scholars hold that these specific words were provided by the evangelist, though with a historical basis.

These women must have been strongly committed followers of Yeshua to have risked their safety publicly to mourn and attempt to comfort a condemned prisoner, something the male followers of Yeshua failed to do, and consequently it is to women alone that Yehsua addressed himself on his *Via Dolorosa*. Clearly Yeshua did what apparently no other rabbi was even concerned to do—he reached out and deeply touched the hearts of many Jewish women, and they responded to him here with reckless abandon. A male disciple of Yeshua might well have recalled this incident with shame, though there is no hint of such shame in the text as we now have it. But how much more likely is it that a woman follower of Yeshua would have had burned on her memory how the women—perhaps she too—rushed out to meet Yeshua on the way to his agonizing and humiliating death, only to have him speak to their need alone, as he reached out to them one last time to show his concern for them in his last minutes: "But Yeshua turned to them and said, 'Daughters of Jerusalem, do not weep for me; weep rather for yourselves and for your children.'"

> As they were leading him away . . . large numbers of people followed him, and of women too, who mourned and lamented for him. But Jesus turned to them and said, "Daughters of Jerusalem,

do not weep for me; weep rather for yourselves and for your children. For the days will surely come when people will say, 'Happy are those who are barren, the wombs that have never borne, the breasts that have never suckled!' Then they will begin to say to the mountains, 'Fall on us!'; to the hills, 'Cover us!' For if men use the green wood like this, what will happen when it is dry?" (Luke 23:26–31)

Was Luke Prowoman or Anti-woman?

Almost everything that has been analyzed up to now has reflected a positive attitude toward women on the part of Luke, his sources, or both. However, some items can be seen as reflecting a somewhat negative attitude when compared with similar passages in Matthew, Mark, or both. It would be well to list them, analyze them individually, and evaluate their overall implications. Ten such passages can be discerned.

(1) Luke 3:23–38. Luke here presents an ancestral genealogy of Yeshua, listing only male ancestors, whereas Matthew includes four women in his genealogy of Yeshua (Matt 1:1–17). However, it was not at all customary to include women in genealogies, so one would have to say, not that Luke is thereby negative in his attitude toward women, but rather that Matthew is especially positive in this instance.

(2) Luke 4:22. "They said, 'This is Joseph's son, surely?'" Again, nothing negative toward women here. But the corresponding description of Yeshua in Mark is as follows: "This is the carpenter, surely, the son of Mary, the brother of James and Joset and Jude and Simon? His sisters, too, are they not here with us?" (Mark 6:3). And in Matthew: "This is the carpenter's son, surely? Is not his mother the one called Mary, and his brothers James and Joseph and Simon and: Jude? His sisters, too, are they not all here with us?" (Matt 13:55). There does seem to be a greater awareness of women relatives in, Mark and Matthew here than in Luke and/or his sources.

(3) Luke 8:19. Luke records that Yeshua's mother and brothers came to see him and that Yeshua responded that those who act on the word of God are his mother and his brothers. Matthew (Matt 12:46–50) and Mark (even more Mark 3:31–35) add "sisters" to the account. Again, this indicates nothing of a negative attitude toward women, especially since Luke does include "mother," but it does perhaps indicate a slightly greater awareness of women on Matthew's and Mark's part than Luke's in this instance.

(4) Luke 9:10–17. All four evangelists record the accounts of the multiplication of the loaves and fishes (Matt 14:13–21; 15:29 38; Mark 6:31–44; 8:1–10;; Luke 9:10–17; John 6:1–13). Three, including Luke, refer only to thousands of men being fed (or to a crowd of thousands), whereas Matthew adds women and children besides. Again, this indicates nothing negative on Luke's—or Mark's or the Fourth Gospel's—part in this account, but rather a greater awareness of women on Matthew's part.

(5) Luke 12:35–37. Luke records a saying of Yeshua about men waiting for their master to return from the wedding feast—nothing negative. However, Matthew's version (Matt 25:1–13) tells of ten bridesmaids waiting. Again, this shows a stronger emphasis on women in Matthew than in Luke.

(6) Luke 14:15–24. Luke records a parable in which the realm of God is likened to people invited to a banquet. However, in Matthew's version (Matt 22:2–10) it is a wedding banquet, perhaps adding thereby a further "feminine" element. Further, in Luke's version one excuse offered for not accepting the banquet invitation, "I have married a wife," suggests that marriage might be an obstacle to responding to God's call.

(7) Luke 14:26. In quoting Yeshua's listing of those relatives who must give way to the demands of discipleship, Luke records not only father, mother, brothers, sisters, and children—as does Matthew (Matt 10:37–38 does not mention siblings, but see Matt 19:29)—but also "wife," perhaps again reflecting an attitude that views marriage as an obstacle to the full following of God's call.

(8) Luke 18:29. A similar listing of relatives left for the "sake of the reign of God" includes "wife" in Luke's version, but not in either Mark's (Mark 10:28–30) or Matthew's (Matt 19:29).

(9) Luke 23:49. Luke mentions Yeshua's women disciples as present at the crucifixion; so do Mark (Mark 15:41) and Matthew (Matt 27:56). However, the latter two mention only the women as being present, but Luke includes in addition "all his [Yeshua's] friends," perhaps slightly diluting the focus on the loyalty of the women.

(10) Luke 24:1–11. In Luke's Gospel several women are the first witnesses to the empty tomb, but no appearances of Yeshua to women are recorded, whereas in Matthew (Matt 28:9–10), the Fourth Gospel (John 20:11–18), and the later added ending of Mark (Mark 16:9–11) they are.

It should be noted first that numbers 1–5 and 9 in no way indicate in themselves anything negative in Luke's attitude toward women, but rather evidence a somewhat sharper focus on women on the part of Matthew,

Mark, or both. Second, numbers 6–8 indicate an attitude that marriage was a burden in seeking the reign of God. Moreover, these three statements are written solely from the man's point of view (i.e., wives must be given up, or, "I have married a *wife*, and so I cannot come"). No mention is made of marrying or giving up *husbands*. This sexually ascetic perspective reflects Paul's attitude toward marriage: that is, marriage is best avoided. His attitude was doubtless influenced by his expectation of Christ's immediate second coming, and this expectation made worldly matters such as marriage less significant (see 1 Cor 7). According to deutero-Pauline sources (Col 4:14; 2 Tim 4:11; Phlm 24), Luke was a longtime companion of and fellow worker with Paul. Perhaps a second influence of Paul upon Luke here can also be seen in number 10. According to Paul's writings, Yeshua did not appear first to the women, as in the three Gospels other than Luke; indeed, according to Paul, Yeshua did not appear to the women at all, unless they were among "the five hundred" (1 Cor 15:3–7). It appears that Luke followed his teacher Paul in this regard also. But perhaps the most interesting, and obvious, point to be noted about all this "negative" evidence of Luke's is that it can be construed negatively only on a basis of comparison with other Gospel accounts of the same event—i.e., *none* of these passages comes from sections of Luke that are unique to him. This means that the source of these "negative" passages within Luke is *not* the Proto-Gospel by the woman evangelist embedded within Luke. This would indicate that the Proto-Gospel source was more consciously and strongly prowoman than Luke's other sources, and Luke himself—another fact that points toward at least the possibility, and more than likely the high probability of a woman evangelist.

Conclusion

In sum it can be said that beyond the evidence that clearly points to the fact that Yeshua himself was a vigorous feminist, Luke's Gospel reflects this feminism most intensely of all the Gospels. In choosing to record all this prowoman material, Luke himself also clearly indicates a very sympathetic attitude toward women. However, his prowoman material falls into two categories: that which is recorded in common with other Gospels and that which is unique to Luke. The former is almost as large (19 passages—17 of them in common with Matthew) as the latter (23 passages). In the commonly recorded passages, sometimes Luke's version highlights women more than the other version(s); sometimes it's the other way around. It would have to be judged that in regard to this commonly recorded material Matthew and Luke exhibit an attitude that is about equally sympathetic toward the cause of women. But in the material special to each Gospel, Luke is giant strides ahead of all the others in prowoman passages. Simply in terms of the number of passages dealing with women, Luke has 23 (practically all actively prowoman) special to him; Matthew 10 (though half of these do not reflect an attitude toward women); the Fourth Gospel has three and Mark none. Again, it is in that Proto-Gospel section of Luke that the feminism of his Gospel really stands out. Thus it is clear that a strongly feminist evangelist was the source of the Proto-Gospel, again enhancing the possibility, indeed, the high likelihood that it was a woman evangelist—"Luka"—who perforce had to remain anonymous, at least in Luke's judgment, for the sake of the credibility of the Gospel in that male-dominated society. In conclusion, take away the woman-sourced ("Luka") material from Luke's Gospel and there is not much more than Mark's Gospel and Q repeated, which Matthew had already produced, that is, *Luke's Gospel would not have been written.*

THE FOURTH GOSPEL

The Fourth Gospel was the last of the four canonical Gospels to be written (probably close to 100 CE). Much of its material is different from material in the other three Gospels, the Synoptics, and it tends to report the teaching of Yeshua in long discourses. It is third in overall length, being about 75 percent of the length of Luke, the longest Gospel. However, the Fourth Gospel contained far fewer accounts that dealt with women or the "feminine"—only nine. On the other hand, several of these accounts were quite long, were important, and were very sympathetic toward women. In fact, these nine passages are 122 verses in length, compared to Mark's 114. (Matthew has 180 verses and Luke 220 dealing with women.) The critical question of the authorship of the Fourth Gospel will be dealt with at length below. However, let it be stated here that according to a scholarly consensus, the author is definitely *not* John the son of Zebedee, one of the Twelve. The strange source of John's name on the Gospel came from Irenaeus in the late second century. He remembered hearing in his childhood from Polycarp (died 156 CE) that John was the author; Polycarp spoke of a certain Presbyter John, whom Irenaeus mixed up with John the son of Zebedee, one of the Twelve.[22] Since the real name of the author was deliberately suppressed, the name John stuck. More of that below.

The Fourth Gospel's Lengthy Passages concerning Women

It needs to be recalled that all five of the lengthy passages in the Fourth Gospel centering on women have already been discussed above:

Yeshua the Wine-maker at Wedding Feast at Cana

The very first thing reported on by the Fourth Gospel—except for Yeshua having been a follower of his cousin John the Baptist, striking out on his own, and gathering his first disciples, who also left John for Yeshua, including the woman "Anonymous Disciple," who will be seen to be the "Disciple Who Yeshua Loved," the evangelist of the penultimate version of the Fourth Gospel—is Yeshua's attending a wedding feast and performing his first life-and-joy-affirming "miracle": wine-making.

Yeshua's Conversaton with a Samaritan Woman

Yeshua broke all kinds of rules by addressing a woman in public, and conversing with a Samaritan as an equal. Further, she was a "serial husband" woman, and yet Yeshua reached out to her as a person worthy of serious conversation; she in return accepted Yeshua's teaching and ran and persuaded many of her townspeople to come out to listen to Yeshua.

Annointment of Yeshua's Feet by Mary of Bethany

We saw that Christian readers of the Gospels engendered a terrible confusion about three different women in the Gospels: (a) Mary of Bethany, (b) Mary Magdalene, and (c) the penitent woman who washed the feet of Yeshua with her tears (not ointment, as did Mary of Bethany). From Luke/Luka's Gospel we learn that Mary of Bethany was also the intellectual who sat learning at the feet of Yeshua the Master—"she has chosen the better part, and it shall not be taken from her."

---

22. Perkins, "The Gospel according to John," 946.

Three Jesus Certitudes

Raising of Lazarus by Yeshua at Plea of Martha, and . . .

Martha did not only "busy herself about serving," it was she who first pleaded for Yeshua to raise her brother Lazarus from the dead, and she was the first to whom Yeshua proclaimed himself to be "the Resurrection." So it was she in turn who first proclaimed Yeshua the Messiah (John 11:27).

Yeshua's Forgiveness of Adulterous Woman

Although scholars are sure that this episode was not first related in the Fourth Gospel, but in Luke/Luka's (Luke 21:28), apparently the early Christian copyists could not stomach the idea of Yeshua not opting for the joy of stoning a woman to death (a wretched custom still practiced by some traditionalist Muslims), and so dropped this episode from their copies of Luke/Luka's Gospel. Fortunately later copyists of the Fourth Gospel rescued it and stuck it in their copies.

Women in Yeshua's Passion and Resurrection

Witnessing an appearance of the risen Yeshua was the key to authority in the beginning of the Yeshua movement. How did Paul, who never met Yeshua, claim to have authority to teach the Gospel? Because he claimed to have seen the risen Yeshua while he, Saul, was on the road to Damascus. That is what gave him the right to call himself an "apostle" (*apostellein*, Greek: "to send"). Several women, preeminently Mary Magdalene, also experienced an appearance of the risen Yeshua and indeed also knew him before his death. This certainly was a major source of their importance in the early period of the Yeshua movement, which eventually became the church. We will see below how this authority led to a second woman being an evangelist, a writer of a Gospel, the Fourth Gospel.

Women at the Foot of the Cross

It should first be noted that there is no record of any women seeking the death of Yeshua; all those in any way involved in promoting Yeshua's death were men. Such noninvolvement of women in the violent death of others was by no means a foregone conclusion in Jewish tradition: Deborah, Jael, Esther, Judith, and Salome, for example, all caused the deaths of men.

Yeshua's Women Followers Created Christianity

On the positive side, the response of women disciples to Yeshua was extraordinary. He taught and fought for them, and they responded by following him to his bitter end, even risking their own limbs and lives. All Yeshua's male disciples deserted him: "Then all the disciples deserted him and ran away."[23] "And they all deserted him and ran away."[24] Luke, almost certainly a later Gospel than Mark and Matthew, said that "those who knew" Yeshua stood afar and watched the crucifixion. Though many scholars believe that the Fourth Gospel's adding a presumed male disciple to the group of women at the crucifixion was unhistorical, it should be noted that with all the other evangelists the Fourth Gospel evangelist did locate the women there. The Fourth Gospel, like Mark and Matthew, listed three women's names; they are not exactly the same ones as those in the other Gospel lists, but Mary Magdalene was there, as she is in all the lists in all the Gospels. This is the only list on which Mary Magdalene is not placed first. In the Fourth Gospel's account, Yeshua's concern to find his widowed mother a home was almost the last thing he spoke of (John 19:25–27; cf. Matt 27:55–56; Mark 15:40–41; Luke 23:49). But more will be said of this important passage below.

Women Testify to Male Disciples about Yeshua's Resurrection

See above for a discussion of the women's testifying about the resurrection of Yeshua to the male disciples. The traditions are extremely various on this matter:

(1) The earliest of the accounts in the New Testament, i.e., Paul's First Letter to the Corinthians 15:5–8, did not even mention the women in connection with the resurrection.

(2) The earliest Gospel, Mark, said the women were frightened, ran away and "said nothing to a soul," though obviously they did eventually say something to someone—how else could the existence of the Gospel account be explained?

(3) In Matthew it simply said the women "ran to tell the disciples," and on the way were met by Yeshua and commissioned by him to "go and tell my brothers"—no indication of the brothers' reaction.

23. Matt 26:56.
24. Mark 14:49.

(4) Luke/Luka, written, like Matthew, between the time of the writing of Mark and the Fourth Gospel, recorded that a whole group of women told the apostles of the empty tomb, "but this story of theirs seemed pure nonsense, and they did not believe them; Peter, however, went running to the tomb."

(5) In the Fourth Gospel, the latest to be written, Mary Magdalene ran and told Peter and "the other disciple"; their response was simply to run and see for themselves, not necessarily implying that they did not believe her, but it seems likely so.

(6) The ending added to Mark's Gospel (Mark 16:1–9), written probably early in the second century, sounds in some ways much like Luke/Luka's account and in some ways like the Fourth Gospel's: "But they did not believe her [Mary Magdalene] when they heard her say that he was alive and that she had seen him."

Furthermore, of the four Gospels' accounts, Mark recorded that an angel in the empty tomb commissioned the women to testify to the male disciples; Matthew did so as well, but also added that Yeshua himself likewise commissioned the women; Luke/Luka mentioned two angels in the empty tomb but recorded no commissioning at all, though in fact the women did testify to the male disciples; the Fourth Gospel reported the presence of the angels, but recorded only Yeshua's commissioning of Mary Magdalene. Thus, three of the four Gospels spoke of a commissioning of the women: one (Mark) by an angel, one (the Fourth Gospel) by Yeshua, and one (Matthew) by both; one (Luke) did not record such a commissioning. In fact, however, according to Luke the women did nevertheless testify, and according to Mark they did not, despite the commission—though the matter is confused here because of the strong possibility of a lost original ending and because the second-century ending did record a testifying by Mary Magdalene.

It is perhaps not possible to speak of an original version of the account of the women's commissioning and testifying. Rather, perhaps it is best to speak of several traditions that fed into the different Gospel accounts and that may or may not have been significantly adapted by the Gospel writers. What is clear is that all three elements—(1) the commissioning of the women to testify to the male disciples concerning the empty tomb, the resurrection, or both; (2) their actual testifying; (3) a disbelieving response to the women from the men—are strongly represented in the Gospel accounts (though not at all in Paul). Mark without the "lost" or added ending is the least supportive of the women's role in these matters; the other three are equally, though differently, supportive. One would have to conclude that the tradition concerning this very significant involvement of women in this most essential matter of Christian belief and their being put down by the men grew so much stronger—either in times after, or places other, or both—than when Paul and Mark wrote that they found a prominent place in the later three Gospels, and in the later ending of Mark (Matt 28:16-20; Mark 16:7, 11; Luke 24:9-11; John 20:18).

The Risen Yeshua Appears to Women

See above for a discussion of the risen Yeshua's appearance first to women (one or more) (John 20:11-18; cf. Matt 28:9-10; Mark 16:9).

Raymond E. Brown noted that essential to the apostolate

> in the mind of Paul were the two components of having seen the risen Jesus and having been sent to proclaim him; this is the implicit logic of I Cor 9:1-2; 15:8-11; Gal 1:11-16. A key to Peter's importance in the apostolate was the tradition that he was the first to see the risen Jesus (1 Cor 15:5; Luke 24:34). More than any other Gospel, John revises this tradition about Peter . . . In John (and in Matthew) Mary Magdalene is sent by the risen Lord . . . True, this is not a mission to the whole world; but Mary Magdalene comes close to meeting the basic Pauline requirements of an apostle; and it is she, not Peter, who is the first to see the risen Jesus . . . The tradition that Jesus appeared first to Mary Magdalene has a good chance of being historical—he remembered first this representative of the women who had not deserted him during the Passion. The priority given to Peter in Paul and Luke is a priority among those who became official witnesses to the Resurrection. The secondary place given to the tradition of an appearance to a woman or women probably reflects the fact that women did not serve at first as official preachers of the Church—a fact that would make the creation of an appearance to woman unlikely.[25]

---

25. Brown, "Roles of Women in the Fourth Gospel," 692.

Three Jesus Certitudes

Interim Reflection

Although the Fourth Gospel had the least number of passages about women (the number of verses was slightly more than Mark's number, however), it took a strongly prowoman stance. As we just saw above, it contained a number of events peculiar to it in which women played extremely important roles: According to the Fourth Gospel, Yeshua performed his first miracle at the bidding of a woman (wedding feast at Cana, John 2:11–12); the first recorded effective woman evangelist was sent out by Yeshua (the Samaritan woman, John 4:5–42); Yeshua revealed himself uniquely to a woman as "the Resurrection" (Martha, John 11:25), and for the first time, in the Fourth Gospel, as the Messiah (the Samaritan woman, John 4:26); Yeshua was proclaimed publicly by a woman (Martha, John 11:27)—rather than Peter—to be the Messiah, and also the Son of God. Likewise, rather than appearing first to Peter, the risen Yeshua was reported by the Fourth Gospel as having appeared first to a woman (Mary Magdalene, John 20:11–18), who then was sent by Yeshua to bear witness to Peter! This latter point, the first appearance of the risen Yeshua to a woman, however, the Fourth Gospel has in common with Matthew, although there the account was not nearly so detailed and moving as that of the Fourth Gospel. Moreover, Yeshua described himself with a very female, maternal, breast-feeding image (*ek tes koilias*, John 7:37–38).

It is perhaps also worth noting that although the account about Yeshua and the adulterous woman (John 7:53—8:11) was clearly not written by the Fourth Evangelist, in the greatest number of manuscripts it ended up being located there, indicating perhaps that many early Christians felt that the Fourth Gospel was so sensitive toward women as to be thought the most appropriate place to locate that orphaned story. The Fourth Gospel contained long accounts about Mary Magdalene and Mary of Bethany—including the accounts of the latter at her own home (John 11:1–44) and as the anointer of Yeshua's feet (John 12:1–8). Perhaps this fact—coupled with the tradition that (incorrectly) considered Mary Magdalene, Mary of Bethany, and the penitent "harlot" of Luke 7:36–50 who anointed Yeshua's feet to be one and the same person—encouraged the early Christians to locate this story of Yeshua's befriending another female sexual sinner in the Fourth Gospel.

In any case, it is clear that the Fourth Gospel was, not quantitatively, but certainly qualitatively, very strongly prowoman. "John gives prominence to women disciples to the point that they seem to be on the same level as members of the Twelve,"[26] states the preeminent scholar of the Fourth Gospel, Raymond Brown.

It is also interesting to note that "in John there is a clear display of female self-confidence: not only in general, but also with regard to female discipleship. John portrays women as speaking far more than Mark, Matthew and Luke. In Mark only five instances of women speaking are recorded, in Matthew women speak nine times, and in Luke eleven times, only four of which occur in stories about Jesus as a grown man. In contrast to the Synoptics, John recorded 22 instances of women speaking."[27]

Who Was the Beloved Disciple?

The Fourth Gospel is the only one that uses the term "the Beloved Disciple" (*mathetes egapa*). Clearly, the Beloved Disciple is the hero of the community of the Fourth Gospel and is the source of the Gospel. (For reasons that will become clear below, I follow Raymond Brown in naming the so-called Johannine community instead the Beloved Disciple community.) The premier scholar on the whole Johannine community (including the Fourth Gospel and the three epistles of John), Brown stated: "The evangelist was an unknown Christian living at the end of the first century in a community for which the Beloved Disciple, now deceased, had been the great authority"[28] Further, although all the other "disciples" were named (and the Fourth Gospel never used the term "apostle"), the Beloved Disciple was always anonymous. If this particular disciple of Yeshua was the beloved one of Yeshua (who leaned on Yeshua's bosom at the Last Supper), and the leader of that community of followers, as well as the source of the Gospel that probed much deeper than any of the other three Gospels into the profound *meaning* of Yeshua and his teaching, the question positively screams: Why was the Beloved Disciple unnamed?

Many answers have been offered to that question. However, one has come to the fore recently with arguments so persuasive that it seems to me to be an "idea whose time has come." The Beloved Disciple, and the source of the Fourth Gospel, was a woman, and the most likely candidate is Mary Magdalene.

---

26. Brown, *Community of the Beloved Disciple*, 76.
27. Boer, "Mary Magdalene and the Disciple Jesus Loved."
28. Brown, *Community of the Beloved Disciple*, 186.

Why? Because by the time the Fourth Gospel was written, as we have it (probably some-time near 100 CE), the apocalyptic period when the expected return of Yeshua was imminent had long passed, and the followers of Yeshua were setting up more institutionalized forms. Statements had begun to appear that increasingly pushed women to the background—statements such as these: "Wives should regard their husbands as they regard the Lord" (Eph 5:21); "Wives, give way to your husbands" (Col 3:18); "wives should be obedient to their husbands" (1 Pet 2:13); "I permit no woman to teach or to have authority over men; she is to keep silent" (1 Tim 2:9); "the women should keep silence in the churches. For they are not permitted to speak, but should be subordinate, as even the law says" (1 Cor 14:33).

According to Raymond Brown, the Beloved Disciple community underwent four phases of development. (In what follows, I summarize Brown's argument except that I cast the Beloved Disciple as a woman, an idea that Brown did not assert.) The Beloved Disciple and her followers initially had a low Christology, that is, they understood Yeshua to be purely human. With the passage of time, the Beloved Disciple and her followers discerned ever deeper meaning in the teachings of Yeshua and moved increasingly in the direction of a higher Christology (that is, they saw more and more of the divine in Yeshua). Brown discerned that a crisis developed in the community in the mid-'80s of the first century of the Common Era when the followers of Yeshua were being forced out of the synagogue by the addition of a required blessing which Yeshua followers who held a high Christology could not in good conscience confess.

Then in phase 2 a division occurred within the Beloved Disciple community: The majority (eventually called the secessionists) stressed Yeshua's divinity and downplayed his humanity. At that time the Gospel as we have it was revised: the high Christology was kept, but the importance of Yeshua's humanity was also maintained. The final redactor, in phase 3, clearly wanted to maintain connections with the *ekklesia katholika*, the "great church," that was emerging, and so perhaps added ameliorating phrases such as "*Kai ho logos sarx egeneto* [and the word became flesh]" (John 1:14).

> This curious history of the Fourth Gospel would become quite intelligible if we posit that the larger part of the Johannine community, the secessionists, took the Gospel with them in their intellectual itinerary toward docetism, gnosticism, and Montanism, while the author's adherents carried the Gospel with them as they were amalgamated into the Great Church. This would explain why Johannine ideas but not quotations appear in the earlier church

writings: because a majority of those who claimed the Gospel as their own had become heterodox, there would have been a reluctance among the orthodox to cite the Gospel as Scripture.[29]

Thus it also became imperative that the gender of the Beloved Disciple be suppressed, lest the Gospel of the Beloved Disciple community be rejected by the great church. In fact, it was not until the middle of the fourth century that the Fourth Gospel was generally accepted by the *ekklesia katholika*, although it had earlier been widely favored by various docetic and gnostic communities. (Docetic communities claimed only divinity for Yeshua whereas gnostic communities focused on Yeshua's divinity and stressed the importance of secret knowledge.) The fourth phase of development within the Beloved Disciple community was marked by the definitive split of the community: the secessionists drifted more and more toward docetism and gnosticism, and the orthodox remained with the great church, and eventually saved the Fourth Gospel for the orthodox church.

Ann Graham Brock has shown that a sort of seesaw relationship existed between Mary Magdalene and Peter in all the documents in which they appeared together, including in the three Synoptic Gospels, and most prominently the pro-Peter Gospel of Luke (despite the argument of this book that its Proto-Gospel had a female author, "Luka") but also very dramatically in the Fourth Gospel, which is almost anti-Peter and surely pro–Beloved Disciple and pro-Magdalene.[30] Beyond that, the authority struggle between Peter and Magdalene persisted in the early apocryphal writings (that is, in those Christian writings that did not make it into the New Testament canon, such as the Gospel of Mary, the Gospel of Philip, and the Gospel of Thomas). I will look at each of the instances where in the Fourth Gospel the term "the Beloved Disciple" occurred.

I am not claiming that a woman, and specifically Mary Magdalene, was the writer of the Fourth Gospel as we have it, but that the Beloved Disciple was clearly a woman—most likely Mary Magdalene—and that hence she surely was the source of the Fourth Gospel and the writer of a Proto–Fourth Gospel, even as our present Fourth Gospel comes from the hand of a final redactor working toward the end of the first century after the death of Magdalene. The end of the Fourth Gospel stated: "This is the disciple [1] who is a witness to these things, and [2] has *written about them*, (*grapsas*), and [3] we know that that witness is true" (John 21:24). Thus, the

---

29 Ibid., 149.
30. Brock, *Mary Magdalene*, 40ff.

Beloved Disciple (Mary Magdalene) wrote the penultimate version of the Fourth Gospel.

First a Disciple of John the Baptist? (John 1:35–40)

The Beloved Disciple was not mentioned specifically in John 1:35–40, but many scholars see a reference to the Beloved Disciple here. The Fourth Gospel tells of John the Baptist standing with two of his disciples and proclaiming Yeshua to be the Lamb of God, upon which the two disciples follow Yeshua. One of them was named as Andrew, and the other was unnamed: this marks the first, anonymous appearance of the anonymous Beloved Disciple. Readers unavoidably ask, why is Andrew deliberately named as Peter's brother, but the other disciple is also specifically referred to, but equally deliberately not named? (This anonymous referring to the Beloved Disciple occurs in the Fourth Gospel eight times!) The answer is the same every time, namely, because the Beloved Disciple was a woman, and, as we have seen above, to reveal that the Beloved Disciple, the source of the Fourth Gospel was a woman would have been to lose the Gospel for the great church. In this case at hand, although is not absolutely certain, it is likely that the Beloved Disciple, Mary Magdalene, was—like Yeshua himself—a disciple of John the Baptist, and that she then became one of the first disciples of Yeshua.

> The next day again John was standing with two of his disciples; and he looked at Jesus as he walked, and said, "Behold, the Lamb of God!" The two disciples heard him say this, and they followed Jesus. Jesus turned, and saw them following, and said to them, "What do you seek?" And they said to him, "Rabbi" (which means Teacher), "where are you staying?" He said to them, "come and see." They came and saw where he was staying; and they stayed with him that day, for it was about the tenth hour. One of the two who heard John speak, and followed him, was Andrew, Simon Peter's brother. (John 1:35–40)

Yeshua's Dinner Companion (John 13:23–26)

Here for the first time the term "the disciple whom Yeshua loved" (*ton matheton on egapa tou Iesou*) was used, and she was described as leaning on Yeshua's breast at dinner. They were obviously using the practice customary in the Roman Empire of reclining on cushions at meal. In fact, Peter called her attention and asked her to ask Yeshua who was going to betray him, after which the Gospel stated that she "fell back on Yeshua's breast and asked him." Clearly Peter was unwilling to ask Yeshua out loud who the traitor was, but Peter felt that Magdalene was close enough to Yeshua, physically and psychologically, to do the asking—and he was right.

(In this scene is another instance of the pairing of Peter and Magdalene—and Peter comes off lower and Magdalene higher.) There is no psychological tension expressed here (as there is in the later Gospel of Mary and Gospel of Philip), but clearly Magdalene has the more authoritative position, above Peter, measured in closeness to Yeshua. How different this is from the Gospel of Luke, where Peter predominated and where Magdalene made her most diminished showing—whether in any of the Gospels or in the works of Paul, who recognized the authority of Peter but did not even mention Magdalene.

Now this description of the closeness of Yeshua and the Beloved Disciple, Mary Magdalene, strikes readers as an extraordinary, intimate closeness. Obviously it also similarly struck Magdalene and the subsequent followers of the community that formed around her, for it was clearly and starkly described in the Gospel here. Further, this scene became so important for the community of the Beloved Disciple that it was reiterated at the very end of the Gospel when Magdalene was again anonymously identified as the disciple whom Yeshua loved, who also leaned on his breast at the supper and said . . ." (John 21:20).

The "Beloved Disciple leaning on Yeshua's breast" became a kind of "branding" for Magdalene and her subsequent community. But in order for her insights into the meaning of Yeshua and his teaching to become accepted and widespread, she, like John the Baptist, had to decrease so that Yeshua could increase (cf. John 3:30). But that period is now passing. Though only a few scholars to date have discerned that Magdalene was the most intimate interpreter of the meaning and teaching of Yeshua, it will, in my judgment, doubtless become an accepted realization, and Magdalene and the other women disciples of Yeshua, such as that intellectual Mary of Bethany, and "Luka" (who might well be Mary of Bethany) will take their rightful places in the Christian tradition.

> One of his disciples, whom Yeshua loved [*ton matheton on egapa tou Iesou*], was lying close to the breast of Jesus; so Simon Peter beckoned to him and said, "Tell us who it is of whom he speaks."

Three Jesus Certitudes

> So, falling back on Yeshua's breast, he said to him, "Lord, who is it?" Yeshua answered, "It is he to whom I shall give this morsel when I have dipped it. (John 13:23–26)

Friends in High Places (John 18:15–16)

In this passage Yeshua has just been taken into custody and the Fourth Gospel had it that Peter "and another disciple" (*kai allos mathetes*) followed Yeshua. Brown and many scholars are convinced that this was the Beloved Disciple, for the Fourth Gospel was always hypercareful to give names and detailed specifics, except when it pertained to the Beloved Disciple—read: Mary Magdalene. The Fourth Gospel noted that the unnamed disciple knew the high priest—a very interesting detail, suggesting that Magdalene was a self-confident, outgoing kind of person. She spoke to the woman watching the gate to let Peter in. Shortly thereafter Peter denied that he ever knew Yeshua, while nothing further was reported about the "other disciple," Magdalene. Once again Magdalene was shown to be superior to Peter—why else was she introduced here in the story?

> Simon Peter followed Yeshua, and so did another disciple. As this disciple was known to the high priest, he entered the court of the high priest along with Yeshua, while Peter stood outside at the door. So the other disciple, who was known to the high priest, went out and spoke to the maid who kept the door, and brought Peter in. (John 18:15–16)

Magdalene, Beloved Disciple, at the Foot of the Cross (John 19:25–27)

On the one hand, this is a very confusing and confused text, and on the other, it is one with an unusually deep meaning. To begin with, there apparently were three women listed as standing below the cross of Yeshua, and all three of them were named Mary. The confusion begins with the fact that verse 25 stated that there were the three women named Mary standing by the cross, and then suddenly verse 26 said that Yeshua saw both his mother and the Beloved Disciple. But *he* wasn't there! How did Yeshua see him? Ramon Jusino has argued that the redactor simply replaced the name of Mary Magdalene with that of the "anonymous Beloved Disciple." Why?

Because the words Yeshua was about to utter were far too central to have safely said to a woman if the "orthodox" of the Fourth Gospel community could hope to have the Gospel accepted by the great church.[31]

Esther de Boer has argued quite persuasively that that, yes, the Beloved Disciple was indeed a woman, Mary Magdalene, but that the final redactor of the final version—the version we have—did not arbitrarily bring in the Beloved Disciple and therefore have to put the word "son" in Yeshua's mouth to fit the disciple's presumed male gender. Rather, she argues that this exchange at the foot of the cross was understood by the head of the Fourth Gospel community (by the Beloved Disciple, Magdalene) as a sort of commission into the deeper meaning of being a follower of Yeshua. De Boer contends that when the Gospel said, "When Yeshua therefore saw his mother and the disciple whom he loved standing there," he was looking at Mary his mother and Mary Magdalene, and he said to his mother, "Behold your son," referring first to himself and then to his alter ego (the Beloved Disciple), who had been with him from the days of John the Baptist, was the intimate at the Last Supper, and was now to be the first of numberless ones loved by him and his Father. Then Yeshua said to the Beloved Disciple, Magdalene, "behold your mother. And from that hour the disciple took her onto his own."

De Boer writes: "The ultimate importance of the scene in 19:26–27 lies in Jesus' invitation to his mother to look away from her dying son to find him, alive, in the Disciple He Loved [Magdalene]. At the same time Jesus' words are a solemn declaration to this disciple [Magdalene]: she may act on Jesus' behalf, as if she were Jesus himself."

> Near the cross of Jesus stood his mother, and his mother's sister, Mary, mother of Cleopas, and Mary of Magdala. Seeing his mother and the Disciple Whom He Loved [*ton matheten hon egapa*] standing near her, Jesus Said to his mother, "Woman, behold your son." Then to the disciple, he said, "Behold your mother." And from that moment the Disciple made a place for her in his home. (John 19:25–27)

This commission was obviously the launching pad for Magdalene, when seen in retrospect, for her becoming the center of a community of followers probing the deeper meaning of the life and teaching of Yeshua. But precisely because the Fourth Gospel was understood as so central to the proclaiming of the good news, the orthodox final redactor felt compelled

---

31. Jusino, "Mary Magdalene."

to suppress the fact that the leader of the Fourth Gospel community, the Beloved Disciple community, was a woman: Mary Magdalene.

A Race to the Tomb (John 20:1–11)

In this section there is clearly confusion as a result of the work of the redactor apparently trying to fuse two traditions. In verse 1 Mary Magdalene went alone to the tomb (in no other Gospel did she go alone), found it empty, and ran to tell Peter and "the *other* disciple whom Yeshua loved" (v. 2). Then Peter and the other disciple ran to the tomb; the other disciple got there first, but did not go in (vv. 3–5). Peter arrived and went in (vv. 6–7), followed then by the other disciple, "who saw and believed" (v. 8). This last statement was clearly important: Peter did not believe, but the "other disciple whom Yeshua loved" (called this in v. 2) did. Both then went home (v. 10). But where was Magdalene? Somehow, after Magdalene initially ran to tell Peter about the empty tomb in verse 2, she next appears in verse 11, back at the tomb, weeping—though nothing has been said in the intervening verses about her return to the tomb.

Then followed the famous scene wherein Magdalene met Yeshua (see below). Some scholars believe that "the other disciple," who ran to the tomb with Peter (vv. 3–5), and who entered the tomb after Peter and believed (v. 8), was in fact the Beloved Disciple. If so, then again in the Fourth Gospel the "Beloved Disciple" bested Peter, both in running and in believing. However, some scholars question whether "the other disciple whom Yeshua loved" was the Beloved Disciple. Why was reference made (v. 2) to the "other" disciple Yeshua loved? Was it some other disciple than the one at the Last Supper and elsewhere? When the Gospel spoke of this *other* disciple whom Yeshua loved, it here used the term *ephilei* (from one of the Greek terms for "love," *phila*) instead of *egapa* (from another Greek term for "love," *agape*). Elsewhere when speaking of *the* Beloved Disciple, the Gospel employed *egapa*. To further the confusion, Yeshua also was said to love Martha and her sister, Mary, and their brother, Lazarus, of Bethany. (In this case *egapa* appears once and *ephilei* twice: John 11:3, 5, 36). Was the "other disciple whom Yeshua loved" (*ephilei*) also a woman, and was this another instance of the Fourth Gospel having a woman disciple besting Peter ("and she believed")?

The confusion clears up easily if we accept the basic premise that the final redactor felt it necessary to suppress the prominent presence of women Yeshua disciples overall. (And he—or *she*?—was, of course, proven correct.) *In the Fourth Gospel an anonymous disciple is always a woman!* In this case "the *other* disciple whom Yeshua loved" was Mary of Bethany, who was with Peter when Mary Magdalene burst upon them with the report of the empty tomb. Peter and Mary of Bethany then ran to the tomb, Mary arriving there first, and also "believing."

Magdalene Again Superior to Peter (John 21:7)

In this postresurrection verse it was the Beloved Disciple, Magdalene, who recognized Yeshua standing on the lakeside speaking to the disciples who were fishing, and she told Peter that it was Yeshua speaking. Readers wonder, why the detail about Magdalene telling Peter that it is Yeshua? Oscar Cullmann notes that "the ambivalent relationship which we have seen in John's Gospel between Peter, the representative of the rest of the original community, and the Beloved Disciple mirrors precisely the double effort of the Beloved Disciple circle: On the one hand, holding on to a conscious independence, and on the other, the conviction of the necessity of a mutual expansion for the sake of the whole."[32] Once again the Fourth Gospel put Magdalene up, and Peter down. Most scholars, in fact, consider this entire chapter 21 a later appendix, "the result of a later redactor's attempt to represent an effort by the Beloved Disciple community to unite with the church at large."[33]

The Fourth Gospel: The Gospel of Magdalene (John 21:1–2; 20:2–4)

If, as most scholars believe, the entire chapter 21 was written by the final redactor of the Fourth Gospel, it is important to note that the whole of it was, as Cullmann suggested, a balancing act between Magdalene, now disguised as the Beloved Disciple, and Peter, the perceived leader of the *ekklesia katholika*. Chapter 21 began by stating that Yeshua showed himself again to several of his disciples, and then named each—except, as 21:2 has it, "two other disciples" (*alloi ek ton matheton autou duo*). Why are these disciples unnamed? A little later in the chapter, as we have seen, the Beloved Disciple is present. Remembering that in the Fourth Gospel an

---

32. Cullmann, *Der johanneische Kreis*, 60.
33. Boer, "Mary Magdalene."

anonymous disciple is always a woman, most likely Mary Magdalene was one of the "two other disciples," and the second one was also a woman. Something was about to happen that was very important for the Christian community, the church—namely, an appearance of the risen Lord, which then made those to whom he appeared "apostles" with the authority and commission to preach the good news, the Gospel—as happened to Paul (who never knew the earthly Yeshua) on the road to Damascus. But this could not be accepted in the church, which issued statements such as, "I allow no woman to have authority over man" (1 Tim 2:12), or, "Women must keep silence in the church" (1 Cor 14:34). Hence, in this final chapter, the work of the orthodox redactor, both the women disciples were neutered.

There then followed the "put-down" of Peter by Magdalene in verse 7. Verses 15–19 were where the final redactor "did obeisance" to Peter, who of course at the time of the redactor's writing was long dead ("signifying by what death he [Peter] should glorify God" [John 21:19]). Then Magdalene came to the fore once more in the guise of the Beloved Disciple, with tension toward Peter still reflected in the language. Peter turned and saw Magdalene—again identified as "the one who leaned on the breast of Yeshua at supper" (v. 20)—and said to Yeshua in rather abrupt fashion, what about this one? (*outos de ti* [v. 21]). Yeshua then proceeded to scotch a rumor that the Beloved Disciple, Magdalene, had not died (vv. 22–23).

Then came the reaffirmation that Magdalene, without being named, was in fact the source of all the community's information about Yeshua and his meaning: "This is the disciple who bears witness of these things" (*Outos estin ho mathetes ho martyron peri touton* [v. 24a]). The final redactor went further and announced that Magdalene wrote a Proto-Gospel, which he, and perhaps others before him, reedited: "and *wrote* these things" (*kai ho grapsas tauta* [v. 24b]). Hence, the Fourth Gospel should in fact not be named the Gospel of John, but the Gospel of Magdalene, even though we have it only in a slightly edited form.

> Later on, Jesus showed himself again to the disciples. It was by the Sea of Tiberias, and it happened like this: Simon Peter, Thomas called the Twin, Nathanael from Cana in Galilee, the sons of Zebedee *and two more of his disciples* [*kai alloi ek ton matheton autou duo*] were together. Simon Peter said, "I am going fishing." They replied, "We will come with you." They went out and got into the boat but caught nothing that night.
>
> It was light by now and there stood Jesus on the shore, though the disciples did not realize that is was Jesus. Jesus called out,

"Have you caught anything, friends?" And they answered, "No." He said, "Throw the net out to starboard and you'll find something." So they dropped the net, and there were so many fish that they could not haul in. The *disciple Jesus loved* [*ho mathetes hon egapa ho Iesous*] said to Peter, "It is the Lord." At these words, "It is the Lord," Simon Peter who had practically nothing on, wrapped his cloak round him and jumped into the water . . . Peter turned and saw the disciple Jesus loved [*ton matheten hon egapa ho Iesous*] followed them—the one who had leaned on his breast at the supper and had said to him Jesus, "Lord, who is it that will betray you?" Seeing him, Peter said to Jesus, "What about him [*outos de ti*], Lord?" Jesus answered, "If I want him to stay behind till I come, what does it matter to you? You are to follow me . . .

This is the disciple who has witnessed this things [*ho martyron peri touton*], has written them down [*kai ho grasps tauta*], and we know that his testimony is true [*kai oidamen hoti alethes autou he marturia estin*]. (John 21:1–24)

Mary Magdalene

It should be noted that Mary Magdalene, i.e., Mary from the town of Magdala, is named in all four of the canonical Gospels. (As we saw, she clearly is not the sinful woman of Luke 7:37–50 or Mary of Bethany.) In every instance (there are a total of twelve in the four Gospels) except Luke 8:2, the reference is in connection either with her being at the crucifixion and observing Yeshua's burial, or with her seeing the empty tomb and the risen Yeshua—the former being mentioned as a preparation to recording the latter. Each time, Mary Magdalene is either named alone or is at the head of the list (with the exception of the special situation of John 19:25, where the focus is specifically on Yeshua's mother Mary). Moreover, all of the lists vary from evangelist to evangelist; no two lists are the same: however, Mary Magdalene is always listed. Scholars conclude that there was a strong and widespread tradition that Yeshua appeared first of all to Mary Magdalene and that she therefore held a place of honor in the early Christian community: this would explain her appearance on all the lists of women in the Gospels, and her being first on all save one.[34]

---

34 See (1) Matt 27:55–56; (2) Matt 27:57–58; (3) Matt 28:1; (4) Mark 15:40–41; (5) Mark 15:45–47; (6) Mark 16:1–2; (7) Mark 16:9; (8) Luke 8:1–3; (9) Luke 24:9–11; (10) John 19:25–27; (11) John 20:1, 15,17, 18.

THE APOSTLE TO THE APOSTLES

As a result of Mary Magdalene's role as one sent (*apostellein*) by Yeshua to witness to the male apostles, as recorded in the canonical Fourth Gospel 20:17, she was the only woman besides Yeshua's mother on whose feast day the creed was recited in the Western church.[35] The term "apostle" in reference to Magdalene occurs often in the well-known ninth-century life of her by Rabanus Maurus: Yeshua commissioned her an apostle to the apostles (*apostola apostolorum*);[36] she did not delay in carrying out the office of the apostolate to which she was commissioned;[37] her fellow apostles were evangelized with the news of the resurrection of the Messiah;[38] she was raised to the honor of the apostolate and was commissioned an evangelist (*evangelisto*) of the resurrection.[39] Even the acerbic Bernard of Clairvaux (twelfth century) refers to her as the "apostle to the apostles."[40]

Rabanus Maurus simply carried on a tradition attested many centuries earlier. Around the end of the second century or the beginning of the third, Hippolytus of Rome also commented on Yeshua's appearing first to Mary Magdalene, and the other women, and spoke of Mary Magdalene, and the other women—and symbolically, Eve—as *apostles* and *evangelists* (proclaimers of the gospel, the *evangelium*). The extant text is in a Slavonic translation, with variations in an Armenian translation:

> Christ himself sent [Mary Magdalene], so that even women become the apostles of Christ and the deficiency of the first Eve's disobedience was made evident by this justifying obedience. O wondrous adviser, Eve becomes an apostle! Already recognizing the cunning of the serpent, henceforth the tree of knowledge did not seduce her, but having accepted the tree of promise, she partook of being judged worthy to be a part of Christ . . . Now Eve is a helpmate through the Gospel! Therefore too the women proclaimed the Gospel [from here on the Armenian translation has a few differences; see below]. But the basic fact was this that Eve's custom was to proclaim lies and not truth. What's this? For us the women proclaim the resurrection as the Gospel. Then Christ

---

35. Jungmann, *The Mass of the Roman Rite*, 70n55.
36. Cf. Migne, *Patrologia Latina*, 112: col. 1474B.
37. Ibid., col. 1475A.
38. Ibid., col. 1475B.
39. Ibid., col. 1479C.
40. Migne, *Patrologia Latina*, 183: col. 1148.

appeared to them and said: Peace be with you. I have appeared to the women and have sent them to you as apostles.

The differences in the Armenian translation are as follows:

> Therefore women too proclaimed the Gospel to the disciples. Therefore, however, they believed them mistaken . . . What kind of a new thing is it for you, O women, to tell of the resurrection? But that they might not be judged mistaken again, but as speaking in truth, Christ appeared to them and said: Peace be with you. Wherewith he showed it as true: As I appeared to the women, sending them to you, I have desired to send them as apostles.[41]

Mary Magdalene in Gnostic Christian Literature

Besides the strong, positive tradition about Mary Magdalene in the canonical Gospels and the orthodox Christian writings quoted above, and others, a similarly strong tradition about her exists among gnostic Christians in the third- or fourth-century Manichean document wherein Mary Magdalene is sent by Yeshua as a messenger *(angelos)* to "evangelize" *(euangelizein)* the male disciples with all possible skill.

Mary Magdalene, Teacher of the Apostles

This tradition of Mary Magdalene's superiority to the male disciples begins even earlier in the apocryphal gospel named after her, the Gospel of Mary, as we saw, probably an early second-century gnostic Christian document. In it, after Yeshua commanded the disciples to go and preach the Gospel and then left them, the men played the stereotypical female role—not knowing what to do and crying whereas Mary played the stereotypical male role—confidently knowing what to do and encouraging the men. At first she succeeded admirably, but then as she expounded her specialized knowledge from Yeshua, jealousy was engendered among the male disciples, particularly Andrew and Peter, who attacked her for thinking that she, a woman, might have better access to the truths of Yeshua than they, the men, did. Mary responded bluntly and was supported by another apostle, Levi, who rebuked Peter for being so hot-tempered and attacking Mary

---

41. Hippolytus, *Exegetische und homiletische Schriften*, 354–55.

Magdalene. In the end they all went off to preach the Gospel, so that Mary Magdalene prevailed.

> But they were grieved and wept sore, saying: "How shall we go to the heathen and preach the Gospel of the Kingdom of the Son of man? If he was not spared at all, how shall we be spared?"
> Then arose Mary, saluted them all, and spake to her brethren: "Weep not, be not sorrowful, neither be ye undecided, for his grace will be with you and will protect you. Let us rather praise his greatness, for he hath made us ready, and made us to be men."
> When Mary said this, she turned their mind to good, and they began to discuss the words of the [Savior].

Peter now says to Mary, "We know that the Savior loved you above all other women." He asks her to recount the revelations that she has received from the Savior, which he and the others have not heard. Mary tells how she saw the Lord in a vision and spoke with him. There follows a lengthy, complicated gnostic conversation between Yeshua and Mary, which is missing in the extant manuscript.

> When Mary had said this, she was silent, so that (thus) the Savior had spoken with her up to this point. But Andrew answered and said to the brethren. "Tell me, what think ye with regard to what she says? I at least do not believe that the Savior said this. For certainly these doctrines have other meanings." Peter in answer spoke with reference to things of this kind, and asked them about the Savior: "Did he then speak privily with a woman rather than with us, and not openly? Shall we turn about and all hearken unto her? Has he preferred her over against us?"
> Then Mary wept and said to Peter: "My brother Peter, what dost thou then believe? Dost thou believe that I imagined this myself in my heart, or that I would lie about the Savior?" Levi answered (and) said to Peter: "Peter, thou hast ever been of a hasty temper. Now I see how thou dost exercise thyself against the woman like the adversaries. But if the Savior hath made her worthy, who then art thou, that thou reject her? Certainly the Savior knows her surely enough. Therefore, did he love her more than us. Let us rather be ashamed, put on the perfect Man, [form ourselves (?)] as he charged us, and proclaim the Gospel, without requiring any further command or any further law beyond that which the Savior said (Gr.: neither limiting nor legislating, as the Savior said)."

But when Levi had said [this,] they set about going to preach and to proclaim (Gr.: When he had thus spoken, Levi went away and began to preach).⁴²

Mary Magdalene, Most Beloved Disciple

In the above citation Peter admits that "the Savior loved [Mary Magdalene] above all other women." He could not bring himself to say that Yeshua loved Mary Magdalene more than him, but a little later Levi does make such an admission: "But if the Savior hath made her worthy, who then art thou, that thou reject her? Certainly the Savior knows her surely enough. Therefore, did he love her more than us." In the early third-century gnostic Christian document *Pistis Sophia*, Yeshua said, "But Mary Magdalene and John, the virgin (*parthenos*), will surpass all my disciples and all men who shall receive mysteries." Beyond these there is a further gnostic Christian apocryphal Gospel, the third-century *Gospel of Philip*, in which Mary Magdalene is said to be called the companion of Yeshua and loved by Yeshua "more than all the disciples." There is also a startling passage in which Yeshua is said to "kiss her often on the mouth." In this gnostic Christian document this action obviously has a spiritualized significance, but still, Mary Magdalene is the recipient of the most intimate favors (graces) of Yeshua.

> There were three who always walked with the Lord: Mary his mother and her sister and Magdalene, the one who was called his companion. His sister and his mother and his companion were each a Mary ... And the companion of the [Savior is] Mary Magdalene. [But Christ loved her] more than [all] the disciples [and used to] kiss her [often] on her [mouth]. The rest of the [disciples were offended] by it and [expressed disapproval]. They said to him, *"Why do you love her more than all of us?"* The Savior answered and said to them, *"Why do I not love you like her?"* When a blind man and one who sees are both together in darkness, they are no different from one another. When the light comes, then he who sees will see the light, and he who is blind will remain in darkness.⁴³

---

42. *Gospel of Mary*, in Hennecke and Schneemelcher, eds., *New Testament Apocrypha* 1:342–44.

43. *Gospel of Philip*, in *Nag Hammadi Library in English*, 135–36, 138 (italics added). See also http://www.earlychristianwritings.com/text/gospelphilip.html/ (Early Christian Writings).

Three Jesus Certitudes

Peter's Jealousy of Mary Magdalene

In the canonical Fourth Gospel, Mary Magdalene, rather than Peter, is the one to whom the risen Christ first appears, just as it is Martha rather than Peter who declares Yeshua to be the Son of God, giving in the Beloved Disciple Christian community a certain priority of Mary Magdalene and other women over Peter. This does not reflect anything negative toward Peter in the Beloved Disciple community, but it does probably indicate a conscious stress on the importance of women, especially Mary Magdalene, rather than Peter, whose importance in the other Gospels was probably known to the final redactor of the Fourth Gospel. As will be discussed further below, it should also be recalled that there are several lengthy and important passages in the Fourth Gospel that focus on women, including Mary Magdalene's first discovery of the empty tomb, her reporting of it to Peter and the others, and Yeshua's appearing to her alone and commissioning her to "go to the brothers, and tell them." It was probably the next sentence (or the tradition behind the sentence) in the Fourth Gospel which said, "So Mary of Magdala went and told the disciples that she had seen the Lord and that he had said these things to her,"[44] that gave rise to the expanded report in the apocryphal *Gospel of Mary* about Mary Magdalene reporting her conversation with Yeshua to Peter and the other disciples. Further, the Fourth Gospel would have been found very attractive by gnostic Christians, for, as they did, it stressed light and life and a very "spiritual" kind of theology—with many long and complicated discourses placed in the mouth of Yeshua. Hence it is not surprising to find gnostic Christians, like the Fourth Gospel, giving a prominence to Mary Magdalene and also speaking of Peter's fits of jealousy toward her.

Besides the male disciples' generally taking offense at Mary Magdalene's favored position with Yeshua recorded in the *Gospel of Philip* (cited just above), and given the specific resentment voiced by Andrew and Peter in the above-cited Gospel of Mary, there is also the extremely vicious attack on women prophets attributed to Peter in the apocryphal *Kerygmata Petrou*. Further, Peter's hostility toward women in general and Mary Magdalene in particular is referred to twice (chs. 36 and 72) in the early third-century gnostic Christian *Pistis Sophia*, and reaches a kind of climax in the statement attributed to him in the third-century gnostic Christian *Gospel of Thomas*, wherein Peter wants to excommunicate Mary Magdalene *because*

---

44. John 20:18.

she is a woman, but Yeshua defends her (in a way peculiar to the later ascetic time). Again the question naturally arises: Was this a protest on the part of some Christian women and their male sympathizers against what they saw to be the rising restriction on women; and even against misogynism exercised by church leaders, who prided themselves on their rootage in the apostles—the chief of whom was Peter—over against the feminism of Yeshua? The solution for many non-gnostic as well as gnostic Christian women lay in becoming a man, a male *(vir)*—that is, celibate. However, the celibate gnostic Christian women were less willing to accept subordination to the male hierarch than were the orthodox catholic women.

> Simon Peter said to them: Let Mary go forth from among us, for women are not worthy of the life. Yeshua said: Behold, I shall lead her that I may make her male, in order that she also may become a living spirit like you males. For every woman who makes herself male shall enter into the kingdom of heaven.[45]

Summary concerning the Fourth Gospel

To summarize, the Community of the Beloved Disciple, as Raymond Brown referred to the community within which the Fourth Gospel, or more accurately, Magdalene's Gospel, was born, stemmed from one of the first disciples of Yeshua: Mary of Magdala. She was most probably a disciple of John the Baptist and became one of the first followers of Yeshua. That means that she was a strong, self-deciding woman. Judging from her Gospel, she also apparently had friends in high places, and obviously was a very intelligent and sensitive person.

Not only did she, along with many others, find Yeshua a very charismatic, deep, and loving person, but Yeshua clearly also found her very understanding and appealing. Even in all three of the Synoptic Gospels she was always mentioned in the list of women following and working with Yeshua, and in all such lists save one (the pro-Peter/anti-Magdalene Luke) was mentioned first. But when it came to her own Gospel, she figured very prominently (along with several other strong women—e.g., the Samaritan woman, and Martha and Mary of Bethany), and was given a starring role in the extended first encounter with the risen Lord. As the Beloved Disciple,

---

45. Gospel of Thomas, in Hennecke and Schneemelcher, eds., *New Testament Apocrypha*, 1:522.

Three Jesus Certitudes

she was also portrayed as an intimate of Yeshua, "leaning on his breast," not once, but twice. If one looks at the early noncanonical Gospel of Mary and Gospel of Philip, one finds that Magdalene is the one that Yeshua "loved above all else," and that Magdalene is Yeshua's "companion," whom Yeshua "kisses often on the mouth."

Because Magdalene was so intelligent and sensitive, she obviously reflected long and deeply after Yeshua's departure, producing thereby his long soliloquies so characteristic of her Gospel, but not of the Synoptics or the Sayings Gospels. She apparently had a good memory and meditated on the deeper meaning of what she recalled of Yeshua's words. This development was reflected also in the Gospel of Mary where Magdalene reported that she heard Yeshua say things in a vision and then was asked by the male disciples to relate them and explain them. Raymond Brown stated that, "The evangelist was a remarkably gifted thinker and dramatist."[46]

This went on over decades, during which a straightforward understanding of Yeshua's words and actions prevailed in the beginning, but with the passage of time and further contemplation, divinity was more and more seen shining through Yeshua, until a very high Christology developed and even led to a split in the community, quite probably after the anchor of Magdalene had passed on. But before she died, Magdalene wrote a Proto-Gospel, a version of the Fourth Gospel preceding the version we now have.

Then, after Magdalene had died and the majority group of her community (secessionists) pushed still further in the direction of divinity in Yeshua (docetism), the orthodox elements strove to be accepted by the great church, and thus edited Magdalene's Gospel, eliminating her name and substituting for it the name "the Beloved Disciple." The secessionists apparently moved further in the direction of the communities that formed the *Gospel of Mary*, the *Gospel of Philip, Pistis Sophia*, and the like, while the final redactor was eventually successful and the Fourth Gospel was accepted by the *ekklesia katholika*, though at the price that until almost the twenty-first century it was largely unknown that Mary Magdalene was the Beloved Disciple and the author of the earlier version of the Fourth Gospel. But now it is beginning to be known.

---

46 Brown, *Community of the Beloved Disciple*, 101.

Conclusion: A Woman—Magdalene—Is the Evangelist of the Penultimate Version of the Fourth Gospel

Clearly the most important person in the Fourth Gospel after Yeshua is the "disciple whom Yeshua loved." She is mentioned several times, at least eight, but always anonymously. Why is her name suppressed? My conclusion, as I have argued, is that Mary's name was suppressed because the she was a woman. But the community around her began to be worried that these profound recollections of Yeshua that she *wrote* (as the final redactor in chapter 21 directly stated) would be discarded because they had come from a woman. As I have shown, misogyny was flooding the larger Christian community, so the Fourth Gospel community felt that in order to save their Gospel, they had to suppress the name of the Gospel writer because she was a woman—Mary Magdalene.

If readers are still skeptical of this argument, I offer what happened to the *Gospel of Mary* as evidence that the final redactor's judgment was correct. This was a document written around the year 125 CE—perhaps from within the community of the secessionists that Raymond Brown wrote of above. This Gospel was almost completely suppressed, and it disappeared almost entirely—until parts of it were discovered only at the end of the nineteenth century and published only in the middle of the twentieth! If the final redactor of Mary Magdalen's Fourth Gospel had not suppressed her being seen as the *disciple whom Yeshua loved* and hence the evangelist of the Fourth Gospel, the now canonical Fourth Gospel would have met the same fate as had the *Gospel of Mary*! Thus, under the misogynist mentality that prevailed by the end of the first century (in blatant contradiction of the deliberate teaching and practice of Yeshua), the final redactor is to be thanked for his (or *her*?) suppressive action. But now her/his task is finished.

YESHUA: THE ORIGIN OF CHRISTIANITY

It seems increasingly clear that a historical figure called John the Baptist had a number of followers, and that some of them moved to Yeshua of Nazareth, especially after John's death. Yeshua was obviously an extraordinarily charismatic person who deeply impressed a number of Jews. His person, teaching, and then his death and the response—the resurrection event, however understood—engendered a variety of follower groups. In fact, from the nineteenth century forward "scholars gathered substantial evidence to show that the early Christian church did not exist as a unified body but rather consisted of distinctive, competing groups that associated themselves with different foundational figures and various theologies."[47]

We can today discern several distinct groups:

1. The oldest is the community that generated the Sayings Gospel, the so-called Q. "Because Q's theology and its written expression is either contemporary with the Apostle Paul's writings or possibly even antedates Paul's, we have in Q one of the earliest writings, if not the earliest writing in Christianity."[48] Scholars have discerned some three phases in the Q community, the first phase coming after Yeshua's death and the last phase ending by its absorption into the community that produced the Gospel of Matthew in the middle 80s of the first century.[49] Doubtless the Q document had been copied many times during the decades of the first century, and even beyond, but after the narrative Gospels were written, and especially after both Matthew and Luke absorbed all the Q material, people stopped copying the Q document and apparently the existing copies eventually disintegrated. Hence, we have no direct copies of it, but have to reconstruct it from its presence in Matthew and Luke.

2. The next oldest is the *Christ*-centered group (as distinct from *Jesus*- or *Yeshua*-centered groups) best represented by Paul and Barnabas. Here salvation was to be found through "the Christ" (*ho Christos*), which was a kind of "salvation from above." It is significant that nowhere in his many letters did Paul quote or try to pass on the teaching of Yeshua. Paul of course often talked about ethical issues, but they were *his* teachings (largely from the widely current Stoic ethics) or what he said when talking about Christ, but nowhere did he write that Yeshua taught such and such (the one exception was when he referred to a version of Yeshua's teaching about divorce, and then rejected it—1 Cor 7:10–12). These communities tended to be scattered around the Roman Empire wherever the six and a half million Jews around the empire were located.

3. After 1945, we slowly learned of a separate Sayings Gospel, the *Gospel of Thomas*, discovered at Nag Hamadi in Egypt. Presumably there was a community behind it as well, for it is different from the Sayings Gospel as found in Matthew and Luke. The presence of both the *Gospel of Thomas*

---

47. Boer, "Mary Magdalene."
48. Havener, *Q: The Sayings of Jesus*, 11
49. Mack, *The Lost Gospel*.

Yeshua's Women Followers Created Christianity

and the Q material suggests that yet other early Yeshua communities might have existed with their own lists of sayings that we have not yet found.

In addition, of course, there were the several different communities that generated our known Gospels:

4. The Gospel of Mark community;

5. The Gospel of Matthew community;

6. "Luka's" Proto-Luke Gospel community;

7. The canonical Gospel of Luke community;

8. Magdalene's Proto-Gospel community

9. The redacted canonical Fourth Gospel community.

At least these early communities of Yeshua followers we know about, and in many ways they are strikingly different, each going off in various directions, depending on what struck them most in their encounter with Yeshua. Even more, some of them sprang from preachers who were not even direct witnesses of Yeshua, such as Paul—and this was reflected in the fact that Paul was not really interested in Yeshua's teachings, for he apparently did not even know them; he was interested only in Yeshua's messiahship of a very special sort, in a sort of cosmic Christ operating from above.

Doubtless one Yeshua was behind all these different responses, but the different responses gave rise to various understandings of Yeshua, to various Christologies. Presumably there was a certain value and validity in each of them, but my arguemnt is that the person Yeshua ha-Notzri is the most inspiring and the foundation of what it means to be a follower of Yeshua (what we have misnamed a Christian). And one very important thing about trying to be a Christian, a follower of Yeshua, of Jesus, is that he was a feminist.

5

Pacifism, Feminism, Women Evangelists
A Virtuous Triangle!

THE THREE THESES OF this book are proposed as three of the most historically founded facts that we know of Yeshua/Jesus. The fundamental reason for their historical solidity is their counterculturality. Nobody in the culture of Judaism or the Roman Empire of which it was a part practiced and advocated pacifism or feminism, or made women essential sources of a mass religious movement—producers of the good news, evangelists. And yet that is what Yeshua did!

The *first thesis* of this book is that Yeshua was a pacifist: that is, he practiced and advocated nonviolence. From what we know of his life (from the four Gospels), he surely practiced and advocated nonviolence. His followers in the first three centuries after his lifetime also advocated nonviolence—for instance, eschewing military service. However, after Emperor Constantine legalized Christianity and made it the *de facto* religion of the Roman Empire early in the fourth century (and when Emperor Theodosius made *de jure* the religion of the Roman Empire by before the end of that century), the practice and teaching of nonviolence was largely set aside. Saint Augustine, also at the end of the fourth century, articulated his just war theory, which was, and still is, largely embraced by most Christians, although some deliberately opt for pacifism, and many more work avidly to promote peace, and point to Yeshua for their justification.

In summarizing the *second thesis* of this book—that Yeshua was a feminist—it should first of all be recalled that Yeshua was not a Christian.

Pacifism, Feminism, Women Evangelists

He was a Jew—indeed an observant, Torah-true Jew, a rabbi.[1] Yeshua stood very much in the Jewish, Pharisaic, rabbinic traditions of his day.[2] But in attitudes toward women Yeshua was very different from his peers. He took an egalitarian, feminist position on women. He was not a social activist organizer like Saul Alinsky, nor was he like Betty Friedan, the founder of the National Organization for Women. Yeshua was much more personalist in his approach. It was his disciples who came after him who developed the organization, the *ekklesia*, the church. Hence it is personal attitudes and actions that can be looked for in Yeshua regarding the place of women as well as all other human issues of import—not organized actions and systematic social implementation of principles. This latter came, to the extent it came, later, with the church, with Christianity.

It is very difficult to discern precisely what in the Gospels is to be attributed to Yeshua and what to the first believing communities, or the evangelists, who are our only sources of information about Yeshua. Nevertheless, Yeshua's extraordinarily positive attitude toward women depicted in the Gospels (especially vis-à-vis the Palestinian Jewish context of that time) ultimately must be attributed to him, though the form and exact wording of many of the specific statements attributed to Yeshua doubtless were reshaped by the evangelists and their sources. The fact that the Gospels—whether written by Jews (probably Mark, Matthew, and Fourth Gospel) or a Greek (Luke), whether for a Greco-Roman audience (Mark) or a Jewish one (Matthew)—all that depict Yeshua as egalitarian toward women argue that this feminism was not dictated by a Greek or a Jewish author or audience. The fact that Matthew's Gospel, the most Jewish of all the Gospels, was quantitatively much more positive toward women than Mark's (in many ways the least Jewish of the Gospels) and almost as much so as Luke's Gospel (probably the only one written by a Greek) eliminates the possibility that the Gospel feminism was projected onto Yeshua either by a Greek influenced by the feminist movement in the contemporary Hellenistic world (Luke) or by an evangelist writing to impress a Gentile audience (Mark). If either of those assumptions were true, then the Jewish Matthew and his Jewish audience, and indeed his Jewish sources, should never have produced the feminist image of Yeshua they in fact did produce. In the end, the strongly prowoman, feminist image of Yeshua projected in the Gospels must find its source in Yeshua. And in this matter Yeshua

1. See Küng and Lapide, "Is Yeshua a Bond or Barrier?"
2. See Aron, *The Jewish Yeshua*; and Fisher, *Faith without Prejudice*.

Three Jesus Certitudes

profoundly differed from his peers—another technically persuasive argument that Yeshua and not the community was the source of that attitude and action.

Yeshua's positive attitude toward women clearly affected the early followers of Yeshua, though patriarchal social structures by no means immediately all fell away. Nevertheless, women did play leading roles in the earliest Christian communities, from Lydia the first European convert (Acts 16:14–15) to the various women evangelists, deacons, and rulers to the apostle Junia (Rom 16:7).

Paul, who never met Yeshua, had an ambivalent attitude toward women, partly positive and partly on the borderline between positive and negative. The deutero-Pauline materials (letters by Paul's disciples but traditionally attributed to him) and the other later New Testament writings became progresssively more negative toward women, veering toward the misogynist. The woman deacon (*diakonos*) of Paul's day became the diminutive deaconess (*diakonissa*) of the fourth-century *Apostolic Constitutions*—a holy order lesser in status than that of the male deacon. As Christianity moved into the age of the Fathers, the status of Christian women became ever more restricted. The Fathers took a uniformly male-superior attitude that often was misogynist. The trend continued into the Middle Ages and up to the most recent times.

What is puzzling here is that although a strong anti-Jewish and pro-Greek trend quickly developed in Christianity as it spread in the Gentile world (unfortunately leading to a rejection of much of Yeshua's and Christianity's Jewish heritage), on the subject of women it was the somewhat more positive Hellenistic stance that was rejected. Why, with such a clear difference in attitude expressed by Yeshua and by some of the Pauline writings, did Christianity's choice go not to Yeshua but to the negative Pauline and deutero-Pauline writings? Apparently the rigid patriarchal system, which Yeshua did his best to dismantle, was so pervasive in the lives of the majority of Christians that they were blind to this choice; they automatically gravitated toward the most restrictive, subordinationist passages of the late New Testament. Christianity early on became so intent on identifying itself by differentiating itself from the world around it that it often vigorously rejected the pagan world—or at least that part of the pagan world that offered women relatively higher status.

One additional partial answer to this puzzle is suggested by Johannes Leipoldt:[3] After the destruction of Jerusalem in 70 CE, many Hellenistic Jews became Christians because they rejected the intensified observation of the rabbinic prescriptions that developed in the Jewish attempt to preserve identity. These Hellenistic Jews, used to less rigorous observance, found in Christianity an environment that was familiar and receptive. They of course brought with them the strongly subordinating attitudes toward women that were then prevalent in Judaism, even Hellenistic Judaism.

Whether or not, or to whatever degree, this may be true, the receding eschaton ("final days") imminently awaited by Paul and the other early Christians doubtless played a major role in the early decline in the status of women in Christianity. As long as the *parousia*, the second coming of Christ, was expected at any moment, the need to develop organized structures in the community of believers was felt very little. But as that expectation faded, the need for structured patterns of community life increased. In an almost inevitable development these second- and third-generation Christians naturally turned to the structures of the societies in which they lived for models to apply to the newly forming church structures. In the Greco-Roman society of the Roman Empire, despite the advances women made in family life, economics, law, and other arenas, women were almost entirely excluded from political life. Hence, in following this Greco-Roman model (e.g., "diocese" and "parish" are originally Roman civil administrative terms) the Church set up authority structures that almost entirely excluded women.

To this was added the pervasive Greek notion of dualism and its offshoot, asceticism. (For a dualist the world ultimately consisted of matter and spirit, and in extreme dualism matter—personified by a woman—was seen as evil, and spirit—personified by a man—as good.) Of course dualism was not exclusively Greek (e.g., dualism appeared in Persian Zoroastrianism and Manicheism). Nor was asceticism. (Essenes[4] and Therapeutae[5] were ascetics.) But dualism and asceticism spread throughout the Roman Empire. Paradoxically these aspects of pagan society, far from being rejected by the newly forming church, were embraced by it—again putting women at a serious disadvantage vis-á-vis men.

---

3. Leipoldt, *Die Frau in der antiken Welt*, 127.
4. Swidler, *Women in Judaism*, 17ff.
5. Ibid., 23 ff.

Thus, three attitudes formative of Yeshua—(1) a service orientation rather than authority orientation; (2) a full, life-affirming stance (eating, drinking, celebrating); and (3) an egalitarian perception and treatment of women—were all significantly reversed by the early Christian church.

Furthermore, a restrictive attitude toward women was also fostered in Christianity by the fact that early Christians in the Greco-Roman world faced the worship of the Goddess in strong resurgence—from the worship of the Phrygian Mater Magna or Kybele throughout Asia Minor and even in Rome to the cult of Isis and her veneration under many other names (Demeter, Athena, Venus, Ceres, Ma Bellona, and so forth). The worship of Mater Magna or Kybele in Asia Minor not only was extremely influential but also often included ecstatic passion, self-mutilation, even self-castration in order to attain complete identity with the Goddess.[6]

Although in fact the most pervasive Goddess worship at the beginning of the Christian era, the Isis cult, did not promote sexual excesses of promiscuity,[7] it was widely rumored to do so, and thus the effect on the early Christians of seeing women priests of Isis was just as negative as if the Isis cult had promoted sexual excess. Edwin O. James stated that "her cultus was the most effective rival to Christianity from the second century onwards, and during the temporary revival of classical paganism in Rome in A.D. 394, it was her festival that was celebrated with great magnificence."[8] James further noted that "the unprecedented victory of the cultus [the cult of Isis] over official opposition and its persistence during the first three centuries of the Christian era are a testimony to the deep and genuine religious emotion aroused in the initiates by the ritual."[9] In fact, her public worship was brought to an end only by Emperor Justinian in 560 CE.

Thus the in-group/out-group mechanism at work within Judaism, intensifying its restrictions of Jewish women, was also at work in early Christianity and had a similar result. However, a special irony of Christian history is that by turning toward the subordination of women, Christianity turned away from its Jewish founder Yeshua and his attitude toward women, for Yeshua was a feminist.

The *third thesis* of this book is that women Yeshua followers were such a major source of the essential information we have about Yeshua

---

6. See James, *The Cult of the Mother Goddess*, 21–22.
7. See Heyon, *The Cult of Isis*, 111ff.
8. James, *The Cult of the Mother Goddess*, 180.
9. Ibid., 177.

(his teaching and his actions, what he thought, taught, and wrought) that whatever religious movement might possibly have developed without this woman-sourced knowledge would at most have been anemic, and would have died almost aborning.

It is obvious that the pervasive positive attitude toward women that Yeshua exhibited excited and attracted them. The contrast between Yeshua's attitude toward women and the attitude toward women in the rest of the culture was startling. Each of Yeshua's actions and teachings that addressed women would have been stunning to them, leading them to remember and treasure such events, and then to pass them on. We have looked at the massive amount of Yeshua material from the Gospels that positively dealt with women, and it is obvious that women experienced, remembered, and passed on these positive teachings and actions.

Even though Mark's Gospel is the least prowoman of the four, it nevertheless features ample material that would have been sourced only by woman. Add to that the massive amount of prowoman material found in Greek Matthew (possibly "Mathea"?)—such that without it that Gospel would have been only a shadow of its current vigorous reality. When we move onto Luke's Gospel, the evidence is overwhelming prowoman—almost all of which appears in the huge Proto-Luke material. This Proto-Luke material inescapably points to having been written or at least sourced by a woman or women, to a "Luka" evangelist. A very likely candidate for Luka is Mary of Bethany, who "sat at Yeshua's feet," who had "chosen the better part."

Then we come to the Fourth Gospel, which, as the final redactor states clearly in chapter 21, was "written [*grapsas*]" by the "disciple who Yeshua loved." This always anonymous, most important person in the Fourth Gospel after Yeshua had her name and sex blotted out precisely because she was a woman! I have shown that the disciple whom Yeshua loved, the evangelist of the Fourth Gospel, was Mary Magdalene.

Thus, take away the Fourth (Magdalene's) Gospel, Luke/Luka's Gospel, much of Greek Matthew (Matthea?), the prowoman portion of Mark, all the women promoters named and unnamed of the Gospel of Yeshua throughout the Roman Empire, you have no Christianity!

Are these three theses related? They are intimately related. First, the connection between the first two: that Yeshua was both a pacifist and a feminist. How are these two characteristics connected? Humans are the most developed of all the beings we know—that is, we are bodies which

Three Jesus Certitudes

can think abstractly and hence chose freely: that is, we are rational and free. This means that humans are potentially capable of perceiving that every human ought to be free up to the point that such freedom would inhibit the freedom of other humans. Given that violence limits human freedom, humans are morally bound to be nonviolent—pacifist—toward others and themselves, short of when not to be violent would cause even more violence. However, since both women and men are full humans, each woman and man must be allowed freedom up to the point where such freedom would inhibit other humans' freedom. The principle that human freedom belongs to both women and men is a central principle of feminism.

This may seem somewhat abstract, but I believe that this connection between pacifism and feminism is nevertheless clear to all modern persons who accept the idea of human rights: Without feminism, half the world's humans would be shorn of their human rights, and this would be (largely still is!) an egregious act of violence against them.

It was nearly two millennia from the time Yeshua lived until the idea of human rights was created (during the eighteenth-century Enlightenment) and ratified in 1948 in the *United Nations Universal Declaration of Human Rights*. Although Yeshua did not use the term *human rights*, the preceding pages make the case that Yeshua was indeed both a pacifist and a feminist, and in that profound sense a forerunner and exemplar of the *de facto* practice of peace and equal rights for women.

These two positions advocated and practiced by Yeshua absolutely guaranteed that his teaching and example would be embraced by that half of the world who were most addressed and liberated by it—women! They were the ones who first really heard and understood Yeshua's message and embraced and promoted his teachings, so vigorously that women became the major source of our information about Yeshua, and thus, the creators of Christianity.

Quite typically, when males perceive the good thing that the women often positively respond to almost reflexively, they grab it, take power, and shove women back. For example, the most ancient human understandings of divinity were always female because it was obvious that new life came from the female; only when the role of males in the production of progeny became clear did male gods begin to appear in human history. The same pattern is present in everyday life. Except for a brief moment of conception, the woman does all the heavy work of creating new life for nine months, and then the man takes all the power.

Pacifism, Feminism, Women Evangelists

It happened again in with the birth of Christianity: The brief moment of conception occurred (the short public life of Yeshua—who was psychologically an androgynous person—when he encountered and attracted especially women to his teaching). This moment of conception led to women gathering the seeds of Yeshua's teaching and action, nurturing them until they bore fruit in the written Gospels. Once the Gospels appeared, the power of the Gospel fruit was largely stolen from women by men!

Slowly nonviolence has been growing in humanity, counterintuitive as that may seem to most—but see the data- and fact-soaked book by Steven Pinker, *The Better Angels of our Nature*.[10] Parallel to the rise of nonviolence has come the rise of feminism, and at the leadership of both nonviolence and feminism have been women—though not exclusively. These women have been joined also by "androgynous" men who have learned, albeit slowly, from women—very much including myself![11]

Thus, all three theses are intimately connected: Yeshua's pacifism, feminism, women evangelists (spreaders of the good news)! Three of the greatest gifts Rabbi Yeshua has given to the world are, first of all, his commitment to nonviolent peacebuilding—his pacifism; second, his countercultural treatment of women as equal to men—his feminism. Third, his core values of mutual and common love—especially for the marginalized—including his pacifism and feminism were all delivered to the world mainly by his women followers—who *de facto* created Christianity.

---

10. Pinker, *Better Angels of Our Nature*.
11. See Adams (a.k.a. Kaplun), *There Must Be YOU*.

Bibliography

Adams, River (a.k.a. Maria Kaplun). *There Must Be YOU: Leonard Swidler's Journey to Faith and Dialogue*. Eugene, OR: Resource Publications, 2014.
Aron, Robert. *The Jewish Jesus*. Translated by Agnes H. Forsyth and Anne-Marie de Commaille, with Horace T. Allen Jr. Maryknoll, NY: Orbis, 1971.
Boadt, Lawrence. *Reading the Old Testament: An Introduction*. New York: Paulist, 1984.
Boer, Esther de. "Mary Magdalene and the Disciple Jesus Loved." lectio.unibe.ch/00_1/m-forum.htm/.
Boer, Esther de. *Mary Magdalene: Beyond the Myth*. Harrisburg, PA: Trinity, 1997.
Borg, Marcus, *Jesus: Uncovering the Life, Teachings, and Relevance of a Religious Revolutionary*. San Francisco: HarperSanFrancisco, 2007.
Bratsiotis, P. "Das Menschenverständnis in der griechisch-orthodoxen Kirche." *Theologische Zeitschrift* 6 (1950) 376–82.
Brooten, Bernadette J. *Women Leaders in the Ancient Synagogue: Inscriptional Evidence and Background Issues*. Brown Judaic Studies 36. Chico, CA: Scholars, 1982.
Brock, Ann Graham. *Mary Magdalene, the First Apostle: The Struggle for Authority*. Harvard Theological Studies 51. Cambridge: Harvard University Press, 2003.
Brown, Raymond E. *The Community of the Beloved Disciple*. New York: Paulist, 1979.
———. "Roles of Women in the Fourth Gospel." *Theological Studies* 36.4 (1975) 688–99.
Charles, R. H. "The Testament of Issachar." In *The Testaments of the Twelve Patriarchs*. http://www.earlychristianwritings.com/text/gospelphilip.html
Cohen, A., ed. *The Minor Tractates of the Talmud*. 2nd ed. London: Soncino, 1971.
Creed, John Martin. *The Gospel according to St. Luke*. London: Macmillan, 1930.
Cullmann, Oscar. *Der johanneische Kreis: Sein Platz im Spätjudentum, in der Jüngerschaft Jesu und im Urchristentum: Zum Ursprung des Johannesevangeliums*. Tübingen: Mohr/Siebeck, 1975.
———. *The Johannine Circle*. Translated by John Bowden. Philadelphia: Westminster, 1976.
Drury, John. *Luke*. J. B. Phillips' Commentaries 3. New York: Macmillan, 1973.
Fisher, Eugene J. *Faith without Prejudice*. New York: Paulist, 1977.
Foerster, Werner. "*Iesous*." In *Theological Dictionary of the New Testament*, edited by Gerhard Kittel, 3:283–94. Translated by Geoffrey W. Bromiley. Grand Rapids: Eerdmans, 1966.
Forman, M. B., ed. *The Letters of John Keats*. 4th ed. London: Oxford University Press, 1952.

Bibliography

Gospel of Mary. *Early Christian Writings.* http://www.earlychristianwritings.com/gospelmary.html/.

Grob, Leonard, et al., eds. *Women's and Men's Liberation.* Contributions in Philosophy 45. New York: Greenwood, 1991.

Gryson, Roger, *The Ministry of Women in the Early Church.* Collegeville, MN: Liturgical, 1976.

Haight, Roger. *Jesus, Symbol of God.* Maryknoll, NY: Orbis, 1999.

Haim Gordon, ed. *Women's and Men's Liberation.* New York: Greenwood, 1991.

Havener, Ivan, OSB. *Q: The Sayings of Jesus.* Good News Studies 19. Wilmington, DE: Glazier, 1987.

Hennecke, Edgar, and Wilhelm Schneemelcher, eds. *New Testament Apocrypha.* Translated by A. J. B. Higgins. Edited by R. McWilson. 2 vols. Philadelphia: Westminster, 1963.

Heyon, Sharon K. *The Cult of Isis among Women in the Graeco-Roman World.* Etudes préliminaires aux religions orientales dans l'Empire romain 51. Leiden: Brill, 1975.

Hick, John. *Evil and the God of Love.* New York: Harper & Row, 1966.

———. *The Fifth Dimension: An Exploration of the Spiritual Realm.* 1999. Reprint, Oxford: Oneworld, 2004.

Hippolytus. *Exegetische und homiletische Schriften.* Die griechischen christlichen Schriftsteller der ersten drei Jahrhunderte 1/1. Leipzig: Hinrichs, 1897.

Homolka, Walter. *Jesus Reclaimed: Jewish Perspectives on the Nazarene.* Translated by Ingrid Shafer. New York: Berghan, 2015.

———. *Jesus von Nazareth im Spiegel jüdischer Forschung.* Jüdische Miniaturen 85. Berlin: Hentrich & Hentrich, 2009.

James, Edwin O. *The Cult of the Mother Goddess.* New York: Barnes & Noble, 1961.

Julian of Norwich, Saint. *The Revelations of Divine Love of Julian of Norwich.* Translated by James Walsh. Orchard Books. London: Burns & Oates, 1961.

Jungmann, Josef Andreas. *The Mass of the Roman Rite.* 2 vols. St. Louis: Benzinger, 1951.

Jusino, Ramon. "Mary Magdalene: Author of the Fourth Gospel?" www.BelovedDisciple.org/.

Kaltenbrunner, Gerd-Klaus. "Ist der Heilige Geist weiblich?" *Una Sancta* 32 (1977) 273–80.

Kittel, Gerhard, ed. *Theological Dictionary of the New Testament.* 10 vols. Grand Rapids: Eerdmans, 1966–74.

Küng Hans, and Pinchas Lapide. *Brother or Lord? A Jew and a Christian Talk Together.* Translated by Edward Quinn. Glasgow: Collins, 1977.

———. "Is Yeshua a Bond or Barrier? A Jewish-Christian Dialogue." *Journal of Ecumenical Studies* 14 (1977) 466–83.

Lapide, Pinchas. "Vorwort." In Leonard Swidler, *Der Umstrittenen Jesus.* Stuttgart: Quell, 1991.

Lapide, Pinchas, and Ulrich Luz. *Jesus in Two Perspectives: A Jewish-Christian Dialog.* Translated by Lawrence W. Denef. Minneapolis: Augsburg, 1985.

———. *Der Jude Jesus: Thesen eines Juden; Antworten eines Christen.* Zurich: Benzinger, 1980.

Leipoldt, Johannes, *Die Frau in der antiken Welt und im Urchristentum.* Leipzig: Koehler & Amelang, 1954.

Mack, Burton L. *The Lost Gospel: The Book of Q & Christian Origins.* San Francisco: HarperSanFrancisco, 1993.

Bibliography

Montefiore, Claude G. *Rabbinic Literature and Gospel Teaching*. London: Mac-millan, 1930.
Nestle, Eberhard, ed. *Novum Testamentum Graece et Latine*. Stuttgart: Privileg. Württemberg. Bibelanst, 1954.
Nyland, Ann. *The Source: New Testament with Extensive Notes on Greek Word Meaning*. Parramatta, Australia: Stirling & Smith, 2007.
Perkins, Pheme. "The Gospel according to John." In *The New Jerome Biblical Commentary*, edited by Raymond E. Brown et al., 942–85. Englewood Cliffs, NJ: Prentice Hall, 1990.
Pinker, Steven. *The Better Angels of Our Nature: Why Violence Has Declined*. London: Penguin, 2011.
Patai, Raphael. *The Hebrew Goddess*. New York: Ktav, 1967.
Paul VI, Pope. *Ecclesiam suam*. 1965. http://w2.vatican.va/content/paul-vi/en/encyclicals/documents/hf_p-vi_enc_06081964_ecclesiam.html/.
Rengstorf, Karl Heinrich, et al. *Das Neue Testament Deutsch*. Vol. 1, Pt. 3. Göttingen, 1968.
Schechter, Solomon, and David Werner Amram. "Divorce." www.jewishencyclopedia.com/articles/5238-divorce/.
Schüssler Fiorenza, Elisabeth. *In Memory of Her: A Feminist Theological Reconstruction of Christian Origins*. New York: Crossroad, 1983.
Sigal, Phillip. "The Halakhah of Jesus of Nazareth according to the Gospel of Matthew." PhD diss. University of Pittsburgh, 1979.
———. *The Halakhah of Jesus of Nazareth according to the Gospel of Matthew*. Lanham, MD: University Press of America, 1987.
Strack, H. L., and Paul Billerbeck. *Kommentar zum Neuen Testament aus Talmud und Mid-rasch*. Munich: Beck, 1926.
Sukenik, E. L. *Ancient Synagogues in Palestine and Greece*. The Schweich Lectures 1930. London: Oxford University Press, 1934.
Swidler, Leonard J. *Biblical Affirmations of Woman*. Philadelphia: Westminster, 1979, 4th printing 1991.
———. *Bloodwitness for Peace and Unity: The Life of Max Josef Metzger*. Philadelphia: Ecumenical Press, 1977.
———. "Jesus Was a Feminist." *Catholic World* 212 (January 1971) 171–83.
———. *Jesus Was a Feminist: What the Gospels Reveal about His Revolutionary Perspective*. Lanham, MD: Sheed & Ward, 2007.
———. *The Status of Women in Formative Judaism*. Metuchen, NJ: Scarecrow, 1974.
———. *Der Umstrittenen Jesus*. Stuttgart: Quell, 1991.
———. *Women in Judaism: The Status of Women in Formative Judaism*. Metuchen NJ: Scarecrow, 1976.
———. "Yeshua, Feminist and Androgynous: An Integrated Human." In *Women's and Men's Liberation*, edited by Leonard Grob et al., 155–77. Contributions in Women's Studies 45. New York: Greenwood, 1991.
———. *Yeshua: A Model for Moderns*. Kansas City, MO: Sheed & Ward, 1988.
Swidler, Leonard J., and Paul Mojzes. *The Study of Religion in an Age of Global Dialogue*. Philadelphia: Temple University Press, 2000.
Tertullian. *Disciplinary, Moral, and Acetical Works*. Translated by Rudolph Arbesmann et al. Fathers of the Church 40. Washington, DC: Catholic University of America Press, 1959.
Vermes, Geza. *Jesus and the World of Judaism*. Philadelphia: Fortress, 1983.

Index

Annunciation, 96, 116
Antisemitism, 8, 21
Apostle to the Apostles, 154
Aramaic Matthew, 20, 82, 84, 94–97, 103, 106, 108, 111
Aron, Robert, 165
Augustine, 9, 29, 30, 76, 77, 164

Barnabas, 3, 13, 163
Basilea tou Theou, 27–28, 34
Beloved Disciple, 143–52, 157–60, 173
Ben-Chorin, Schalom, 24
Benedictus, 118, 120
Bethany, 62–65, 68, 125–26, 137, 142, 147, 150–51, 153, 159, 169
Bethlehem, 101, 120–21
Billerbeck, Paul, 7, 67
Borg, Marcus, 56
Boer, Esther de, 143, 149, 151, 162
Bratsiotis, Panagiōtou, 77
Brethren, Church of, 36, 156
Brock, Ann Graham, 145
Brooten, Bernadette J., 36
Brown, Raymond E., 53, 141, 143–48, 151, 160–61
Bultmann, Rudolf, 19

Calvin, John, 76
Cana, 55–56, 137, 142
Canon law, 35
Catholic, 19, 21, 29–32, 35, 48, 62, 159
Christianity, 1–4, 7, 13, 14, 16, 23, 29, 46, 56, 62, 74, 76, 82, 83, 161, 162, 164–71

Church, 3, 7, 9, 13, 18–21, 23, 28–30, 32, 35–36, 38–41, 45, 48, 56, 62, 71–72, 76–77, 83, 91, 131, 138, 141, 144–46, 149, 151–52, 154, 159–60, 162, 165, 167–68
Circumcision, 120
Constantine, 7, 29, 164
Cullmann, Oscar, 151

Deir Semit, 63
Diakonissa, 166
Didascalia, 45, 71, 130
Divorce, 17, 37, 54, 59–62, 90–92, 96–97, 114, 162

Egypt, 26–27, 101, 162
Elizabeth, 114–20, 122
Epiphanius, 39, 131

Feminism, 1–4, 7, 24, 33–72, 104, 109, 112, 132, 136–59, 164–65, 170–71
Fisher, Eugene J., 165
Fourth Gospel, 2, 20, 45, 47, 51–53, 55, 64, 82, 84, 94–95, 104, 106, 108, 111–13, 121, 126, 129, 134, 136–52, 154, 158–61, 163, 165, 169
Fuller, Reginald H., 109

Galilee, 41–42, 60,117, 88–89, 102, 105, 117, 131, 152
Genealogy, 98–100, 111, 133
Gnostic, 9, 42, 56, 83, 144–45, 156–59

Index

Greek, 5–7, 10, 12–17, 21–23, 26, 28, 33, 35, 40, 42, 45, 61, 76–77, 79–82, 84–85, 89, 92, 94–97, 108–12, 132, 138, 150, 165–67, 169
Gregory I, Pope, 64
Gregory Nanzianus, 77
Gryson, Roger, 41, 131

Ha-'adam, 73, 79–81
Haight, Roger, 17–18
Hannah, 12, 115, 118–19
Havener, Ivan, 162
Hennecke, Edgar, 157, 159
Herod, 87–102, 108, 115, 121
Herodias, 87–88
Historical Jesus, 4, 18–19, 21–24, 109
Human rights, 2, 170
Hick, John, 76–78
Hillel, 15, 60–61, 90–92
Holy Spirit, 71–73, 84–86, 96–97, 115–17, 130
Homo sapiens, 78–79
Hippolytus, 153–55

Interpretation, 8–10, 61–62, 71, 76, 8
Irenaeus, 76–77, 136

James, Edwin O., 168
Jerusalem, 25, 27, 35, 49, 53, 57, 60, 63, 101, 121–23, 128–29, 132, 167
Jew, 5–9, 12–15, 19–27, 31, 35–42, 46–47, 51–52, 61–69, 73–74, 87, 89, 91–92, 101, 106, 109, 113–15, 122–23, 125, 128, 130, 132, 138, 161–62, 165–68
John the Baptist, 9, 30, 84, 86–88, 95, 114, 116, 120, 124, 137, 146–47, 149, 159, 161
John XXIII, Pope, 14
Josephus, 26, 35–36, 40, 61, 87
Julian of Norwich, 128
Just war theory, 29, 30, 164

Käsemann, Ernst, 19, 109
Kaplun, Maria (River Adams), 171
Keats, John, 78
Küng, Hans, 22, 165

Landgraf, John, 63
Lapide, Pinchas, 22–23, 165
Latin, 5–7, 11, 14, 21, 41, 75, 77–79, 83, 85, 95, 118, 120, 131, 154
Lazarus, 43, 64–65, 138, 150
Leipoldt, Johannes, 167
Lessing, Gotthold Ephraim, 18
Love, 85
Luka, 46–47, 68–71, 82, 88, 97, 106, 109, 114, 123–25, 132, 136–38, 140, 145, 147, 163, 169, 175
Luke, 2, 11–13, 15, 20, 23, 25, 28, 30, 32, 41–44, 46–51, 53, 57–59, 63–64, 66, 68–70, 73, 82, 84, 87–88, 91–98, 100–101, 104–6, 108–43, 145, 147, 153, 159, 162–63, 165, 169, 173
Luther, Martin, 76
Lutheran, 3

Magnificat, 11, 118–19
Marcion, 41, 130–31
Mack, Burton L., 162
Mark, Gospel, 20, 25, 42–43, 46–48, 50–51, 57–61, 62–65, 69, 82, 84–97, 103–8, 109–13, 121, 126–27, 133–36, 139–43, 145–46, 153, 160, 163, 165, 169
Martha, 43, 52, 63–68, 125, 138, 142, 150, 158, 159
Mary, 11, 22, 43, 51–52, 56–57, 62–69, 72, 82, 86, 96–97, 99–102, 114, 116–19, 121–26, 133–61
Mary Magdalene, 22, 52, 56, 64, 82, 125, 137–43, 145–63, 169
Matthew, 2, 12, 23, 46–47, 61, 64, 70, 82, 84, 87–113, 116, 120–21, 126–28, 133–36, 139–43, 162–63, 165, 169, 175
Maurus, Rabanus, 154
Mennonites, 30
Messiah, 14, 23–25, 27, 37, 52, 87, 98–99, 117, 121–22, 128, 138, 142, 15 163
Metzger, Max, 31
Middle Ages, 10, 18, 86, 166
Midrash, 37
Mithraism, 2, 83

Index

Montefiore, Claude, 60, 110
Nazareth, 117, 121, 124, 161
Nietzsche, Friedrich, 81
Nyland, Ann, 61

Origen, 39, 77

Pacifism, 1–2, 7, 24–32, 164, 170–71
Pagan, 72, 89–90, 92, 106–7, 166–68
Palestine, 34, 37–38, 62, 67, 91, 99
Passion, 84, 94, 104, 138, 141, 168
Patai, Gabriel, 127
Paul, 14, 35, 67, 79, 82, 121, 135, 138–39, 141, 147, 152, 162–63, 166–67
Pax Romana, 29
Peace, 25, 27, 29–32, 37, 44, 48, 54, 59, 155, 164, 170–71
Perkins, Pheme, 137
Person, 2, 7, 9, 14, 28, 32–34, 38, 42–46, 54–55, 58, 61–62, 64–65, 67–68, 72–73, 78, 85–86, 89, 107, 117, 123, 125–26, 128, 131, 137, 142, 159, 161, 163, 165, 167, 169–71
Pharisee, 44–45, 53–54, 57, 61, 64, 69, 70, 72, 90–91, 97, 165
Philo, 36–37, 61, 106
Pilate, Pontius, 14, 27–28, 41, 107, 111, 130
Pinker, Steven, 171
Polycarp, 136
Prodigal son, 55, 69–71
Prophet, 12, 40, 44, 49–50, 53–54, 58, 87, 93, 97, 122, 127–28, 158
Prostitute, 53, 55, 64–65, 99, 105–6, 111, 130
Proto-Fourth Gospel, 2, 82, 145, 152, 160, 163
Proto-Luke, 2, 70, 82, 109, 114–15, 125–28, 130, 135–36, 145, 160, 163, 169
Pseudepigrapha, 23

Q, 84
Quakers, 30
Queen of Sheba, 97

Quest for the historical Jesus, 4, 18–19, 21–24, 109

Rabbi, 9, 15–16, 21–22, 27, 34–35, 45–48, 52, 60–61, 63, 65–68, 82–83, 90–92, 109–10, 114, 132, 146, 165–67, 171
Ranke, Leopold von, 18
Reign of God, 27–28, 34, 42, 55, 59, 65–66, 98, 101, 105, 111, 117, 120, 134–35
Reimarus, Hermann, 18
Rengstorf, Karl Heinrich, 114
Resurrection, 16, 42–44, 52, 56, 82, 84, 94, 103, 138–42, 151, 154–55, 161
Roman, 7, 14, 16–17, 21, 25–29, 35, 44, 85, 89, 91–92, 106–7, 121, 131, 147, 154, 162, 164–65, 167–69

Sabbath, 46–47, 57, 126
Salome, 87–88, 103, 138
Salvation, 5–7, 18, 128, 162
Samaritan, 51–53, 137, 142, 159
Schechter, Solomon, 90, 92
Schneemelcher, Wilhelm, 42, 157, 159
Schweitzer, Albert, 19
Scripture, 4, 7–9, 16, 18, 23, 34, 41–42, 45, 68, 77, 129, 145
Shammai, 15, 60–61, 90–92
Silas, 2
Simeon, 121–22
Sotah, 90, 96
Spitaler, Peter, 16
Sukenik, E. L., 36
Swidler, Carmel, 75
Swidler, Leonard J., 1, 3, 11, 15, 20, 23, 31, 34, 40, 42, 52, 60–61, 67, 69–70, 72, 83, 87, 131,167
Synoptic Gospels, 16–17, 46, 48, 55, 66, 84, 93–95, 107–8, 113, 136, 143, 145, 159, 160

Talmud, 22, 34–35, 37, 67, 96, 114, 132
Tax collector, 55, 69–70, 72, 105
Tertullian, 39
Theodosius, 7, 29, 164
Timothy, 2
Trinity, 72–73, 85–86

Index

Tübingen, 19, 24, 63

Via dolorosa, 132
Vietnam, 31, 75
Virginal Conception, 96, 99, 101, 116
Visitation, 117

Widow, 37, 43, 49-51, 118, 122, 124-25, 139

Woman evangelist, 52, 109, 113, 118, 124, 126-27, 130, 135-36, 142
Women, 1-4, 7, 16, 20, 25, 31, 33-49, 51-56, 58-63, 65-70, 72, 74, 79, 82-89, 91-171

Yahweh, 5, 79, 119, 127

Zechariah, 115-18, 120, 122
Zealot, 25, 28